THE SERVANT OF ALL
Archbishop Nathaniel Popp

30 Years of Leadership
1980 – 2010

Ian G. Pac-Urar
Editor

Polycarp Books
PolycarpBooks.com

Cover Photos: I. Pac-Urar, Dan Ursache

ISBN 978-0-9829182-0-3

Copyright © 2010
The Romanian Orthodox Episcopate of America
Reprinted 2011
All rights reserved

Published by Polycarp Books
inquiries@PolycarpBooks.com

Printed in the United States of America

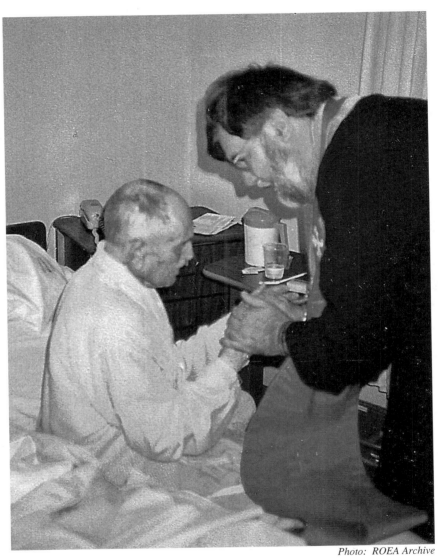
Photo: ROEA Archive

The Servant of All

Table of Contents

Foreword: Metropolitan Jonah

Pastoral Writings

1. Take Up Your Cross and Follow Me 1
2. Floods, Why Turn Back Your Flow? 6
3. Pentecost Bears Laborers Who Bear Fruit 12
4. The Lord Working Among Us 16
5. God So Loved the World 20
6. Are Orthodox Parochial Schools the Answer? 24
7. The Sower is Our Savior 29
8. Mission Sunday: A Penny Nail 32
9. The Dance of Life 34
10. Death of an Author: Burial of a God 37
11. Stewardship in the Church Through the Ages 41
12. Mission Sunday 45
13. Pastoral Letters 1991, 1992 48
14. Editorial: The "Time Honored Stag" 53
15. The Incarnation and Independence Day 57
16. Stealing from the Church 62
17. Women in the Church Congress 66
18. Paschal Pastoral Letter 1999 69
19. Orthodox Christians: Modern Iconoclasts? 75
20. Letter to All the Clergy 79

Youth

21. Teen Time and the Holy Spirit 84
22. Thanks, Church School Teachers! 88
23. With God, All Things are Possible 90
24. To the Participants of the Bible Bowl Tournament 94
25. School Days, School Days, and the Bell Tolls 97
26. Where Have All the Flowers Gone? 101

Feasts and Fasts

27. Housecleaning of Our Soul 106
28. The Presentation of Christ: Cooperation with God 111
29. Pastoral Letters 1985, 1986 115

30	Pentecost: Gift of Renewal	122
31	Excerpts from the Sunday of Orthodoxy	126
32	Apostles of Christ	132
33	The Stones and Stars Speak Out	136
34	Christ's Baptism: Our Renewal	141
35	The Resurrection Fast or Great Lent	147
36	Dearly Beloved in Christ	150
37	Veneration of the Mother of God	154
38	Pastoral Letters 1987, 1988	158
39	Theophany: Baptism of Faithful and of Homes	164
40	Give Thanks to the Lord For He is Good! Alleluia!	167
41	The Star of Bethlehem: Fact or Fancy?	169
42	Resurrection Pastoral Letter 1993	174
43	The Great Paschal Fast	178

Historical Notes

44	One-Year Retirement Anniversary	182
45	Restoring the Lady	185
46	Solia's 50 Years: A Sketch	189
47	The Annunciation in American History	197
48	Archbishop Valerian: Bishop, Man of Prayer	200
49	Memorial Day "Weekend"	204
50	1970-1988: Eighteen Years of Autocephaly	208
51	Archbishop Valerian Remembered	211
52	Fifth Anniversary: Archbishop Valerian	214
53	1993 Church Congress: Legislative Session	218
54	65th Anniversary of the Installation of Bishop Policarp	224

Romania

55	A Letter to the President of the United States	230
56	When, Romania?	233
57	The Plight of Job	236
58	"An Entire Nation Stood Up, As One Man"	241
59	Romania's Orphans	244
60	In the Light of the Resurrection	248
61	Prayer on the Occasion of the First Anniversary of Romania's Revolution	251
62	An Appeal for "Help for Romania"	253
63	Episcopate? Patriarchate?	256
64	Poems from Communist Prisons	260
65	New Iron Curtain: Made in America	264

66	Return of A Pilgrim	266
67	The Dialogue with the Romanian Patriarchate	273

The Unity of the Church

68	In Limbo, But Not Willingly	280
69	An Orthodox Never-Never Land	284
70	"To Be or Not to Be"	288
71	Thoughts on the Unity of the Church in North America	296
72	One Bishop in One City or One Synod in One Nation	302
73	Old Europe and New World	310
74	Double or Nothing	314
75	Unity Among the Followers of Christ	319
76	Not Revolution, Nor Indefinite Evolution, But Action	324
77	An American Orthodox Communion	328
78	Jerusalem! Jerusalem!	332
79	Phyletism or Ministry?	336
80	An American Church? No! The Church in America? Yes!	341
81	Universal, Geographic Ecclesiastic Jurisdiction: Is Such a Concept Orthodox?	346
82	This is the Day Which the Lord Has Made! Today!	351
83	Orthodox Unity in the Light of Apostolic Reconciliation	356

Appendices

I. Address to the 2007 Episcopate Congress 361

II. Resurrection Pastoral Letter, 2010 372

III. Archbishop Nathaniel *by Alexandru Nemoianu* 377

IV. Archbishop Nathaniel Popp *by V.R. Fr. Vasile Hategan* 380

V. A Celebration of Our Faith *by Fr. Remus Grama* 383

Editor's Note

In this volume, the reader will find a range of articles, letters and addresses selected from among the vast body of writing produced by His Eminence Archbishop Nathaniel over the course of his thirty-year archpastorate. The texts cover a wide range of topics, as befits the wide-ranging demands of the Episcopal throne. There are letters to presidents, patriarchs, and children. Often, His Eminence uplifts and inspires us; sometimes he admonishes, and that sternly. In one place, he explains the unity of the Body of Christ; in another, he cheers a Bible Bowl team. He fiercely defends the unique identity of the American community of Romanian Orthodox faithful, even as he insists that all be done in harmony with the Universal Church. Photographs show him entertaining royalty and also repairing an orphanage fence. Nowhere will the reader find the Archbishop writing about himself, his own accomplishments or his personal difficulties.

From the first selection, "Take Up Your Cross and Follow Me" (1982), through the closing Paschal Letter (2010), we hope the reader will gain a glimpse into the heart and mind of this shepherd who has given his life to be the "servant of all" (Mark 9:35).

In earlier years, His Eminence was known as "Father Nathaniel" and "Bishop Nathaniel." For the sake of simplicity and with only a few exceptions, we have used the forms "His Eminence" and "Archbishop" throughout, without regard for the actual date of his elevation to that dignity.

This book was produced by the efforts of a tiny staff with great love. Archdeacon David Oancea, Chancellor of the Romanian Orthodox Episcopate of America, extracted thirty years' worth of articles, letters and photographs from the Solia archives. Pamela Deal and Ann Whaite retyped the raw material into a draft manuscript. Preoteasa Nicole Mitescu, Dr. Violet Leathers and Dr. Noel Leathers worked under an unbelievably short deadline to proofread the text and rid it of errors. I am grateful to all for their enthusiasm, joy and complete affirmation of the value of this project. The errors that remain are mine alone.

IGP
Fairlawn, Ohio
September 2010

Foreword

This anthology marks the 30th Anniversary of Archbishop Nathaniel's tenure in the Romanian Episcopate of the Orthodox Church in America. We warmly congratulate him and his flock for their constancy and perseverance, their love and devotion, in bringing the Gospel of Jesus Christ to the American continent, and for his tender care for his beloved Romanian people.

Archbishop Nathaniel is the Senior Hierarch, after the Metropolitan, of the Orthodox Church in America. Not only is he a fountain of wisdom and treasure house of experience, he is one of the most constant and stable voices calling for the unity of Orthodoxy in America. His work and his vision have inspired many to seek for the unity of all in Christ, in a united synod of a fully autocephalous Church. His vision is one that transcends, but does not denigrate, the tremendous contributions of the various ethnic communities that make up Orthodoxy in America. Each person, each community is precious and has something to contribute.

There are many areas in which Archbishop Nathaniel has labored hard and long, first and foremost to establish the Romanian Episcopate and to accommodate the multitude of new immigrants, to include and integrate them, and to lead his flock into a common mind and vision of the Church. He has not let the specific ministry to the Romanian people deter him from his vision for the whole Church in America. Each community, in its particularity, is a microcosm of the whole; just as each person is a unique image of God: of infinite value, to be guarded and cherished, and encouraged. Archbishop Nathaniel has fulfilled for his flock the roles of teacher and spiritual guide, leader in times of trouble, and prophet announcing a new day in the relationship of the Church and state in Romania. In times of trouble, he defended his people and their rights. While honoring the ancient traditions, he has brought his people into their new American homeland and united them in the American Church.

While in touch with the life of the Church in Romania, and having restored normal relations, he has trodden a path which preserves the integrity of his vision for his Church in America: a church defined not by ethnic loyalties, but by the Gospel of Christ; not nationalist diaspora, but a local church, with unity in Christ as the fundamental criterion. He does not allow any division between Orthodox Christians according to human criteria, but emphasizes the ancient principle of how the Orthodox Church is organized, by territory. Thus, neither nationalism nor ethnicity, neither race nor language, can be principles of the organization of the Church. The only criterion is faith in the Gospel of Jesus Christ, as incarnated in the Orthodox Church.

There are many areas of Episcopal labor that have grown to thrive under the leadership of Archbishop Nathaniel. His work with youth and camp programs, the development of the clergy, educational programs and institutions, have all borne fruit. His outreach to Romania in its time of financial crisis, and continued dialog with the Church in Romania, are a model for the other Churches in America of what the relationship of a daughter to Mother Church can be.

As Metropolitan, I look to Archbishop Nathaniel for advice and wisdom, and a sober and honest appraisal of whatever problem is at hand. I have profoundly appreciated his support and guidance, and his participation in the most difficult decisions of the Holy Synod. Even when the decisions facing us have been extremely complex, the Archbishop is able to keep them in perspective. I am deeply grateful to God for him!

May the Lord grant him a long and peaceful life, health, salvation and furtherance in all good things, and many years as our friend and colleague, and co-struggler in the ascetic task of leading the Church in these troubled times. May his vision be constantly renewed, so that all around him may benefit from his wise guidance and counsel. May the Lord grant him Many Years!

+*JONAH*,
Archbishop of Washington,
Metropolitan of All America and Canada

Pastoral Writings

1

"Some people say we need a 'good persecution' to set us straight and make us aware of our true relationship and indebtedness to God. It seems rather that we ought ourselves, with God's grace to do something about our apathy. We must make decisions to stand for what we propose to adhere to, to what we believe in."

(September 1982)

Archbishop Nathaniel, early in his archpastorate, became known for his calls to action. He calls "indifference" the one enemy of Christians. The responsibility for indifference lies not with the world or with unbelievers, but with the Christian himself. Here, His Eminence presents the command of Christ to "Take up your Cross," as a call to active witness in the world and to struggle against indifference. Those who hear His call and know His love cannot do otherwise.

"Take Up Your Cross and Follow Me"

Jesus the compassionate Lord, the healer of every illness and restorer to life, bestower of sight and sound, pastor of the wandering and scattered, presented an ultimatum: *"If anyone wants to be a follower of mine, let him renounce himself and take up his cross and follow me." (Mark 8:34)*

I often wondered how Christ spoke those words before his own crucifixion. Perhaps these words were later introduced by the writers of the Gospels, I thought. How could Jesus say that someone would have to take up his cross and follow? Was it prophecy, or after the facts?

To "take up the cross" in those days, however, was an expression known to all the Jews. It meant to lay one's life down for the pure faith in one God and his commandments.

The presence of the pagan Romans, their idolic emblems placed throughout the land and in the Holy Temple, their indifference to and mockery of Jewish traditions and laws and rejection of belief in one God was unbearable for the people who had to live under their rule.

Men and women, children, too, like the Maccabees, felt the sting of this domination and the affront to the thing most precious to them: their faith. They banded together to preserve their ways and to fulfill the duties of worship as prescribed by Moses.

In his ultimatum, Christ, in effect, was inviting his disciples and listeners to persevere in their faith. It was a call to resist even to the point of dying at the hands of the foreigners rather than be affected by their influence. The same invitation holds true for us today. We are not oppressed in America as they were in Palestine; we are not subject to dictators as to our religious life, nor are we so terribly mocked or insulted for our Christian way of life.

We must, however, be aware that each of us must always side with God. Our every breath should remind us of him, and our every effort should be to resist the world which rejects him.

The attractions of the "world" are all those things and ways which steal us away from our God, which make us ignore him and which slowly, but steadily build walls between us and him, except for that which we ourselves build.

We should feel a tension between ourselves and the limitations of the world, for we are children of the light and must fight against Satan and all those who would deny the love and even the existence of God. We must, as followers of Christ, feel the weight of the cross; if we do not, then something is not right in our lives.

Today, the one enemy prevalent among us is not the pagans, but an attitude in our own being: indifference. With every freedom available to us, with all the possibilities open to us, we Christians reflect an image of "indifference," of "lukewarmness".

Some people say we need a "good persecution" to set us straight and make us aware of our true relationship and indebtedness to God. It seems rather that we ought ourselves, with God's grace to do something about our apathy. We must make decisions to stand for what we propose to adhere to, to what we believe in.

Taking up our cross is a positive action, which must be thought about and demands an awareness of doing good in the presence of God. To carry the wood of the tree of obedience is to expect difficulties and to be seen as "different". We recognize that we exist to tell others about God and to do everything in his name and to his honor.

The cross is a reminder not to make ourselves too comfortable on earth. We are pilgrims, overnighters, checking in for a while, but still on a journey towards the future life.

The cross, which we symbolically wear, piously, reverently, in whose shade we lay our dead and which we raise over the tops of our places of worship, is alive with power! It is not "just" a sign. It is a source of life, renewal, decision and action. The arms reach from one end of the universe to the other, from the root planted firmly in the earth to the topmost part, which draws heaven down to us. The cross is the pivot, the center of the universe.

The feast of the Lifting up of the Holy Cross, September 14, is a great feast of the people of God. It allows us the opportunity to communally venerate the instrument of obedience, which we must also bear, and to give thanks for the trophy of our salvation.

In the service of the day, the cross is lifted high over our heads to remind us of "him who has his home in heaven". It is lowered to touch the ground to remind us that we are ashes and will return, oh, ever so shortly, "to the earth we came from". It is horizontally shown from right to left, as a reminder that all belongs to the one focal point of existence, to God himself who is creator, savior and sanctifier.

A Christian cannot be a follower of Jesus without carrying his cross in obedience to the new Adam, the Lord who lifts us from the pit of pride. Pride makes us believe that there is nothing further for us to know, to do, to grow in God. We apathetically feel that once baptized, chrismated, receiving the Precious Body and Blood of Christ, that we are perfect. How far from the truth! Pride makes us rest on our laurels: pride of helping in the kitchen, on the council, in the classroom. These are the only expressions of our love, but our love can always become more intense, more pure and profound.

The calling of a cross-bearing Christian is to let others know of "the marvels of our God." To be among those who "bring the good news to those far and near," that is, to those who know the Lord but are indifferent and to those who do not yet confess him, this is our role. We must be so filled with burning love for the Lord that we shine like stars, are consumed by love for him and thrust ourselves in the thirsty world which yearns to hear the glad news that there is a personal God who loves us and in whom alone our souls find peace.

The cross reminds us that it is not easy to be a Christian. The Savior himself implied that with his invitation to follow him. To be a follower of the Son of God means to imitate him, in trust and faith, so that he can lead us to salvation. This is not a birthright bestowed because of our family's past religious affiliation; it is a gift from the Holy Spirit. It is not an inherited, innate blessing as from some ethnic origin, but a gift to be incorporated into the new people of God, his Church.

Jesus freely bestows salvation on us, and we must reflect this in our work, the fruits of his presence in us. It is up to us to reflect the fruit of this gift. Our cross may be too heavy, because we have not remembered that we ought first to carry his cross which is of love for the Father and obedience to him as the source of all. It is by knowingly and lovingly carrying the cross, that we reject the false limitations of this world and its pseudo self-sufficiency. Our lives make sense and become daily renewed in Jesus if we allow him to reign in our hearts and to once again help us bear the weight of this life, of the cross.

September 14 is a holy day, an eventful day, and an invigorating day. In observing the finding of the true cross and presenting it to the faithful, we are encouraged to again realize the length of the forgiveness of our God and the depths of his compassion: *"God so loved the world that he gave his only-begotten Son that whoever believes in him will not perish but will have everlasting life"* (Jn. 3:16).

Part of that mission of the Son was to bear our sins, to die in behalf of all of us so that when we do come to recognize our transgressions, we would return to God, following the path marked and traced by the cross borne by our savior. We cannot be indifferent to such a love, which was lavished on us long before we loved in return.

Now that we recognize his love, we cannot be apathetic toward it. Now that we hear his call with a clear mind, we cannot linger. Now that we feel his presence in our heart, we cannot choose to ignore him. He holds us in his hands and pours his graceful Spirit into our lives, and we must be changed.

The Exaltation of the Holy Cross is one of the outstanding feasts of the community of believers. Let's not ignore it. Let us rather observe it properly and hear the words to bear the cross. If we renew our baptismal calling, which reminds us to follow Jesus through his death and burial, we will take courage in knowing that we shall be raised by him to a life which does not end.

*Blessing the Faithful,
Fairlawn, Ohio, 2009*

2

"This is a reason for celebrating the Theophany with Bible readings and blessing of water. We are refreshed, renewed, reminded of God's actions in the past and of his promises, which are to come. We recall, as we pray in the Liturgy, 'everything you have done for us, those things known and unknown which have been done for us."

(January 1983)

The winter of 1982-83 saw tragic floods in the southern United States. As Auxiliary to Archbishop Valerian, His Eminence took on the problem of tragedy in nature, instructing the faithful in the wonders that God has performed with water through the ages. This article links the floods of that season to the floods of ancient times and shows us the power of water to transform all creation by God's grace.

Floods, Why Turn Back Your Flow?

The media have shown us the tragic results of unprecedented amounts of rain in some of our southern states. Unable to carry off the flow, the banks of the rivers are erased from the landscape, and the waters penetrate homes, businesses, hospitals, and churches.

In such instances, nature does not respect intelligence, power, money, or innocence. It also seems that mankind, caught in the throes of such tragedy, knits together in resisting, in rescuing, in rebuilding.

The history of man is replete with the role of rivers and water. First of all, all forms of life would immediately cease should water disappear from the face of the earth. Second, rivers have been highways of every form of encounter: economic, social, and unfortunately, warfare.

Flooding brought silt, which made the land fertile. It appeared to give life to the nation. Many rivers and bodies of water were regarded as "divine", among them the Nile, the Tiber and the Euphrates. Rivers were also rapid transits for the ancient peoples, bringing new ideas and exchanges of civilizations. For all the problems associated with water, the positive aspects always outweighed the negative.

For the Christians, the Jordan River is THE River. Yes, there are other bodies of water and places whereat water played an important role, but for Christians, the Jordan is a "fountain of life".

Let's return to some of the Biblical passages which are read in January for the Theophany. On this day we read the Bible and bless water. The two go hand in hand. Human life is not an abstraction. Water, that simple element, plays a major role, and it is humanly possible to recognize this dependency and to give thanks to God for it. We also recall the role it has played and will play in our lives.

Look at the history of water and see to what marvelous use it has been put. In Genesis *(1:1-13),* water is created by God. It is mentioned no less than nine times in this first book of holy writing. Water was created "good". It was also "good" for the Israelites who escaped the pursuing Pharaoh through traversing the waters of the Sea of reeds *(Exodus 14:15-18).* Through Moses who held his hands out like the form of the cross, God parted the waters and gave the people escape. Baptism is also like this: by immersing into the waters in God's name, we pass through the limitations of human existence and are given the gift of eternal life.

We sometimes do not like to recognize that life will also have some bitter moments. Trials and rededication are necessary aspects of our human spiritual, and conjunctively, physical growth. The people who escaped Pharaoh became unhappy that the road to a new life was not easier. They felt betrayed by God who did not yet "brush away every tear". They "murmured" against Moses who, as God's chosen leader, had led them into the testing of the journey to peace and stability in a promised land.

When they came to watering places, thirsty for that simple element of water, they discovered the water polluted and unfit to drink. Exodus *(15:22-16:1)* relates the care of God who provided a simple remedy to change the bitter to sweet water: Moses was told to throw a certain kind of wood into it; and, this being done, the water became potable.

In the service of blessing of water, the priest dips a wooden cross into the waters, reminding us of this Bible episode. The cross of Jesus sweetens the bitterness of our limited human life, for it promises unending possibilities of growth.

On Theophany, the priest, as the leader of the community, takes water from a tap, and according to the Bible, gives thanks for it. It is dedicated to God, offered to him in remembrance of all the times that water had an important role in the spiritual growth of his people. By our recognition of the specialness or sanctity of the water, we confirm our belief that everything good comes from above, from the Father of all light, and we offer thanks, worship and glory to him. We drink the "Jordan" water, bless and dedicate our homes to God by sprinkling with it. We also wash our wounds with it. These simple actions take on added meaning if we realize the tremendous history, holy history, of water in the spiritual development of humanity.

In reading the Bible passages, we refresh ourselves with the various events which took place referring to water, God's use of it, and his presence among us (Theophany), and his plans for the world to be harmonious.

The services of the Church include these readings: matins, vespers, the hours, the Liturgy; they all incorporate the various passages into our liturgical life of praise. In January, we are reminded of renewal because of the baptism of Christ in the Jordan, of dedication by participating in the Jordan waters blessed in church, of the call of all mankind through the mystery of holy Baptism.

Looking through the readings, we are "flooded" by the plan of God's love and mercy toward man. We learn that nature obeys the hand of God and owes its allegiance to him alone. Faith is put to the test and rewarded. The wounds of illness and the corruption of death are all washed away by water dedicated by and to God.

Another time in history, waters parted to create a pathway over which God's people walked. Joshua, with the Ark, stepped into the Jordan River, and the waters reversed themselves because of the presence of God's word in them. Remember that the Ark held the stone tablets of the Commandments. The waters reverted, because they worshipped their creator, as the first commandment states: You must worship the Lord God alone. *(Joshua 3:7-8, 15-17)*

Not only does God provide for his entire people, but also for his elected prophets and holy ones. Elijah threw his mantle on the Jordan River, and it divided to let him and Elisha pass over. When Elisha became heir to the work of Elijah, he, too, was blessed with the same power. The mighty Jordan recognized the creator in the creature who spoke in his name. *(2 Kings 2:6-14)*

Waters also heal. Naaman, a foreigner from Assyria, sought help to be healed of his leprosy. Elisha the prophet, moved by God, told him to wash seven times in the Jordan.

Naaman, proud man that he was, expected a much greater remedy. He felt that the prophet should merely say words and heal him. God wants us to work with him. He may part the waters, but we must lift the cup. He will fill them with power, but we must believe and apply them. Only in the persistent washing of seven times did Naaman find healing. We sometimes are directed to "keep on" but fail to pursue to the seventh time. The word of God is power, but he can also use what he has made "by his own hands" to fulfill what he promises *(2 Kings 5:9-24)*.

The great Isaiah called the people to change, renew, and dedicate themselves. "Wash! Clean yourselves!" He called them not to physical washing, but to a purified understanding of life and their human actions as people of God. Who doesn't feel better after having showered or washed? How much cleaner and finer ought we feel after having been washed in the water of Baptism? Of Confession? Of the precious Body and Blood of Christ? *(Isaiah 1:16-20)*.

Jacob had crossed the Jordan River in search of a new life. He had a simple wooden staff as his support. When he returned, he had a large household and many possessions. Passing over the Jordan can also symbolize the fruitfulness and blessings bestowed on those who trust in the call of the Lord *(Genesis 32:1-10)*.

Moses was discovered in the waters of the Nile. They were like a baptism to him, for he received a new life after he was lifted from among the reeds. The Bible says that the baby Moses wept when his basket was opened. Maybe it was the sunlight and the sudden noises around him which caused this. But the daughter of Pharaoh was moved by his fright and tears. God is also moved by our cries in this life of changeabouts, sudden reversals, intrusions of illness, and catastrophe. Like Moses, we are calm in the quiet safety of the arms of God. *(Exodus 2:5-10)*

Water was also used as a confirmation of calling. Gideon could not believe that God would use him to help his people. He "put God to the test". He asked for dew to fall on a sheep's skin and not on the ground around it. This happened. He asked for the reverse to know that God had really prescribed this event. This happened: the dew fell on the ground around the fleece. The dew confirmed the will of God. "Into each life we are also called to "do the will of God". Our proof is in receiving the mystery of holy Baptism, Chrismation, and the Eucharist. *(Judges 6:36-40)*

Can fire burn wet wood? Can flames fuel itself on water? Hardly so, and yet, as proof of God's will and as a display of truth in contrast to falsehood and error, water was used for this purpose. Elijah poured quantities of water over his wood, three times with four barrels. He called on God to show that the natural properties of opposites, fire and water, would obey the true God. Flames did come from heaven and were fueled by water, and by this sign the people were strengthened and rejected what they knew to be untrue. *(1Kings 18:30-39)*

A similar event took place through the prophet Elisha as recorded in 2 Kings *(2:19-22)*. There was no water in Jericho and the ground produced nothing. Moved by God, Elisha went to a spring and threw salt into it and proclaimed that the land was no longer barren and death was banished because of the increased flow of water.

We see in this that salt, which stymies growth, became the instrument for growth. Death became the instrument for life when Christ died on the cross. The barren experience of dying becomes a rich and fertile event of renewed existence.

Isaiah reminds us, in our final reading for the feast, that God does not forget our needs and has appointed a contract with us. He will have mercy on us and lead us to springs of water. This means that all our needs are given to us. Our worries are our own.

Because God has promised, we cannot doubt. If we are weak, we must strengthen ourselves.

This is a reason for celebrating the Theophany with Bible readings and blessing of water. We are refreshed, renewed, reminded of God's actions in the past and of his promises which are to come. We recall, as we pray in the Liturgy, *"everything you have done for us, those things known and unknown which have been done for us."*

The problem remains: the flooding in our country; why? The problem of suffering and disaster is a part of our life on earth. We can make attempts to control nature's ways and we have. We can bear with one another when we are struck by such events. As long as we are not in the fullness of paradise, we continue to "toil and sweat to make a living", to exist. But the sweetness in life comes from knowing that in every event, God's hand is present, lifting, holding and sustaining us as we strive to be good and to keep good all which he has made in our behalf.

3

"A seminary is, in fact, the place where the seed of faith is nourished for a special purpose; it is cultivated and fertilized to bear fruit like that of the day of Pentecost. A seminarian is a unique being for he exists for a short time only, and this is a step, a stage in the process of preparation for a change, a transfiguration into a laborer in the ripe field of the Lord, a fisher in the rich depths of the sea of life."

(June 1983)

In this discussion of the meaning of Pentecost, then Auxiliary Bishop Nathaniel reminds us of the origins of the Feast and its importance for those who will bear fruit in the present-day vineyard of the Lord. Always practical, His Eminence uses the occasion to make us aware of the importance of seminaries and the students who will one day serve the Church and her flock as priests. By supporting the seminaries, we too can become partakers in the work of bearing good fruit.

Pentecost Bears Laborers Who Bear Fruit

The day of Pentecost is a feast celebrated in ancient Israel to offer the first fruits of the harvest to God in thanksgiving. This holiday was also a signal that the year ahead would be a good one or lean, depending on the abundance of the harvest. The more the fruits, the happier the celebration.

For us, the harvest of the fruits of the year is far removed. Thanksgiving Day is more of entertainment and visiting than an offering of the work of our hands to the Almighty. We may indirectly realize that a frost in California will cause a hike in price for citrus products; a flood in the Midwest may well increase the cost of a McDonald's hamburger. Generally, we have not the same joy over a harvest as the ancient and even present day rural societies. We do not know what it means to watch our food supply dwindle, to open a "Mother Hubbard's" cupboard. Pentecost celebrations in America are not harvest celebrations.

Our Church schools find it useful to tell our children that Pentecost is the "birthday" of the Church. We know by heart the scene of the apostles being bathed with tongues of fire, filled with courage and committed love to the risen Lord and his message. Pentecost does signal a beginning, a first step on a new journey of preaching the Gospel of salvation. What was newly born in the depths of the apostles was not belief but the desire and need to share that faith with others. The apostles were on fire to give others the same holy joy that overflowed from their own selves. Pentecost is a road marker on the journey of mankind toward heaven; a sign of the vibrant direction in which man's relationship to his God had recently taken through the working of Jesus Christ.

The disciples, touched by the presence of the Holy Spirit, were the first fruits of a new harvest. Christ often used expressions such as "catch of souls" and "harvest of souls". He brought home the idea that God is as concerned for man's perfect existence as man is concerned about his physical subsistence. God's concern for man is always primary. On Pentecost, men responded and put the things of God foremost and the sharing of these as essential.

One of the blessings of our age is the institution we call "seminary". Its name derives from the Latin and has the meaning of sowing and reaping. A seminary is, in fact, the place where the seed of faith is nourished for a special purpose; it is cultivated and fertilized to bear fruit like that of the day of Pentecost. A seminarian is a unique being for he exists for a short time only, and this is a step, a stage in the process of preparation for a change, a transfiguration into a laborer in the ripe field of the Lord, a fisher in the rich depths of the sea of life.

Seminaries are relatively new in the Orthodox Church, as they are in most Churches. In days gone by, the needs of specific communities were served by a ministry passed from father to son. Little training was necessary. The service of the sacramental life was continued through the cultivation of simple faith long implanted and nourished by relevant traditions.

The obvious reason for seminaries is to train individuals for service to the flock to which the hierarch assigns them and to also "go out" and make new disciples, cultivate new fruit. This demands a more systematic pursuit of Scripture and Tradition and a basic grasp of other sciences. The priest of today studies another seven years beyond high school education. The laborers in the streets and metropolitan cities of today must serve both the present membership of the Church and reach out into the world bustling around and absorbing his people.

The life of the Church is one of sharing, a movement outward. The disciples, indeed, began to minister to the Jewish community; but through Paul and others, the mission begun on Pentecost gained momentum and was not stymied by the restrictiveness to serve within ethnic limitations. The spring of water gushing forth eternal life, which Christ mentioned to the Samaritan woman, cascaded into new lands, irrigating the hearts of new people who had not known the one true God nor his Son, Jesus Christ. New fruits upon new fruits were added to the pantry of the Holy Spirit, the kingdom of God.

The celebration of the mission of the Church, motivated and strengthened by the presence of God the Holy Spirit, is a daily celebration; for as Christians, we must bear fruit continuously, or be withered up. The annual celebration of Pentecost, this year is preceded by the SEMINARY DAY, June 19th. Those who are ordained to serve the community must be responsive to the total call to go out and preach. Those who, through their choice of profession and vocation, chose not to be ministers of the Word, must support the work of the seminaries. How can we expect to "bless the feet of those who bring the good news" if we do not make the roads? In other words, how can we hope to share the Gospel unless we support those who have dedicated their lives to the outward mission of the Lord?

Everyone is a partaker in the gift of the seal of the Holy Spirit; everyone is called to produce good fruits. By sharing with the seminaries, we uphold the purpose of God and fulfill ourselves. Our celebration should increase year by year, not because of the fruits of the earth, but because of the increase of laborers in the field.

Consecration, 1980

4

"Our Diocese is blessed with an exciting future in the Lord: we have many new and dedicated priests; there are numerous brothers to be welcomed into our midst from Europe; the established parishes are on the verge of conscientious and dedicated efforts to reach out to others; missions are in the planning stages and the older parishes may be revived. Even though the membership of certain parishes was affected by the changes in local economic variations, the movement to 'open the doors' and wax strong is evident."

(January 1985)

In his first few months as ruling bishop of the Romanian Orthodox Episcopate of America, His Eminence rallied the faithful with calls to action like the one presented here. Economic uncertainty was an issue in 1985 just as it is in 2010, and the new bishop exhorts the flock to rise above their fears and join in working with the Lord Himself to bring about His Kingdom. His words are written at the beginning of an era of the most vigorous growth and expansion since the founding of the Episcopate itself.

The Lord Working Among Us

Quickly following in the echoes of the carols and "colinde" of the season of Christ's birth are the familiar lines of the tropar of Theophany: "At your baptism"... "In Iordan botezându-te tu Doamne", alerting us to the fact that "another year" has begun.

The visit of the priest varies from parish to parish, but always included is a recitation of prayers, the tropar and, through sprinkling of the "Jordan Water", the house and family are rededicated to service to the Lord.

After such intense preparation for Christ's birth, New Year and the Baptism, we should be able to carry on our lives with renewed effort and strength. We have celebrated these events as family, friends and co-workers, and the honest desire to be filled "with peace and good will" is easily nourished.

Using this momentum, this upbeat, this crest, we can continue our sincere efforts to work together, witnessing to the Lord Jesus and his Gospel. We must be on our guard, however, not to let up nor suffer from the "post-holiday hum-drums"! If, in fact, we did receive the message in our hearts and if, truly, we sang of the birth and baptism of Christ with our "whole soul and our whole mind", we can continue through the days preceding the great and holy Pascha.

Some practical things to do are to earnestly read the Scriptures on a daily basis; to participate in the church education programs and to attend all services. What a marvelous gift to the infant Christ it is, to be sure that we are in church before the service begins; be in our place in the choir loft in advance of the service; to take part in the auxiliary meetings with the intention of progressing spiritually and to give full financial support to the good programs of the Diocese and the parish!

Our Diocese is blessed with an exciting future in the Lord: we have many new and dedicated priests; there are numerous brothers to be welcomed into our midst from Europe; the established parishes are on the verge of conscientious and dedicated efforts to reach out to others; missions are in the planning stages and the older parishes may be revived.

Even though the membership of certain parishes was affected by the changes in local economic variations, the movement to "open the doors" and "wax" strong is evident. We are able to search out for those who have moved from the former parishes and to seek to establish new communities.

There could be an increase in the number of "Supporters of the Episcopate". The mission program is expanding and in need of shoring up. The Department of Publications is in the process of reprinting the *Holy Liturgy* and *Holy Icons*. A new bi-lingual book, *Holy Baptism* is on the desk, awaiting the assurance of publication. This is a time to re-evaluate our habits of giving to the Church.

A new summer program for the education of cantors is being planned to be held at the Vatra. The purpose of this course will be to familiarize individuals, men and women, with the structure of the services of the Church and to provide some practical means of assisting the priest.

The Commission on Religious Education (C.O.R.E.) is busy with revamping the education courses held during the summer; and, as an added bonus, it is preparing aids for parochial adult education courses. Retreats for married couples are being anticipated so that the experience of the ARFORA and AROY may penetrate to couples and families.

With all the possibilities before us, there is no time to lose. We need to concentrate on the months ahead. Our Lord himself said that once we put our shoulder to the plow, we have to go on.

The year before us marks the fiftieth anniversary of the enthronement of His Grace, Bishop Policarp Morusca as hierarch of our Episcopate. From that time on, the Romanian Church in America has grown and thrived, even under dire pressures and negative conditions. When the new bishop was no longer among his flock, the Church continued, nourished by those few years of his presence until a new ruling bishop, Archbishop Valerian, took his place at the helm and guided the Ark through turbulent but nevertheless progressive years.

In our service to the Lord, he wants, first of all, that we become truly "his". A lamp that has no oil burns dimly; salt that has no flavor is useless; an axe that is dull does not cut, and so, without pouring Christ in the lamps of our hearts, they flicker, uncertain; without participating in the holy sacraments of confession and communion, our minds are insipid and our life bland; without reading the Word of God, the sword of defense against this world, our life is a waving of empty gesture in the air.

The Scriptures remind us that it was with "the Lord working among them" that the early community grew. It was dedication to the Lord and Savior that gave courage and power to the followers of Jesus Christ. Their witness was one of intense love for one another and for others; the message was not hidden nor locked up. It was, in fact, because of sharing that the authenticity of God's presence was certain, for the numbers increased who praised his name!

All of the programs, parish facilities, and literature are placed before us as gifts from a generous and loving Lord. We must make good and constant use of them. 1985 should be a year like no other, because it is a year of grace given to us by the Master. Each month, week, day, hour and second comes from above; and in those precious timeslots, we cooperate with the Lord. Another year has begun and we have been enlightened; let us live in the light of his presence, strengthened by the Holy Spirit who leads us, step by step to the throne of the Father in the Kingdom which is coming.

Working Among Us: Taking a Break From Fence Repair, Project Mexico, 2001

5

"Orthodox Christianity is born from the side of the Crucified Lord and empowered by the overshadowing of the Holy Spirit. The Church is not one of the many such institutions, another marble in a sack of many marbles. The church is the unique Body of Christ, the fountain of the sacraments and Way to salvation. She is the custodian and teacher of Truth; she breathes and lives it and must necessarily share it with others. The Church is dynamic."

(October 1985)

Even in the first months of his archpastorate, His Eminence worried out loud about the state of his churches. Admittedly beautiful and traditional in design and appearance, the building, he tells us, is not to be confused with "the Church." In this article, Archbishop Nathaniel tackles the thorny problem of nostalgia for "old world structures" and the Gospel imperative to build vibrant, dynamic communities that witness to the true Faith in the New World.

God So Loved the World

When considering writing about the change of seasons and, in particular, about autumn, it came to mind that the harvest season is particular to some areas of the nation but not to others. Some of our communities experience the change of color of the leaves, the accumulation of snow and other signs of regional differences. Others have a more or less stable season and climate.

What is universal to our parishes, whether they are located in California or Rhode Island, Assiniboia or Miramar, is the celebrations of holy days of the Church calendar. We all participate in the feasts of Christ's birth, his baptism, transfiguration, crucifixion and resurrection, the coming of the Holy Spirit and other events in the plan of salvation.

These celebrations are, however, expressions of our faith, our Orthodox faith, which we share with others who are not necessarily in our own diocese. Like scattered seeds cast across the American continent, Orthodox parishes bear witness to our trust in God and our hope in salvation. These communities have sprung up, here and there, wherever the faithful have gone to search for work to live.

Oftentimes, the actual structure of the church is unmistakably "Orthodox," complete with unique features such as special shaped roofs or domes, slanted crosses, or a multitude of them. These edifices are even well known by the citizenry as being "Orthodox" churches, although they do not know what that title means. It becomes "that" church instead of "the" church.

One wonders if, in the past, we have not paid a great deal of attention to reproducing replicas of church buildings while neglecting to reproduce the spiritual life that shaped the old-world structures. I am not saying that there is not a definite "orthodox" shape to a church following liturgical needs and function. My concern is that while we have built monuments to a country of origin, we have much to do to deepen the faith and life-style of the Orthodox faith on the American continent.

It seems to me that we are not a little afraid of the working of the Holy Spirit in the Church, which means, in each of us and collectively. We have been so very concerned about being recognized as a "major" faith, that we have been content to sit on our faith like a hen on an egg and wait for it to hatch "in time".

Orthodox Christianity is born from the side of the Crucified Lord and empowered by the overshadowing of the Holy Spirit. The Church is not one of many such institutions, another marble in a sack of many marbles. The Church is the unique Body of Christ, the fountain of the sacraments and Way to salvation. She is the custodian and teacher of Truth; she breathes and lives it and must necessarily share it with others. The Church is dynamic.

The "new world" is not any newer than the rest of the globe; it may be more fertile, however, for the germination and growth of the Gospel. What other nation has such material wealth and shares it so freely? What other nation is moved by scenes of earthquake, drought, war and springs into compassionate action? What other nation needs THE ANSWER, Jesus Christ, than the one which is calling out to us and to which we do not share nor spring into action to invite to embrace our faith? Orthodox Christians in the Americas must be dynamic!

We now boast of politicians who are Orthodox, of corporate heads who share the same "cup of salvation," of educators and societies, fraternities and publications, but we continue to act like "outsiders." Are we not cold to the spiritual needs of others and fall short of total sacrifice and dedication to our Lord? Do we not continue to build marvelous "old world" structures and fail to build up the Body of Christ in a new environment?

In July, at our annual Church Congress, the delegates viewed a special, very special, videotape about the "death of a parish". It created a ripple, a whisper of concern, a nodding of the head, a vote for limited financial assistance "beginning in January". The need for spiritual growth and for financial giving was recognized but not acted on. Collectively, we acknowledge the needs, but individually we are sluggish in responding. But time marches on and with it, our younger generation which longs to see a vibrant and dedicated community, sacrificing as it is capable of sacrificing; sharing as it has an abundance of spiritual wealth to offer.

Our Episcopate has been blessed with unique opportunities such as never before. We are being called on to reach out to the newly arrived, to the lost generations and to our neighbor. The fields are ripe with those who are seeking Christ, and we have workers but we need supporters who will give financial backing that bears witness to the conviction of the truth of our Faith and of our call to share it with others.

Books must be printed, programs recorded, films registered and the feet of bearers of the Good News set to walking. The closing of the parish in Erie, Pennsylvania was the seed for a "Mission Fund". Without replenishing, it will shrivel and dry up and the plants newly sprouted, the various missions and evangelization, will be aborted monuments to our lack of concern, our indifference, our failure to act.

The harvest time of this earth reminds us that there is a harvest time called for by the heavenly Father; in enjoying the fruits of the earth, we should be concerned to bear the fruits of a spiritual life.

In every issue of the SOLIA, there is a section given over to financial reports. Let's "beef-up" the donations to the "Mission Fund". The command of Christ, to "Go forth and make disciples of all nations"...even America, is to us. To reap, one must plant; to grow, one must nourish; to be saved, one must share.

There are already too many "orthodox" style churches empty or abandoned or sold, because they are in the "wrong" areas! Where, in the name of God, is the wrong area for Holy Orthodoxy? When have we shared too much? The icon of Orthodoxy in America is tarnished by our inwardness. We do not deserve the title of "major" faith but "hidden" Church. To be called the children of God, we must act like our heavenly Father: "God so loved the world that he gave his only-begotten Son." We love the world ... and what have we given?

6

"Our young people are the leaders of tomorrow. They are the politicians, the physicians, lawyers, teachers, workers, and church leaders. Can we possibly continue to leave the formation of these young minds and hearts in the hands of strangers whose philosophy of life, whose actual indifference to the reality of God is contrary to ours? Yes, they will be the leaders. Yes, they will be Americans. But, will they be Orthodox American leaders?"

(January 1986)

The creation of Orthodox Christian day schools is one of the many initiatives supported by Archbishop Nathaniel from the beginning of his archpastorate. In this early appeal to his flock, His Eminence lays out the dilemma facing the Church in America: huge parish complexes are testimony to the dedication of the faithful, yet they function only one or two hours each week. His Eminence calls clearly for a united Orthodox drive to establish an Orthodox parochial school system.

Are Orthodox Parochial Schools the Answer?

For centuries, Orthodox Christianity has adapted to the particular political situation in which she found herself preaching the Gospel of salvation. Where the government was Orthodox, the Church was supported by the State, and she usually maintained a school system, which was an accepted part of society and even reflected the political basis of the nation. The Church also existed under conditions where Christianity was a minority religion and a non-supportive government would not allow for separate religious schools. In such instances, the Church taught her youth through the services in the local parish and the consistent vigilant control by the family. Being part of a minority and subject to pressure from the general society outside also added strength to the individual's loyalty to Church and family.

Church education systems were not unique to Orthodox Christianity. In parts of Western Europe, Roman Catholics, Lutherans and Anglicans were also State supported and maintained school systems supervised or controlled by that particular church. Then, too, the Church-State relationship was close and schools were an accepted part of that State.

On arriving in the "new world," these various churches had to face that fact of re-evaluating a religious education system which would be entirely separate from and, perhaps, appear in opposition to the State; and, which would be supported entirely by the faithful who were at the same time taxed for an already existing public school system with its "non-religious" philosophy of education. The financial burden was great and the sacrifices would be many; pressure to disappear within the melting pot of "equally valid" would be tremendous. All of them, excepting Orthodox Christianity, did opt in favor of their own religious school system as the preferred way of life.

Roman Catholics set up parochial schools, one for each parish; Lutherans, Anglicans, and later, other denominations such as the Seventh-Day Adventists, set up complete education systems which were totally maintained and fashioned by the church body. These systems could be said to have been established for one of two reasons: either in opposition to the philosophy of education which guides the public school system, or as a matter of positive choice for a system of education which recognizes the reality of a supreme, personal, Triune God.

At a glance, our public school system appears to be under the direction of the local superintendent whose own "philosophy of education" may even be at variance with the ideas of the local populace, and of an elected board of education whose members may not even have any such philosophy. In the end, it appears that parents, in fact, have very little to say, or input into the education of their own children. The power of the vote is long in reversing negative aspects.

Can we Orthodox, however, honestly state that our present Orthodox education system is effective? Is it, indeed, the best for our children? The "Sunday Schools, Saturday Schools, Church

Schools" which offer a maximum of two hours per week cannot be the shaping, dynamic force necessary to educate, confirm, and support our youth in facing the tremendous pressures of choice in 21st century America. Perhaps, in borrowing these systems from others long ago, it was a temporary measure, but one that also set us back.

It ought to be determined if, in fact, the Orthodox Christian family, the celebrated "microcosm of the Church", at this point in Orthodox American history is the shaping force it must be. Or is the local parish, for that matter, as influential as it must be? According to a recent survey, those personalities immediately recognized by children, our children, too, are: Santa Claus, Ronald McDonald and the "Easter" Bunny. Jesus Christ is conspicuously not at the top of the list. Obviously, our children are not immigrant children isolated in the ghettos of the past; they are third and fourth generation or, even if "new comers", are much more rapidly absorbed into the American mainstream than were our grandparents and parents. The Church and home do not, honestly speaking, counterbalance, or overcome, the influence of our materialistic society.

Our church schools are weakest where they ought to be the strongest: at the high school and college levels. The college ministry is strapped and plagued by problems created from the local parochial situation. Church schoolteachers testify to the truth that once a child, male or female, become of driving age or is "too old for that kind of stuff," they disappear from the classroom.

The previously listed denominations not only have strong elementary and secondary systems but also rejoice in colleges and universities. An expected reply will state that they are more numerous and can afford the luxury. The fact is, these churches have opted for the future instead of the present. Their preference ran in favor of educating their children.

We do have large complexes, classrooms, offices, halls, kitchens and absolutely staggering maintenance bills for buildings which are put to use one or two days a week out of seven! Utility bills, insurance, maintenance continues, but the actual practical use of our structures is negligible.

The establishment of an Orthodox parochial school system would necessarily need Orthodox cooperation. This is more feasible in metropolitan areas. There are, however, localities and even States where Orthodox Christians reside in proportionately large numbers, which would allow for parochial schools.

While all the benefits for this system are not yet enumerated, a primary one is that the support and guidance gained by our youngsters from a parochial school system would outweigh the sacrifices and financial obligations we may tend to raise in opposition to the need. This is not a luxury but a necessity.

Peer-pressure would become peer-support. The self-image of being part of the second largest Christian body in the world would be raised from the present isolation of being "one of many" even within the framework of Orthodoxy in America.

Our young people are the leaders of tomorrow. They are the politicians, the physicians, lawyers, teachers, workers, and church leaders. Can we possibly continue to leave the formation of these young minds and hearts in the hands of strangers whose philosophy of life, whose actual indifference to the reality of God is contrary to ours? Yes, they will be the leaders. Yes, they will be Americans. But, will they be Orthodox American leaders?

We need not fear loss of ethnic identity. In fact, the parochial school would have a place for language, custom, and history. The school system would, in fact, be the key to preserving what is good and precious of a more universal Orthodox history.

Financing an Orthodox parochial system is not really the problem. Commitment to the future of Orthodoxy in America is the key. The handwriting on the wall tells us that our children deserve and must have the best education. Sacrifices and money must be offered to secure this.

We have left behind those "old world" conditions whereby the entire society pressures and shapes an Orthodox ethnos as a matter of political reality and expediency, nor are we pressured by some external enemy of political or religious identity. In America, we have the freedom we celebrate, and it really means obligation and responsibility, which we either shoulder or under which we shall fall. Our children are a large part of a society which some see as a field for proselytism, for personal gain, for cultivating tomorrow's consumerism market. Others are much more concerned about our children than we appear to be.

In the past, inter-Orthodox cooperation (a strange phrase found in the yet unpublished dictionary of American Orthodoxy) has shown up in the limited participation in processions, choirs, operation of picnic groves, some education programs, incomplete clergy and hierarchal associations. That one area in which our united interest hopes, the youth, has not received the attention due its importance.

We laud the support, those present committees and their efforts in the area of limited education programs, but these results are just that, limited. They are "scotch-tape" remedies. Looming behind the intended serene facade of these "united" efforts is the fast-falling sand of the hourglass of need. The cloud of general ignorance of the faith, the isolation of it to one hour in church, the compartmentalization of the faith to a prayer before meals and an occasional baptism looms high on the horizon of tomorrow.

Is there, in fact, an Orthodox Christian witness and lifestyle authentic in America? Does it truly exist in the home? In the societies? In the parish? We all know that "Orthodox Easter" and "Orthodox Christmas" (which one?) are listed in the Hallmark datebooks and on pass-me-out calendars from the local insurance companies, but have we really "arrived?" Are we "accepted?" And do we want to be part of the general "it's-all-the-same" status? We cannot continue in our separate ways nor bask in the wanton luxury of jurisdictional separatism.

This year, the Statue of Liberty will be 100 years old. Her torch has been lighting the way to religious, political, social and material benefits to our grandparents, parents and others. This "Mother of refugees" as she is poetically called, must stand for more than worldly goods and material comfort. She must stand for truth and look out on an authentic Orthodox lifestyle.

Orthodox Christianity has been in the new world over 200 years. The cross was lifted high in Alaska. The faith still continues there, but under pressure of the day, no less than in the "lower 48". Our calling is to live a lifestyle in America that is a continuity of the apostolic faith. The way to share our faith and to work out our salvation for the life to come is to join together in the absolutely necessary work of establishing an Orthodox parochial school system.

7

"Sometimes, we too, must re-read the parable of 'The Sower' and apply it to ourselves and our diocese...He has not finished speaking or calling. He speaks by the Holy Spirit and through the body of people who respond to his preaching, the Church. The Holy Spirit is that warmth, that necessary moisture, the nutrients that cause growth in receptive souls and hearts."
(September 1987)

At the beginning of the new Church Year, His Eminence reflects on the state of his diocese and the people in it. He asks the hard questions that arise from the parable of the sower: What sort of ground are we? Do all the activities of the diocese and its organizations lead us to salvation, or do they merely distract us? Are we really being transformed into the icons of Christ that we were meant to be? Again and again, Archbishop Nathaniel brings us up short, facing our own responsibility to receive the Word of God and nurture it in our own hearts.

The Sower is Our Savior

This month's issue of SOLIA has many articles about our Church life: the Religious Education Courses, Camp Vatra, AROY Convention news, ARFORA Spotlight, Brotherhood activities. There are the usual administrative matters of birth, death and marriage records, finances, invitations to parish events and some featured articles, Monastery Pilgrimages, "Being the Salt of the Earth," "The Healing Power of the Wounds of Christ."

A religious newspaper, and that is what SOLIA is, the official organ of the Diocese, is the means by which the Bishop keeps in contact with all the faithful and clergy. Its pages of photos, news and articles should live up to the parable of the "good seed."

Sometimes, we too, must re-read the parable of "The Sower" and apply it to our Diocese and ourselves. Are we the hard path that is so crass that the real message of our Lord bounces off of us? Are we the rock which follows "tradition" but without the Spirit of the inner truth of our Church life? Are we the false patch of weeds which pretends to be "Christian" but in reality our interests and our "kingdom", our "treasure is far from the message which our Lord Jesus Christ preached to us? He came for a purpose, to save us. It was not as a "good will visit" or as a "warning" that he came but to call us to respond. He is not an ambassador nor an officer but is Savior. He came to redeem, to gather together, and to collect whomsoever belongs to his Father.

He has not finished speaking or calling. He speaks by the Holy Spirit and through the body of people who respond to his preaching, the Church. The Holy Spirit is that warmth, that necessary moisture, the nutrients that cause growth in receptive souls and hearts.

The parable of the Sower is happening now, and we fall, personally and collectively, into either the category of productivity and salvation or fruitlessness and damnation.

Let's read the news in the SOLIA. Let's read about ourselves and how we occupy our time. Let's read between the lines and draw from what our hearts and souls feel, and paint a picture, an image, an icon of our own lives and present it to our Lord. How do we occupy our time? With what activities? With what fruit?

Will he say: "I recognize you! Welcome into your Father's glory!" or will he state, "Depart from me! I do not recognize you, or your life or your lack of responses to my invitation to salvation!"

Before you take that journey of inner self-reflection and paint your self-icon, you must, we all must, read the wonderful gospel account of the Sower, Jesus God-man who came from the heights of glory and power to plant in the hearts of all men the seed of hope of eternal life and the promise of forgiveness of sins. There are four kinds of souls described in the parable. Take the time, make the short pilgrimage to your heart: read this four times, slowly and in the presence of the All-holy Trinity, Father, Son and Holy Spirit dwelling within you who are the temple of God!

*With His Grace, Bishop Irineu
and some of the faithful,
2007 Episcopate Congress,
Vatra Romaneasca*

8

"Although we hear of financial instability, of depression, of caution, these words cannot affect our financial support for the mission, for evangelization of America. They are not words to frighten the heart of the Orthodox Christian who wants to share something with the church for the service of the Lord."

(February 1988)

"How much should I give? How great is your love for your Savior?"How much can I give? As much as your heart directs!"Who should give? Every person, tiny or mature, the young and elderly, for we are all the church and must lend our strength to God's work."

(February 1989)

Short and to the point – these no-nonsense appeals for Mission Sunday appeared in 1988 and 1989. Their messages are timely after twenty years. Each is less than a half-page long in its original format.

Mission Sunday: A Penny Nail

This is the final copy from many different drafts. The reason for the number of starts? They were too caustic or too wordy, too laudatory or dull.

The topic is MISSION, and there is no subject more wonderful or beautiful to believers, because it is the implementation of the command of our Lord and Savior, Jesus Christ: *"Go out and baptize all nations...make disciples."* You and I are the recipients of other missionaries, of long ago or more recent times, who also wanted to SHARE THE GOOD NEWS and the LOVE OF GOD FOR MAN.

Yes! We really do have missions today, and we really do evangelize today. The process goes on in every parish in a particularly local way. The Diocese, which is the LOCAL CHURCH, reaches out, not in the name of one town or area, but in the name of all the parishes and the Diocese, in the name of Christ.

The work of salvation goes on in the parish life, and the spread of the GOOD NEWS goes on in the life of the Diocese. Parishes generate funding locally through the parish activities, but the Diocese must appeal to the parishes to support the wider movement of mission and outreach. The Diocese has no catering, "fish fries," or money making events; only the appeal to the faithful.

How much should I give? How great is your love for your Savior? How much can I give? As much as your heart directs! Who should give? Every person, tiny or mature, the young and elderly -- we are all the CHURCH and must lend our strength to God's work.

When the collection is made in every parish in our Diocese, we should consider that we are extending our hand to Christ and his message, to the saints who gave their lives to the Lord, to ourselves; for in sharing the Golden Promise of eternal life, we reach out to the world and for the world to come.

Too many words, too few deeds. "For want of a penny the nail was lost; for want of the nail the shoe was lost; for want of a shoe the horse was lost; and, for want of the horse the battle was lost." Christ has won the battle by his power, but we must still be sure the message is carried. Let the donation we make for **MISSION SUNDAY** be our nail in the race for salvation! Let's not lose the Kingdom of heaven for WANT!

9

> "The celebration of the Resurrection is a celebration of a change within us. It is an acknowledged dedication to Christ as God that changes us, lifting us above the crest of the waves of the cares, the shortness and the sorrows of this life to the rock of stability and trust in the presence of God in our world, in his guidance and wise direction."
>
> *(April 1988)*

In this opening editorial for SOLIA, Archbishop Nathaniel reflects on the "Dance of Death" that characterizes our daily lives. He lifts up the example of the apostles, who themselves had to deal with the same daily pressures, demands, fears and hopes that face contemporary man. He takes us out of the fearsome 'Dance of Death' into the gladness of the Resurrection, where we can begin the 'Dance of Life,' hand in hand with our Lord.

The Dance of Life

In centuries past, in those times often referred to by some historians as the "middle ages", there was a strange fascination with death. Plagues, wars, and the "grim reaper" were constant themes of conversation even at the table. Pictured on walls of castles, frescoed on vaults of cathedrals and woven into tapestries was the dance which all must learn: the Dance of Death.

Centuries have passed, walls torn down, medicines discovered, but still our world is not the rejoicing place it ought to be. Our days reflect much of that medieval concern and preoccupation. Stirred up by the clouds of nuclear wars, economic failures and egocentric self-interest, the Dance of Death seems to be piped through our streets. This is in part because we are too identified with this life, with present needs and with futile pursuit of an evasive utopian society conceived by social scientists devoid of belief in anything other than man's own powers.

Then too, as Christians we sometimes celebrate the Resurrection as an historical event, but then we fail to make its message change our lives and our direction. If we embrace the meaning of the feast and apply the promise to our life, we could radiate the joy of the day everyday and everywhere. The Resurrection of Christ was an historical happening, but its power lies in the possibility to change our hearts today.

Among the disciples as they first heard of the empty tomb, there was a great excitement. An exuberant thrill pierced their humble, frightened souls as they heard report after report that: The Lord is risen! A mixture of joy and awe, relief and hope swept over them as they realized the power of the words of the Lord Jesus, the promise of resurrection extended to them. No dull heart was found among them! Men, women and children were bursting with the joyful implications of the empty tomb, the sepulcher that had held Life Itself.

They had to continue to work and get through each day. No sweat was wiped off their brow, no labor foreign to their hands. They were still as much a part of this earth and its toil as before, except the chains of finality, of being held by the fear of death were broken, and no longer were they afraid of life, nor the Dance of Death. Not one of them was unready then and there to burst forth and sing and dance in the streets and by-ways of proud, staid, cold Jerusalem, the haughty capital that rejected her King and Savior. Taken up in earnest by St. Stephen, the Dance of Life, the Dance of the Resurrected One quickened and continues, whirling through ages, skipping through our days, unraveling, bounding over the centuries until it halts triumphantly before the great and awesome judgment seat whereat the lively dancers, led by the Holy Spirit, will bow before the Lord Jesus, the first to leap from the grasp of death!

The celebration of the Resurrection is a celebration of a change within us. It is an acknowledged dedication to Christ as God that changes us, lifting us above the crest of the waves of the cares, the shortness and the sorrows of this life to the rock of stability and trust in the presence of God in our world, in his guidance and wise direction.

There is a single historical resurrection of our Lord Jesus Christ, but there is also a daily spiritual resurrection in us. Like the disciples, we too are called upon, invited, welcomed to take the initial steps of this dance which plays through our lives, echoing in our hearts, reflected in our words, thoughts and deeds, the Dance of Life whose strains ring out: *Christ is risen from the dead, trampling death by death and bestowing life on those in the graves!*

10

"Man, of himself, by himself is for himself, and when he rejects the Word for words, the Image for the imagined, Grace for disgrace, he is indeed a murderer of God in himself, a self-defacing pot. The craftsman always recognizes his work; alas, the work does not always choose to reflect the master. Man, however, is not another piece of "planned obsolescence"."
(March 1989)

When an Islamic court ordered the execution of British novelist Salman Rushdie for offending Islam, Archbishop Nathaniel used the event as a springboard for this wide ranging discussion of such disparate characters as the Emperor Hirohito and Norman Mailer. As always, His Eminence ends by bringing us face to face with Christ, "the Author of the Book and of life."

Death of an Author: Burial of a God

The Western World has recoiled in humanistic horror from the order of Ayatollah Khomeini to execute novelist Salman Rushdie. Members of the Common Market recalled their envoys from Iran in protest. A writer portrayed the revered founder of a religion as an imposter, thus choosing to offend Moslems throughout the world.

Mr. Rushdie's work provoked so much consternation among Moslem nations that he succeeded to unite them in solidarity, a feat unachieved when it came to unity of action in the petroleum production. The consensus judgment calling for the death of the "blasphemer" should have been expected: Mohammed was insulted; Moslems must avenge, or let us say, "defend" the prophet. There is an admirable consistency in their action. Even those larger differences between the sects disappeared in defense of the prophet.

Although "The Last Temptation," the work of Nikos Kazantzakis, caused some ripples in America and the Western World, there was no unified outcry of protest. Some "Christians" were not at all offended; some lashed out in counter offense at the producers, actors, and their associates. There was no unified voice or act in "defense" of Jesus of Nazareth. The heavy pall of humanism suffocated a unified Christian response.

Meanwhile, royalty and officials gathered in far-off Japan to march together behind the weeks-old corpse of Hirohito, Emperor of Japan, a "god" being put to rest. Among them, our own newly inaugurated President took his place, marching in step with others to pay homage to a "god" man. The presence of Mr. Bush may be honoring the Japanese people, but the dead emperor still personifies the nation, much like the Caesars were "divine" representatives of the Roman people.

Shinto rites, hidden behind veils so as not to offend, were chanted and now the son of the emperor assumed, in the eyes of many of his "subjects," the mantle of divinity of his father. Another "god" continues the line.

Mohammed never claimed to be divine, merely the humble prophet of the divine; Hirohito claimed to be divine but did not promise his people eternal life. He lived in the "forbidden city" because he was a "citizen," lived a scholarly life and died and was buried with his ancestors, and with his ancestors will his bones and flesh turn to dust.

Someone once said, "The only two interesting topics to discuss are politics and religion." Man is ultimately concerned both with who governs him in this life and who governs in the next. Because there is a belief in the next life, it is important to defend what one holds to be objective truth, and if religion and politics come into opposition on earth, the believer should cast his lot with the ruler of the world to come.

When Christ came, he clearly stated that the Kingdom of God is among us and that no one rules (or is elected) without the knowledge and intention of his Father. It may be that men appear to govern but "the world is the Lord's and the fullness thereof." There can be no doubt that this world and the next are one, that there is one Ruler and one Truth. Men may choose to enter the ranks of the wrong or losing army, but the Victor has already claimed his honor.

One of America's modern writers, Norman Mailer, in protest to the Iranian threat claimed: "Our religion is our words, good or bad, nice or naughty (I am not quoting exactly)! We can say what we want and that is what religion is for us!" Really! Has objective truth come to be just the shattered shards of Western man's disillusionment with his fallen self? Is the unified adherence to a religion bad because it does claim objective truth? Moslems could not agree with Mailer, nor can Christians for that matter.

Humanism has so permeated our society that where two or three gather together there is only subjectivity, no objectivity, because the gathering is in the name of man, not of God. Hirohito's reign and councils have proved to be void of spirit (one may argue for great material gains, if so inclined) and his divinity an empty cocoon. He will continue to rest, dead among his ancestors. He made no promise to rise nor to raise up, nor to be raised.

A man-god is honored and a prophet dishonored -- such is the fickle road of man: Christ is "recrucified" but overcomes the cross; such is the path to God.

Not all that long ago, the Inquisition forced Jews to "accept" Christ or die because of him. The "crusaders" debauched the sanctuaries of the Church with prostitutes laid out across the holy altars. The end result of the "Renaissance," the "Age of Reason", the "Age of Enlightenment" has brought us death in humanism, rejection of Absolute Truth and deeper inner darkness. Man, of himself, by himself is for himself, and when he rejects the Word for words, the Image for the imagined, Grace for disgrace, he is indeed a murderer of God in himself, a self-defacing pot. The craftsman always recognizes his work; alas, the work does not always choose to reflect the master. Man, however, is not another piece of "planned obsolescence".

Mr. Rushdie! When you play with fire, be prepared to be burned!

Mr. Hirohito! When you claim what is not yours, be prepared to return it!

Mr. Ayatollah! When you accept the prophet but not the Fulfillment of the Prophecies, be prepared for the Prophet!

Mr. Christian! When you no longer bear the sweet yoke, prepare for the "surrender and to be yoked with death"!

We are all authors in this life; we are all buried as "gods". The difference is that there is one Book of Life and one God who is the author of the Book and of life and who is also the Destroyer of death. Let us walk in his procession to arrive at eternal life; let us embrace his word that we may have life on this earth. "Grant us, O Lord, our request for knowledge on this earth and unending life in the age to come."

11

"Christians have always shown their love for the Savior by surrendering to him their lives, their talents and finances. This is, in a few words, stewardship; returning to God all he has bestowed and receiving from him his grace to use his gifts wisely for his service and service to neighbor."
(July 1990)

Archbishop Nathaniel reviews the Episcopate's commitment to assist the newly liberated people of Romania, and reminds us that stewardship is the work of all the saints, past and present.

Stewardship in the Church Through the Ages

In trying to choose a cover for this month's issue of SOLIA, the editors had planned to use a photo of the Congress, quite appropriate for this issue.

Considering the activities of the Clergy Conference, the Episcopate Council and the Congress itself, and knowing the general theme of charity, or service to others and stewardship, we settled on an icon of the "Fellowship of the Holy Physicians."

Christians have always shown their love for the Savior by surrendering to him their lives, their talents and finances. This is, in a few words, stewardship; returning to God all he has bestowed and receiving from him his grace to use his gifts wisely for his service and service to neighbor.

Throughout this year's Congress, presentations were made about medical assistance given by the Episcopate to Romania. With the establishment of the Physicians Advisory Council in Detroit to help the Episcopate in what direction to serve those needs, a new organization came about: National Association of Romanian American Physicians (N.A.R.A.P.).

Dedicated to serve others and to share knowledge and give support to others in the profession, the NARAP will reflect the high calling of physicians and their service to mankind.

Returning to the icon on the cover, we reflected on a few of those famous doctors whose names are repeated through the ages for intercession and remembrance. In the various services of the Church, their names are repeated to remind us that Christian stewardship is not merely giving money but service, time and talents.

The communion of saints is not a magical calling on dead spirits but on reflecting on exemplary lives and in recalling that, in fact, they are alive in Christ and await the resurrection, enjoying now some taste of paradise. If one is dead and there is not resurrection, then they no longer exist. The saints, however, are alive in Christ, and being alive can also hear our prayers, much as we hear one another. Their physical ears may be closed to sound, but their souls respond to our cries.

The first of the physicians, the patron of doctors and artists, is St. Luke the writer of the Gospel; he is "Luke the Evangelist." Born in Antioch in Syria, Luke, a Roman, was an outstanding physician of his city. When he heard the Christian message, he embraced the Physician of Souls and Bodies. He was the traveling companion of St. Paul on his second missionary journey as reported in the Acts of the Apostles. Paul called him the "glorious" physician. His life was eventful, traveling to many cities and using his medical knowledge to serve the brethren. One of the rare few, St. Luke died peacefully at age 84 in Thebes, in Egypt.

Another of the famous saint physicians is Panteleimon who was born in Nicomedia in Asia Minor in 275. His father was a pagan, his mother a Christian. He was a student of one of the most skilled physicians at the imperial court, Euphronios. Working with his teacher, he became known at the court and won the respect of Emperor Maximian. At the time, his practice was outstanding, his healing truly miraculous, and he felt good about his career. Another Christian, Hermolaos however, reminded him that true healing comes from above and that the physician works with God who grants the cure. Realizing this, Panteleimon worked even harder. However, his Christian character was noticed and he was forced to choose between Christ and pagan deities. He was cruelly tortured and beheaded at the age of 29, in the year 304. His feast day is July 27.

Physicians are always respected and always sought after. In this case, there were two, and brothers at that. Cosmos and Damian were born in Asia Minor in the early years of the Church. Born of wealthy parents, given a good classical education, they continued in studying medicine. They agreed, as brothers and physicians, that "healing comes from the Most High" and this, coupled with their skills and piety, made them sought after.

Cosmos and Damian opened up what we would call a clinic and refused payment from rich or poor. They bear the title of "Unmercenaries" for not accepting payment. Like St. Luke, their lives of stewardship to the Church and mankind ended peacefully. Their Feast Day is November 1.

Another of the physician saints and unmercenaries is St. Sampson, not the one of the Old Testament but of the New. A native of Rome, born in the 6th century, Sampson was related to the Emperor Constantine. He had a liberal education by his family. He chose to follow medicine and was observed to be very skilled. He chose to turn his family's estate into a kind of hospital and hospice for the physically incapacitated and mentally ill. He hired a staff and then endowed the hospice with funds from his inheritance.

He traveled to see the city his uncle had raised as the new Rome, Constantinople, going as a tourist. He remained there and was moved to begin his profession on seeing the great number of poor and sick. In time, those who knew him brought him to the attention of the authorities, and when the Emperor Justin, the builder of St. Sophia, was deathly ill, Sampson was called to minister to him. The ruler benefited from his skill and in payment set up a hospital larger than the one Sampson had established in Rome. He continued to work there until his peaceful death on June 27, 598.

Another aspect of Stewardship is that of using relationships well to God's glory. In this instance, the wife of the Emperor Diocletian was a noblewoman who had a sense of obligation to the

Roman people. In her rounds of attending the people and making observations for the Emperor, she heard about a certain young soldier who was being unusually tortured. She visited the man in his cell and heard his story, and she herself was converted by his dedication to the Lord of Hosts.

Embracing this King of kings, Alexandra, the wife of the Emperor, went to her husband and asked him to stop the torture. Angered beyond words at her audacity to use her relationship as empress, he ordered her imprisoned and executed unless she gave up her new faith. She refused and was to be executed with the young soldier. She died in her sleep in prison; the soldier was executed: his name, George.

The stewardship of the saints is a reminder to us and should encourage us to give, too, of all we have to God.

12

"Let us be careful to not think that the mission of the Church is to set up parishes or build churches; it is to save souls."
(February 1991)

With the fall of communism came a flood of immigration to the United States and Canada, and an explosion in the number of missions across the continent. Here, His Eminence reminds us of the true mission of the Church in the world.

Mission Sunday

The very reason for us to exist as a special body called "Church" is to live a new life based on the Lord Jesus Christ and to invite others to also accept him as the basis for their lives. We even identify him as the head of the body and ourselves as limbs that act in his name and live our daily life in awareness of being in his presence.

We have all "put on Christ" like a garment and must have values and a response to life in a unique and powerful way. If we do not believe that we are "different" from others, then we are the same; if we are the same, then we are not Christians, followers of Christ who came to remind us that the ways of man have fallen short of the ideal which God has established. To return to an ideal life, a new life, a life based on Christ and his promises, is a call to a higher existence; but one which is open to all who respond to Christ's invitation to "Follow me!" to those who can also exclaim: "You are the Son of God!"

We are told in Scripture that, "Unless someone tells me, how do I know this way?" In other words, men are seeking the ideal life in Christ but have not been able to identify it without help. Help is twofold: it comes from someone announcing the Good News and from the Holy Spirit who moves the soul to accept this as true. Elsewhere we are told by God: "I loved you even before you loved me . . . I have chosen you; you have not chosen me." God aches to love all mankind, but each person must respond to that love; and, that love must be proclaimed.

Let us be careful to not think that the mission of the Church is to set up parishes or build churches; it is to save souls. We are gathered into local units of believers called "parishes" or "churches," but we do not erect a building and then go out and look to fill it! We build a spiritual temple of souls, of individuals, and then to house that group into local worship units, we can erect buildings. A church building can cease to exist, but the individual human soul has the gift of eternal existence! "What can a man give in exchange for his soul?" As glorious as any house of worship may be, it is of stone and mortar; the human soul created in the image and likeness of God is the most glorious temple in which God is present.

Gone are the days when the faith of individuals was determined by a ruler; gone are the days when nations became Christian with one mass baptism. In the new world, in particular, the individual is surrounded by a multitude of choices or decision to not believe. The body of faithful in the new world must both "tell others" of the promise of Christ by word of preaching and teaching but primarily through the way of life. "See how they love one another!" was the identifying tag on early Christians.

On Sunday, February 24, on the Sunday of Orthodoxy, we are called to remember our true mission in life and to share it with others. The service of vespers on this day is not meant to be kept under a bushel but to be a clarion of the promise of Christ and a statement of truth. How can we be comfortable in attending that service behind closed doors and not bringing the meaning of it into our homes, social and public forum? This Sunday was selected to push us, to encourage us, to wake us up to the real meaning of Church, of Life, of Gospel, of Self.

The Reverend Clergy should preach a simple sermon on the call to follow Christ! Let the pious faithful reflect on their dedication to the Lord and inspect their Christian existence.

We carry the message of the Gospel into the world about us, and to do so we need to send messengers and the message. On this Sunday, a very special collection must be taken to promote the efforts of our Holy Orthodox Church to preach the good news and to go out and bear witness. There is no donation as worthy as that given in God's name to tell others about his love. There is no amount large enough or any too small. But when the collection is made, double the amount which you had first in your mind decided to give. Let your heart and soul respond: "What can I offer to the Lord for all he has done for me?" Double your gift not because you want to receive more, because God gives everything we need. Give because your heart wants to share and to bring others to the Gospel, to a new life and to eternal salvation.

As the collection passes by, let every hand put something into the work of the Church's Mission, both old and young, all members of the family, for each soul will be judged; and besides, each hand has its own wallet.

May God continue to bless us with earthly blessings, give us the promised kingdom and preserve us from the temptation to withhold our meager money from this holy work.

13

"Man cannot heal himself alone; he needs the appropriate Physician, and only God is the one who knows the depths of man's heart and his wounds. Thus it was the Lord Jesus, who is true God, who was born of the Virgin Mary and who thus is also true man, who in his flesh redeemed us, his brothers and sisters in the flesh."

(December 1991)

"Let us, too, like Christ offer ourselves and one another to those who still sit in darkness and who do not yet know the Lord Jesus; and, let us become to them the angel seated on the tomb, crying out to the world around us: Christ is risen from the dead, and he is the savior of the world!"

(April 1992)

In these two Pastoral Letters of the 1991-1992 season, His Eminence radiates the joy of the feasts, and calls us to do likewise. Pastoral letters are meant to be read aloud in the churches at the Festal Divine Liturgy. The writer's exuberance shines through the many quotations and references, and uplifts the listener.

The Nativity of our Lord and God and Savior Jesus Christ, 1991

"The Word of God, Jesus Christ, on account of his great love for mankind, became what we are in order to make us what he is himself."   St. Ireneus: Against Heresies

Dearly Beloved in Christ:
    Christ is born! Let us glorify him!

Once again, God has allowed us to come to these holy days in which we celebrate the birth of his Only-begotten Son and anticipate the revelation of the All-holy Trinity at the Jordan. Thanks and glory to him for this moment!

St. Gregory of Nazianzus exhorts us to keep this feast by recalling it as a "healing," a "re-creation" whereby we are restored to our heavenly Father as his beloved children and heirs to his kingdom. The need for healing and restoring, for a re-creation of what had been damaged by sin and error is present in all generations. Christ died once on the cross but for all generations. All generations need his healing.

"What was the purpose of the Incarnation," states St. Ambrose of Milan, "but this – that the flesh which sinned should be redeemed by itself." The great love, of which St. Ireneus speaks, is echoed in the words of St. Athanasius the Great. "By becoming man, the Savior was to accomplish two works of love: first, in putting away death from us and renewing us again; secondly, being unseen and invisible, in manifesting and making himself known by his works to be the Word of the Father, and the Ruler and King of the universe."

Man cannot heal himself alone; he needs the appropriate Physician, and only God is the one who knows the depths of man's heart and his wounds. Thus it was the Lord Jesus, who is true God, who was born of the Virgin Mary and who thus is also true man, who in his flesh redeemed us, his brothers and sisters in the flesh. What went astray gets into the right path; fallen flesh is healed in itself. Who went astray, Adam, is led back and re-created in the person of Jesus Christ, the new Adam, the Physician of our bodies and souls.

Returning to St. Ireneus's theme, we hear from the lips of St. Peter that God "has given us the guarantee of something very great and wonderful to come; . . . you will be able to share in the divine nature." (2 Pet. 1:4) From our simple humanity, we are promised to be lifted up to the heights of sharing in God's own nature. Thus, not only are we given immortality, as St. Athanasius said, but we are renewed here and now; we are healed, participating in the divine nature.

Again, St. Gregory reminds us that man needed " . . . a stronger remedy, a greater aid – the Word of God Himself. He assumes the poverty of my flesh that I may assume the richness of his Godhead. He partakes of my flesh that he may both save the image and make the flesh immortal." Thus, by taking on our human flesh, our wounded nature, and uniting it to the divine nature which heals, creates, restores, Jesus Christ, the Word of God, has broken down the wall between heaven and earth, between the Creator and the created, between the Father and his children.

Indeed, we celebrate this holy feast of the Birth of our Lord and God and Savior, Jesus Christ, as the beginning of the restoration of man, of the healing of his wounded nature, as the day of giving glory to God as did the angelic choir, the shepherds and wise men. We also celebrate that we must live our life "according to the Christ we have received, Jesus the Lord" (Col. 2:6). We must actively participate in our healing, in the re-creation not just of man, but of the universe co-working with God as he leans down from heaven, and we stretch upward from the earth. As sons and daughters of the Most High, we are called to share with others this news, this good message of peace from above and good will on earth.

The news is old from the fall of Adam that a savior would come; it is fresh because Jesus came in the fullness of time, and what we celebrate is not a past event but an ongoing action which generates new life and hope to all mankind. The words of the Archangel Gabriel to the Blessed Virgin resound as fresh today as yesteryear: "You are to conceive and bear a son and you must name him Jesus," (Luke 1:32) " . . . because he is the one who is to save his people from their sins" (Mt. 1:22).

To him, with the Father and the Holy Spirit be eternal glory!

Paschal Letter 1992

To the Pious Clergy and Faithful of the Romanian Orthodox Episcopate of America
"Rejoice, O people, and be glad! The angel seated on the stone of the tomb announced the news to us, saying: Christ is risen from the

dead. He is the savior of the world and has filled everything with a fragrant aroma. Rejoice, o people, and be glad!
Praises, Tone 2, Bright Monday

Christ is Risen!

Dearly Beloved in Christ:

This holy and festive celebration is ours! It belongs to those who believe in God and in the resurrection of the Lord Jesus from among the dead. God has been merciful to us and blessed us, and he has shown his face to us again. Let us rejoice, indeed, and be glad in spiritual joy and with heavenly gladness.

St. Gregory Nazianzus reminds us: "We were created to be happy. We were made happy when we were created. We were entrusted with Paradise that we might enjoy life," *(2nd Paschal Oration)*. God in Three Persons, Father, Son and Holy Spirit, created man in his image and likeness, and we were made to be happy! *(Gen. 1:26 f)*.

He continues, however, explaining how it was that we were cast out of that paradise: "We were cast out because we transgressed. We needed an Incarnation of God, a God put to death, that we might live. We were put to death together with him, that we might be cleansed; we rose again with him, because we were put to death with him; we were glorified with him, because we rose again with him."

The author of Romans states: " . . . people are without excuse; they knew God and yet refused to honor him as God or thank him . . . they have given up divine truth for a lie and worshipped and served creatures instead of the Creator" (1:21/24); and, "Both Jew and pagan sinned and forfeited God's glory, and both are justified through the free gift of his grace by being redeemed in Christ Jesus who was appointed by God to sacrifice his life, so as to win reconciliation through faith" (3:24/25).

Jesus Christ, "the Word was with God and the Word was God" (Jn1:1), was himself immortal and could not die; but, says St. Athanasius, "he took to himself a body such as could die, that he might offer it as his own in the stead of all, and as suffering through his union with it, on behalf of all" (Incarnation #20). "The Savior came to accomplish not his own death, but the death of men," says St. Athanasius. Thus, the sacrifice of our Lord Jesus reconciled us to God whom we had refused to honor or thank, and bestows on us the right to once again rejoice and be glad!

From St. Cyril of Jerusalem, the Holy City of the Lord, we are reminded: "Let mourning be turned into gladness and lamentation into joy; and let our mouth be filled with joy and gladness, because of him who after his resurrection said: 'Rejoice'!" (Resurrection Sermon).

So we see that the resurrection is like a new creation for us, and the happiness once lost has been restored. But only those who know Christ crucified can know Christ resurrected, and only those who know of the resurrection have true joy and gladness in their lives.

Dearly Beloved:

Let us reflect the joy of this day not only at this moment but through the days of our lives. Let thoughts and our hearts rest on the treasure given us, reconciliation with God and the gift of eternal life. Let us, too, like Christ offer ourselves and one another to those who still sit in darkness and who do not yet know the Lord Jesus; and, let us become to them the angel seated on the tomb, crying out to the world around us: Christ is risen from the dead, and he is the savior of the world!

Truly He is risen!

14

"It is outrageous that a woman should be forced to walk down a church aisle to approach a man standing, waiting for her and who has just experienced the debauchery, the drunkenness and whoring which is the usual central part of such a misogynist event as a Stag party. This usually takes place the very night before the ceremony!"
(March 1993)

On occasion, a leader is called to abandon euphemism and suggestion. Here His Eminence denounces, in no uncertain terms, the unchristian and demeaning practices common at stag parties.

Editorial:
The "Time Honored Stag"

Couples are busy preparing for upcoming marriages, including making arrangements with the parish priest for the Sacrament of Holy Matrimony. In addition, there are many other preparations for wedding attire, photographs, orchestra and reception. Often, these preparations are confused with being the primary preparation for the wedding.

The requirements of the Church are very simple. It is these other civilities, which are considered to be the important part of a wedding, which demand the most time, money and can sap one's energy. Some of these preparations seem to be incumbent on the bride, others on the groom.

If we can be honest, we would recognize that these preparations can become out-of-hand, demanding so much from a couple that the actual day of the wedding is almost a "trial" or "endurance test." Life becomes a marathon of "getting through the wedding!" Parents' lives are affected, too: "We can't do anything this year; we're having a wedding!"

We don't deny that preparations are necessary and hospitality is proper and fine. Let's even remind ourselves of the Lord's own joy at being present at the wedding in Cana of Galilee along with his mother and his disciples. His first public acts revealing his divine powers and compassion took place in the presence of that blessed young couple (whose names we do not even know). Weddings should be wonderful! Marriages should last!

The Orthodox Sacrament of Holy Matrimony and its ritual are steeped in meaning and are full of the power of the All Holy Trinity. However, the Orthodox in America have been greatly influenced by other traditions which have their basis in their own meaning and concept of marriage; some are harmless but others are downright poisonous!

One such custom is "Giving the Bride Away." The father takes his daughter on his arm to the altar and "gives" her to her husband to be. In Western Europe, this meant that the father was the guarantor of his daughter's virginity and he took care of her, she depended on him and he bears her on his arm to the very last moment. That is also why he lifts the veil and may kiss her good-bye. He is "taking the wraps" off her, so to speak, showing her in public as marriageable and pure. She was guarded and kept safe until this moment. The father walking the bride down the aisle is a part of this same "guarantee" ritual.

Wearing white is also part of that culture; white is a symbol of purity, virginity. In Eastern Europe, wedding garments were usually colorful and were prepared by the bride herself years in advance. There was no question that she was virgin. Clothes, however, made no difference. In other words, the Church makes no demands on the bride to wear this or to wear that; to spend this much or that. This is a personal and subjective decision.

On to the point of this article! Although we Orthodox do have our own bridal procession with the groom and bride coming together into the church, and although we do have a fixed ceremony, some clergy try not to "rock the boat"; and, they might "bend" to allowing other traditions. We have long experienced that, among other sacramental occasions, a wedding can create havoc in the ranks of the parish's families and friends because of the insistence of the family on incorporating other than Orthodox traditions.

One of the pre-marital events with which the groom is solely involved is the Stag. It is, however, one of the more important events that few attend and yet which certainly can have a negative effect on a marriage. The title of this article is "The Time Honored Stag." The use of the adjective, 'time honored' refers to practice and not to value. There is no honor in a stag party. If there is one non-Orthodox wedding-related event which has been adopted in America, which should be rejected and abolished, the "STAG" is it!

It is outrageous that a woman should be forced to walk down a church aisle to approach a man standing, waiting for her and who has just experienced the debauchery, the drunkenness and whoring which is the usual central part of such a misogynist event as a Stag party. This usually takes place the very night before the ceremony! How can a serious man expect his wife-to-be to lift her veil to him who has just come in from whoring? How can a father-in-law be so hypocritical as to give his daughter over to a person who has sleep in his eyes, has booze on his breath and whose mind and heart are in a state of confusion?

Furthermore, what kind of person could think to arrange such activities for the groom who is about to join himself to the woman of his life, to be united in one flesh and spirit and to whom he will shortly and in public promise fidelity? The groom's "Best Man?" "Friends?" Come on! There is no honesty there!

There are horror stories locked in the hearts and minds of countless men who later regret what happened on the Stag night, and they have no way to forget this. They bear in their lives the scars of unfaithfulness from the beginning, and their wives must also carry much hurt. Yes, they can confess their sins. But how can one repent beforehand, and if there is repentance, there cannot be sinning! The night before? A week before? Pre-planned whoring?!

Even if there is no whore as part of the night's activities, there are films, stories, drink and other activities which are not appropriate to the pre-wedding event. There is no consideration given to honest preparation for the Sacrament that is about to be bestowed. Sincerely, though, something similar can probably be said about the bride's lack of spiritual preparation for the Sacrament on the day previous to her wedding.

How can an Orthodox believer, a Christian, plan such a despicable event while anticipating the Holy Sacrament? This is an outrageous thing and one that must stop. God cannot be mocked. These "normal" premarital preparations are mere indications that we are sometimes more concerned over the externals than the substance. Do we want to be guilty of abusing the sacraments which God himself has established for us?

The high rate of divorce and instability in modern marriages attests to a lack of trust, love and respect between the partners. A Stag is an event that reflects a pre-existing basis for this lack of honesty between the promised pair.

Unrealistic? Anachronistic? Un-American? Priggish? It seems to me that we should all reflect on the baseness of this "dishonorable" stag event, that we must consider, first things first, and the kingdom of God. Do we really want our marital unions to be Holy? Do we not know that God is present wherever we are, even at a Stag? Would we invite our bride to be present at this event? Why not, if we are about share everything

Some traditions we can live with; some kill us. Let's be more serious and reject the stag as stupid and stagnant!

15

"We are to live our lives where we find ourselves and to do so in the cognizance of the real presence of God. The Romanian proverb, "The person sanctifies the place," rings true. We must offer back to him our lives lived according to those commands: offer back to him our places of habitation, recreation, and work, not just the obvious offering of dedicated places of worship."

(July 1993)

His Eminence's words in this article call us to sanctify the nation in real, lived ways. He holds up the mission of the Church before us, and reminds us that her mission is real, here and now for us, just as it is real for all persons in all nations.

The Incarnation and Independence Day

From our vantage point at Vatra Romaneasca during our annual Church Congress, it is difficult for us to ascertain how the rest of the country celebrates Independence Day. Are there parades? Fireworks? Picnics? Is it a time of reflection on freedom and liberty and the "American Dream"? Does the Fourth of July still have the mystique and power to create a wholesome sense of national spirit and unity among the myriad citizens of various ethnic origins? Is it just a holiday and a day off work?

Most of our debates at the Church Congress may appear to have to do with "Us" and "Ours". In fact, the reality of the problems of the rest of the nation seem to not be a part of our Church Congress considerations nor for that matter of our everyday lives. We are concerned with OUR parishes and national auxiliaries, with the rights and duties of OUR parishioners, council members and auxiliaries.

Does this mean that the Church and our organizations are, in fact, "detached" from the everyday world, the "real world" in which we live, and indifferent to its needs?

With the Incarnation of God into our human world, and the refining of the Ten Commandments into the basic, "Love God First" and "Love Your Neighbor As You Want To Be Loved," the Church is plunged into the necessary sanctification of our world and the resolution of its problems through this message.

We are to live our lives where we find ourselves and to do so in the cognizance of the real presence of God. The Romanian proverb, "The person sanctifies the place," rings true. We must offer back to him our lives lived according to those commands: offer back to him our places of habitation, recreation, and work, not just the obvious offering of dedicated places of worship.

Underlying this restored and refined view of life is the true concept of freedom and liberty, of duty and responsibility based not on flexible and fluctuating human political or philosophical decisions, but on the sublime fact of the Incarnation of Jesus Christ and the true liberation he bestowed on humanity through his cross and death. True freedom is freedom from all sin that distorts God's plan for us. The Church, as his body, must proclaim this freedom.

While political freedom and material growth are gifts to be appreciated; and, when good, can be ascribed to the grace of God working in people of good will, these mundane realities and earthly blessings must be seen in light of the lasting gifts bestowed by the Incarnation.

True freedom enables us to go forward and empowers the Church to share this knowledge of God's plan of restoration of all mankind through grace. True freedom does not allow for walls or barriers, human weakness or intellectual superiority. It acknowledges only the power of the Holy Spirit which penetrates all walls, real and erected through prejudices; the power which elevates that which is weak and reduces human sophisms to muteness by the experienced depth of God's compassion and love toward all peoples, all nations, all times.

In this issue of SOLIA, we read of the power of God at work in believers, in individuals and parishes, in the diocese and the Church universal. We can see that the work of the Church and at the Congress will not be enacted in isolation. Reflecting on the theme of America's political liberty celebrated on the Fourth of July, we need to remind ourselves of the two-sided gift of freedom and responsibility, of duty and love, of individual and collective oneness of purpose from God himself, the gift which has been bestowed on us, true and lasting freedom and liberty and which we celebrate daily in our lives as Christians, bearers of Christ.

Political changes in government, in Romania, have allowed the Church to re-establish her previous and wider scope of activities of educating, serving the needy and bringing to the fore, the call of Christ to sanctify the nation. We know that these political steps are meager, and we look to and are vigilant for more developments. The Episcopate continues her support of the Romanian people through the Department of Assistance and Help for Romania as can be read in the article by V. Rev. Richard Grabowski.

On the other hand, the letter of our Holy Synod calls for a ceasing of all political aggression in the former Yugoslavia where religious differences are being used as an excuse against citizens even though the hierarchs of the Orthodox, Roman Catholic and Muslim faiths have spoken out against the war. Sanctification of a particular nation must include all its citizenry.

"A Long Way Home" is the account of a man and his family to find the Orthodox Way, the Worship, the Praise of God as the true basis for life and the unfolding of day-to-day existence in the presence of the Almighty. Fred Farnow's pilgrimage to the altar of Orthodox Christianity is one which sheds light to those searching and which enkindles in those who have the "Pearl of Great Price", the radiant luster of their faith.

A short article, "Bishop Policarp's Gramata Comes Home," induces a sort of nostalgia for the "beginnings", for those early formative and hopeful years of the Episcopate under its first spiritual shepherd. Although there were good and dedicated priests and laity who, in the beginning, established the parishes, it is a fundamental principle that without the hierarchy, the Church is not the Church. The Holy Synod of the Orthodox Church in Romania sent Policarp as the first bishop for Romanian Orthodox outside of Romania. His house arrest kept him from returning to his flock. The return of Policarp's gramata to the Vatra by its "protectors" signals a perception of normalcy in the making, of picking up loose threads to weave a new fabric of fraternal cooperation and ecclesiastical recognition.

Radu Gyr's poem "DAYS", the 8th in our series of *Poems from Communist Prisons,* could well have been written by many who, although not physically imprisoned, are spiritually incarcerated, without hope, without the freedom through faith in the Lord Jesus. One may be bound behind bars, but one's faith can give free flight to the soul to the uppermost realms; one tied to sin and hopelessness is dragged to darkness, despair.

The Romanian language section has an article by Fr. Nicolae Barsan, a regular contributor to SOLIA. "Love for Neighbor" is as necessary for New York City, where Fr. Nicolae resides, as it was for Jerusalem, Samaria and is for the world today. This is the unique kernel of the Christian faith: to love God first and to love one's neighbor and even one's enemy as one wishes to be loved, treated, respected. A tangible witness to one's freedom in Christ is the ability to love one's neighbor and one's enemy for the sake of the name of Jesus.

Also in Romanian, "The Power of Holy Unction" tells of a recent exorcism, January 24-29, 1993, of a woman possessed. The holy fathers of the Monastery of Sihastria served the holy mystery over this woman. Throughout the services, the argumentations of the demons left little doubt of their fear of the power of Christ Jesus over their powers of darkness. Are there demons today? Do we Orthodox Christians really believe that evil spirits exist in persons and are not figments of the imagination or "folk tales or myths?" This article reminds us that Satan is real, that he does not sleep, nor is he myth or folklore.

The work of transfiguring the world goes on through the efforts of each of the faithful, through the power of the sacramental life, through the presence of the Holy Spirit. With or without governments' support or non-interference; with or without a homogeneous citizenry, the Gospel ferments and raises, lifts and transfigures. The Incarnation of the Lord Jesus Christ is the basis for the Independence Day celebration. If the founding fathers were not all "theists", they certainly were aware that good will and human talents transform the political world; and, this is part of the plan of the Almighty, to use good will and human talents as a springboard for a restored world. For those who do believe, we know that whatever is done is done by knowledge of God; and, whatever we do, we do in synergy with him.

16

"We all steal from God and from the Church; some steal time, by not ever giving of ourselves for the benefit of the Church. Some steal the beneficial activities of the Church by participating in what others organize but not offering our own talents and assistance. Some steal salvation, thinking that they will be saved only through baptism and without good works."

(April 1994)

The problem of theft in the churches is taken up in this article. Far from pretending the problem is nonexistent, His Eminence faces it squarely and openly, denouncing stealing as sin against Christ Himself.

Stealing from the Church

Among the Ten Commandments given by God to Moses on Mt. Sinai is that one which states very simply, "You shall not steal" (Ex. 20:15). Stealing is loathsome; it is underhanded, dishonest, unkind, unprofitable, and selfish. No one likes a thief nor does anyone want to be associated with a thief.

In Acts of the Apostles, Chapter 5, the account is given about a husband, Ananias and wife, Sapphira, members of the apostolic community who commit fraud, a form of stealing and lying. The story is worth reading in its entirety.

"There was a Levite of Cypriot origin called Joseph whom the apostles surnamed Barnabas. He owned a piece of land and he sold it and brought the money, and presented it to the apostles.

There was another man, however, called Ananias. He and his wife, Sapphira, agreed to sell a property; but with his wife's connivance he kept back part of the proceeds, and brought the rest and presented it to the apostles. 'Ananias,' Peter said, 'how can

Satan have so possessed you that you should lie to the Holy Spirit and keep back part of the money from the land? While you still owned the land, wasn't it yours to keep and after you sold it wasn't the money yours to do with as you liked? What put this scheme into your mind? It is not to men that you have lied but to God.'

When he heard this Ananias fell down dead. This made a profound impression on everyone present. The younger men got up, wrapped the body in a sheet, carried it out and buried it.

About three hours later his wife came in, not knowing what had taken place. Peter challenged her, 'Tell me, was this the price you sold the land for?' 'Yes,' she said 'that was the price.' Peter then said, 'So you and your husband have agreed to put the Spirit of the Lord to the test! What made you do it? You hear those footsteps? They have just been to bury your husband; they will carry you out, too.' Instantly she dropped dead at his feet. When the young men came in they found she was dead, and they carried her out and buried her by the side of her husband. This made a profound impression on the whole Church and on all who heard it" (Acts 4:36, 5:1-11).

After each death, the Scripture states: "This made a profound impression on everyone present," and, "This made a profound impression on the whole Church and on all who heard it."

The Scripture account is not made up; it is not a "lesson" story fabricated for us. From the concern for details given by the author, we can ascertain that this really took place.

St. Peter's main concern was not about the funds but about the spiritual "death" of the couple. In lying against the Church, in cheating the Church, they sinned against God and thus put their eternal salvation into jeopardy. They had committed a form of spiritual "suicide."

I believe that what made the impact on the listeners is that the couple died before they could repent. The early Christians understood that people do break God's commandments and that God, in his great mercy, calls each to repent. The listeners were impressed, however, that this couple did not have "time" to repent; the "luxury" of "doing it tomorrow" was not theirs!

Perhaps this account should be read more often in Church.

If the Church were a mere social club, then misappropriation (the nicer word we use for "stealing") would be an insult only to fellow members. But the Church is the extension in time and space of Christ; and, the insult and affront of stealing is against the Lord who was himself sold by one of his own apostles for thirty pieces of silver!

We all steal from God and from the Church; some steal time, by not ever giving of ourselves for the benefit of the Church. Some steal the beneficial activities of the Church by participating in what others organize but not offering our own talents and assistance. Some steal salvation, thinking that they will be saved only through baptism and without good works.

Some actually steal goods from the Church: from the collection plate, from the kitchen, funds from established accounts. How can the Church protect herself from herself, that is, from her own members?

Like St. Peter, we need to say, 'Why?' We need to be careful neither to put the Spirit of God to the test nor to make light of our eternal salvation. We put God to the test by saying, "I'm not going to die if I do such and such a thing!" and "I'm not so important that he cares about what is happening here at this moment, this place, this act." God does care.

God is just, and his love for his Church knows no bounds as we know from the fact that "God so loved the world that he gave his only begotten Son, so that whosoever believes in him will not perish but have everlasting life" (John 3:16). The Lord Jesus died on the cross and redeemed mankind out of love, not out of obligation.

In Scripture, it says that God loved us before we could ever love him. He chose us; we did not choose him. Such love, such concern demands a dignified, honest, loving response.

Perhaps, in the end, our belief in the afterlife is not strong? Perhaps, we believe that our actions are not precious to and seen by God? Perhaps, we have become so much a part of the world, which does not know the Ten Commandments, that we, ourselves, see them as "old fashioned", and even "anachronistic?"

Let us take this time of the Great Fast to make use of the right moment in which we can repent. Let us reflect on the value of what we desire and where our heart finds its true interest. Let us be peaceful in the knowledge that God gives us all we need, and we can provide for ourselves and respect him, his Holy Church and one another without stealing from the Church.

May these holy days bring you the sweetness of joy in the Lord.

17

"The By-Laws clearly state that 'By virtue of his or her baptism and chrismation, an individual is a member of the Holy Orthodox Church ... To become a voting member of a Parish, a baptized and/or chrismated Orthodox Christian man or woman...'."

(October 1995)

The issue of women's participation and voting in parish assemblies and the Episcopate Congress continues to demand attention. In 1995, His Eminence reminded the faithful that voting rights do not belong to men alone.

Women in the Church Congress

Years ago, the Episcopate Congresses made certain that on the parish level the youth of the Church were "ex officio" represented at the Parish Council meetings in the person of the AROY local chapter president. Likewise, the women of the parish were represented, "ex officio", by the president of the ARFORA auxiliary.

On the Diocesan level, the Congresses insured that all the women of the Episcopate were represented by the president of the ARFORA, "ex officio", on the Episcopate Council.

The By-Laws clearly state that "By virtue of **his** or **her** baptism and chrismation, an individual is a **member** of the Holy Orthodox Church ... To become a **voting member** of a Parish, a baptized and/or chrismated Orthodox Christian man or woman...".

We reviewed the parish mandates for delegates and alternates for the Church Congress 1995-97 and found the ratio of

men and women delegates and alternates elected to represent their parishes as follows:
> **37 US parishes:**
>> 15 women delegates (two are preotese) of 74;
>> 22 women alternates (two are preotese) of 74;
>
> **Total of 37 from a possible 148.**
> **10 Canadian parishes:**
>> 6 women delegates of 20;
>> 7 women alternates of 20;
>
> **Total of 13 from a possible 40.**

From a **possible 94 delegates,** there are **21 women;** from a **possible 94 alternates,** there are **29 women;** Total **possible 188 delegates and alternates,** there are **50 women.**

The number of women counted at the **1995 Congress** representing **US parishes** were **8**, one of whom is a preoteasa; for the **Canadian parishes, 4**; a **total of 12 delegates** plus three for the ARFORA. **"Grand" total of 15 women voting in the Congress of a possible 94** male/female delegates.

Perhaps women do not readily accept nomination to be delegates; perhaps they are not even nominated. Is the low ratio due to the fact that there are fewer female voting members in the parishes?

According to general health statistics, women do outlive men, indicating that the actual number of female members should be higher than the number of males.

The scope of this editorial is to remind individuals and parishes that any woman, 18 and older, has the right to become a voting member in any parish; and, as such, is eligible to be elected as a delegate or alternate to the Church Congress. No parish may deny voting membership to any person because they are female. On the contrary, every parish should make the effort to increase membership, making an active drive to invite every 18 year old to become a "voting member" of the parish.

The practice of "family" membership is not acceptable, if this means that a woman may not vote in any parish assembly. Some parishes allow two votes but consider the dues to the Episcopate as being "one," a "family" membership. Double standards, for sure! Some individual families think that it is enough if the male partner of the marriage "pays dues" and votes in the name of the family. In all cases of membership in a parish and thus, in the Diocese, the Episcopate By-Laws prevail.

We need to take a mature Christian view of financial support of the Church: "cutting corners" is not such a Christian attitude. Every Christian is responsible for supporting the Church with time, talent and treasure. By refusing to individually support the Church, we are refusing to help in the Lord's work, the same Lord from whom we demand that he listen to our needs and goals and **answer them! Now!**

With the new By-Laws, Article III, Section 2, "Lay delegates and Alternates...cannot be elected either as Delegate or Alternate Delegate for a third consecutive two-year term." Perhaps the time has come when more women will become voting members, thus broadening the possible number of women eligible for delegate election and participation in the Church Congresses and Episcopate Council.

We invite the women of our diocese to reflect on the privileges available to them through the Episcopate By-laws, privileges reflecting an honest Scriptural and traditional basis of more active membership in the Church.

18

"This is why our life in the Church, the communion of all believers in the one Body, is so important. We are strengthened by one another in the unity of the faith, worshiping together with one voice and one mind not only during the holy services, but in the service of our daily life. "Let us offer ourselves and one another to Christ our God." This is why there must be peace and harmony in the Church, for the Holy Spirit unifies, but the self-love in us thrusts us toward division and disunity."

(April 1999)

His Eminence points to the Resurrection as the manifestation of God's perfect love for us. He warns us against our own imperfect, often misdirected love, and calls us all to unity in the Faith and harmony as we work out our own salvation, preaching the Gospel by the example of our own lives.

Paschal Pastoral Letter 1999

To our beloved clergy, monastics and pious faithful of our God-protected Episcopate, Grace, mercy and peace from God and from us our fatherly love and hierarchal blessing.

Christ is risen! Truly, He is risen!

Dearly Beloved:
On this wonderful day of days and festival of festivals, all creation is celebrating the triumph of humility over pride, of righteousness over sin, of light over darkness, of love over hate, of life over death, of immortality over mortality. We are celebrating God's gift to his creation, the restoration of the fallen world. At the first creation, the All-Holy Trinity, Father, Son and Holy Spirit,

out of love, created all that exists. A fundamental gift from God to man was the endowment of free will which included willful service to God. God is love, and love does not force. The response to love, however, is embracing the other with service, to "do unto others as you would have done to you."

Adam chose not to serve the God who loves but exult himself, placing himself before his creator. Thus, pure love was thwarted by self-love, and self-love is the foundation of human sin. "Sin entered the world through one man, and through sin death, and thus death has spread through the whole human race because everyone has sinned" (Romans 5:12). Sin means to place oneself before others, and in particular, before the Creator, Savior and Sanctifier.

The result and inheritance of Adam's sin has been mortality to his descendants and disorder in the natural world. The enemy of mankind is death itself, but death will not exist forever. "After that will come the end, when (Christ) hands over the kingdom to God the Father...and the last of the enemies to be destroyed is death, for everything is to be put under his feet" (1 Corinthians 15:24, 25).

Belief in a resurrection was not invented in the apostolic age. Some ancient peoples believed in one form or another of an after-life. In the Hebrew tradition, many of the prophets spoke of the resurrection as an event to come, while others who were empowered by God through their intercession before the Throne of the Almighty, resurrected the dead.

Remember Ezekiel's prophecy of the dry bones in chapter 37:3, 13: "(God) said to (Ezekiel): "Son of man, can these bones live?' I said, 'You know Lord God'...And you will know that I am the Lord God when I open your graves and raise you from your graves, my people." Recall what Isaiah foretells in chapter 26:19: "Your dead will come to life, their corpses will rise; awake, exult, all you who lie in the dust, for your dew is a radiant dew and the land of ghosts will give birth."

But not only is there prophecy in the Old Testament time but actual resurrections by those chosen by God. Elijah speaks of his raising the son of the widow of Zarephath in Sidon. "Lord God, do you mean to bring grief to the widow who is looking after me by killing her son? ...The Lord heard the prayer of Elijah and the soul of the child returned to him again and he revived...'Look,'

Elijah said, 'your son is alive.' And the woman replied, 'Now I know you are a man of God and the word of Yahweh in your mouth is truth itself'." (3 Kings 17:20-24)

The successor to Elijah, Elisha, also raised the dead. "Elisha then went to the house, and there on his bed lay the child, dead. He went in and shut the door on the two of them and prayed to the Lord...When (the mother) came to him, he said, 'Take up your son'." (4 Kings, 4:32, f)

The power given to the prophets was the power of the Son of God who himself has the power to raise the dead. Luke the Evangelist states: "...it happened that a dead man was being carried out for burial, the only son of his mother and she was a widow...When the Lord saw her he felt sorry for her...and he said, 'Young man, I tell you to get up.' And the dead man sat up and began to talk, and Jesus gave him to his mother" (7:14).

Just days before his crucifixion, Jesus raised Lazarus who had been buried four days. "Meanwhile a large number of Jews heard that (Jesus) was there and came not only on account of Jesus but also to see Lazarus whom he had raised from the dead" (John 12:9).

Thus, we come to understand that our own belief in the resurrection has come through the ages. Now, Christ himself, who raised the dead, allowed himself to be put to death so that he could encounter death as an innocent man, free from sin, and by his just state free us from the authority, the power, the sting of death.

In seizing Christ, death took that which was not its to take and thus its "right," its "privilege," was destroyed, because the right of death over man was due to man's guilt. Christ was guilt-free, and thus death was guilty of injustice. Christ was obedient to the Father, sin-free and thus, as a new Adam, he gave to those who believe in him the right to be born anew, to become sin-free through baptism and to be death-free in observing his commandments and returning his love.

As the seed which is dry has the potential of life after it has been cast down into the earth, so, too, we who are of the earth have the potential of eternal life after the universal resurrection. "I tell you solemnly, when all is made new and the Son of Man sits on his throne of glory, ...and everyone who has left houses, brothers, sisters, father, mother, children or land for the sake of my name will be repaid a hundred times over, and also inherit eternal life" (Matthew 19:28-29).

Thus, today, we rejoice for we have been re-routed from the contorted path toward annihilation to the certain expressway to eternity. "For God sent his Son into the world not to condemn the world, but so that through him the world might be saved" (John 3:17). The Kontak Hymn of Tone 7 wonderfully encapsulates the expression of universal rejoicing in Christ's victory over Adam's sin and mortality's claim over mankind:

"The dominion of death can no longer hold man captive, for Christ descended, shattering and destroying its powers! Hades is bound. The prophets together rejoice, for the Savior stood before them and said to those who believe: O you faithful! Come out to resurrection!"

There will be, before being clothed with immortality, a judgment of worthiness. Christ warns us: "Do not be surprised at this, for the hour is coming when the dead will leave their graves at the sound of his voice; those who did good will rise again to life; and those who did evil, to condemnation" (John 5:28-29). "Then (the Son of Man) shall answer, 'I tell you solemnly, insofar as you neglected to do this to one of the least of these, you neglected to do it to me.' And they will go away to eternal punishment, and the virtuous to eternal life." (Matthew 25:45-46)

"Brothers, put it this way: flesh and blood cannot inherit the kingdom of God; and the perishable cannot inherit what lasts forever...the dead will be raised, imperishable, and we shall be changed as well, because our present perishable nature must put on imperishability, and this mortal nature must put on immortality" (1 Corinthians 15:50, 52-3).

Inasmuch as we bear in us the tendency to be self-centered, whether we are married or single, with offspring or barren, we must be careful of self-love or exaggerated, distorted love for others. True belief in God's word and promise can be stymied in our hearts. We can become so concerned for success in this world and engrossed in the material life that the resurrection of our Lord, which is the promise of the universal resurrection, can become to us a matter of indifference, insignificance, and we may be living in denial of it. In this manner, we are also living in denial of our own resurrection.

Belief in the resurrection demands of us patience and the effort of renewal, return to God, restoration of his image in us. We are called to work out our salvation by our faith and life in Christ empowered by his grace in the Sacramental life of the Church. We hold that all humanity will be resurrected to eternal life or eternal damnation, the choice being made by each of us in this earthly existence.

This is why our life in the Church, the communion of all believers in the one Body, is so important. We are strengthened by one another in the unity of the faith, worshiping together with one voice and one mind not only during the holy services but in the service of our daily life. "Let us offer ourselves and one another to Christ our God." This is why there must be peace and harmony in the Church, for the Holy Spirit unifies, but the self-love in us thrusts us toward division and disunity.

The Church, the Body of Believers whose living head is Christ himself, cannot be thought of as merely an association or a building or institution, but as a living organism, which renews, restores, and cleanses its members on a continuous basis. There is no moment that is not precious to our salvation, and there is no action that does not weigh heavy on this reality. Neither mediocrity nor indifference has a place in the Church. "I have this complaint to make: you have less love now than you used to" (Rev. 2:4).

It is to be strengthened as one that together and aloud we recite the Symbol of faith, said by the entire body of worshipers, for we all confess: "I look for the resurrection of the dead and the life of the world to come! Amen!"

"Christ God, the giver of life, with his life-creating hand, raised all the dead from the depths of darkness. He bestowed resurrection on the human race for he is the Savior, the resurrection, the life and God of all."

Christ bestows resurrection, which is a gift. Because of our free will, we may accept or refuse this gift. We know by faith that the universal resurrection is a predicted divine act, one which is not open to anyone as a choice. It will happen. One can choose to be with God or not, to be in light or to plunge into darkness, to be alive in Christ or remain dead in oneself. We acknowledge that we are still in warfare with our self and with the fallen world in which we live. Satan is not dead, but he has no power other than that which we forfeit to him. "The prince of this world is on his way. He has no power over me..." (John 14:30).

Jesus Christ has conquered. We have heard the good news. We trust in the truth of this notification, and we must patiently and with grace live our lives in anticipation of our own death and burial in prelude to the universal resurrection and restoration to the Father through Jesus Christ.

Today the scoreboard is on our side; we are the winning team; our captain has led us to victory. This is the only race, the time of our life. This is the only cheer, that "Christ is risen!" This is a sure thing that he will come again, and this time to judge the living and the dead. It is a day of rejoicing, a day of good cheer! Together with those who have gone before us let us cry out: Praise the Lord for he is good, his love is everlasting and his mercy is to the ends of the earth. Hallelujah! Christ is risen! Hallelujah! Truly, he is risen!

19

"Instead of being an object of veneration and honor, the Holy Icon has become a "decorative" form, which is interchangeable with any secular symbol or image. It is used to "enhance" some announcement, to draw attention to a "churchy" event but disregarded as a representation of the Holy. In time (if it is not already among us), the disregard for the Holy Icon as a representation of the Incarnation and transfiguration of our world will affect our veneration and honoring of Holy Icons in our churches and on other objects of respect. We will have unwittingly become modern iconoclasts."

(February 2005)

Always a teacher, His Eminence reminds us of the centrality of holy icons to our lives and our spirituality. He warns us against trivializing these affirmations of the Incarnation itself, and calls us to be vigilant against the gradual but steady decline of our own witness to the True Faith.

Orthodox Christians: Modern Iconoclasts?

Orthodox Christians are knowledgeable about the period of iconoclasm. Each year, we gather on the first Sunday of the Great Paschal Fast to celebrate the restoration of icons in the public life of the Church. Clergy and faithful carry holy images in processions, and we anathematize those who reject the teaching of the Church concerning holy images as stated by Saint John of Damascus.

The origin of iconoclasm, or the policy of destroying icons, goes back to the early sects who refused to accept the teachings of the Council of Nicaea in 325. To them, the Christ was a mere creature who was adopted by God. The principle of their theology was that there is conflict between matter and spirit: the first is evil, the second good. Therefore, the Incarnation (Jesus born in the flesh of the Virgin Mary) was not understandable to them.

When the Moslems found themselves in the majority, they pressured the Christians who venerated icons to destroy them. The Emperor Leo III...was mistaken about his theological views on the Incarnation and he, too, was anxious to rid the Church of "materialism". He also had political reason for wishing to suppress the veneration of icons so that he could employ those heretical eastern provinces (of the Roman Empire), and at the same time he hoped to pacify the Moslem and Jewish elements within the empire.

The campaign against icons in the eighth century was very systematic and violent. From 754 to 843, the campaign against icons continued. The Holy Fathers of the Church, meeting in Nicaea stated: 'The icon is to be venerated and honored but not worshiped. Worship is reserved to Him Who is the subject of faith, God Who is Divine Nature. There is nothing inherent in the wood or the stone which is honored; it is rather the person represented who is revered through the image represented." (Holy Icons, ROEA Press 1989*)*

Through the centuries, icons have been relatively limited, because they were hand painted or fashioned. In the last one hundred years and more, however, due to the possibility of mass production of paper imaging, prints of icons have been made available in numberless copies. Today, Church institutions, profit-making corporations and parishes all produce images on letterheads, bulletins, advertising, and other mass media.

Instead of being an object of veneration and honor, the Holy Icon has become a "decorative" form, which is interchangeable with any secular symbol or image. It is used to "enhance" some announcement, to draw attention to a "churchy" event but disregarded as a representation of the Holy. In time (if it is not already among us), the disregard for the Holy Icon as a representation of the Incarnation and transfiguration of our world will affect our veneration and honoring of Holy Icons in our churches and on other objects of respect. We will have unwittingly become "modern iconoclasts", having after centuries rejected the Council of Nicaea of 787 and joined ourselves to those whom we "anathematize" in services on the "Sunday of Holy Orthodoxy" (established in 843).

Is there not a major problem when, in fact, the multitude of these images are thrown into the garbage at the institution and home? How is it that we venerate icons and honor them but at the same time cast them off as so much refuse? Is this not a modern form of iconoclasm, and is it not the practice of "pious and orthodox" Christians? Which family preserves parish bulletins printed in bulk by profit-making firms? Do they not end up alongside coffee grounds, tin cans and chicken bones?

This gradual but wholesale disregard for holy icons as mass-produced and distributed undermines the veneration of Holy Icons as part of the honoring of the Incarnation. We have allowed ourselves to be duped into following modern methods of "advertising" at the cost of honoring the very "product" or better stated, the object of expression of our faith.

Of course, there are those who will say that these bulletins and letterheads and mass distribution of images "teach" and "incite" us to know more about the faith, the feast days, the saints. In all likelihood, if our clergy and faithful would attend the holy services, they would hear and sing the feats of those whose images we momentarily honor and then desecrate. This is a dilemma of the Church of our days; living and passing on the faith which was "once and for all times delivered to the saints," and protecting and being attentive to the manner in which we express it and hand it on to the next generation.

Yes, the very magazine in which this article will be presented reflects this same issue: a cover often showing a feast or saint of the Church, articles adorned with iconographic embellishments.

Multiply this throughout the Orthodox world, in church schools with crayon drawings and wall calendars!

It seems that the Church must consider this matter and take more interest in this issue. One does not see Jewish synagogues or temples now adorned with images or iconic representations, nor do you see any mosque in North America embellished with representations. Have the Orthodox Christians become so crass as to be indifferent to the very images which were once historically desecrated by others and still are, as is evident in Kosovo and other Christian places of worship and residence, and have themselves become "Modern Iconoclasts"?

20

"The existence of the Romanian Orthodox Episcopate in North America is not one of a ghetto. Our clergy and faithful are part of these societies which, each one, has a Christian basis . . . As clergy, let us respond to the real needs of our faithful whose lives are integrated in society and who need our guidance in living authentic Orthodox Christian lives."
(November 2007)

In this brief letter to his clergy, Archbishop Nathaniel reminds them of their mission to the greater society as well as to the small flock entrusted to them. His Eminence's words reveal a love for the parishes and faithful under his care and a paternal concern for the salvation of all.

Letter to All the Clergy from Archbishop Nathaniel

Dear Father,

In anticipation of the forthcoming feasts, we pray that you and your loved ones are greatly blessed with the peace and joy of celebrating the Nativity of our Lord and God and Savior, Jesus Christ and the great feast of the Holy Theophany of the All Holy Trinity which will soon follow.

This letter is being sent to all clergy; and, although it is general in tone, we believe that it can convey our thanks to each of you for your pastoral efforts in the vineyard of our Lord, that is, the Episcopate.

Frequently, we look through the photos and list of clergy given in the SOLIA Calendar, and we are reminded of each of you and your pastorate. So, even though we do not make personal contact with all of you; nevertheless, we are bound through prayer and commemoration on the holy diskos.

You will note that at the end of each calendar year, there are many changes in photos and names. Some of our clergy have fallen asleep in the Lord; some have transferred to other dioceses; some have returned to Europe; others remain in the same parish, continuing a long service to that particular community. Our brotherhood is always in a state of flux, but our service to our Lord remains constant.

Inasmuch as our Episcopate encompasses The United States and Canada, we are unable to visit all the parishes and missions each year or even every few years. His Grace, Irineu, assists us in these visits and in giving advice to you and the faithful. We have sent out a written reminder to the parishes that will be celebrating a fifth-year anniversary so that we can accommodate the requests of these communities by establishing dates for celebrating the particular event. May our Lord continue to bless us and make even more fruitful our service to the Episcopate.

A year does not go by without some conflicts in a parish/mission. As clergy, it is our calling to keep peace in the community and to speak out in gentleness and truth to the faithful. Sometimes, there are problems generated in the Parish Council; sometimes, there are conflicts with individual parishioners; there are also external pressures, which cause unrest in the parish. Whatever and whenever these conflicts occur, we as the spiritual leaders by our example are the ones who must work to resolve the issues. May God give us patience, truthfulness and love necessary to keep or bring our communities to live Christian Orthodox witness through his grace and our personal witness.

The existence of the Romanian Orthodox Episcopate in North America is not one of a ghetto. Our clergy and faithful are part of these societies, which, each one, has a Christian basis. This gives us the foundation upon which to bear an even stronger witness to the apostolicity of our faith, both to our own faithful and to the local community in which our parishes are located. Society demands that we serve not only the flock entrusted to us, but looks to us as clergy to play a positive role in the greater society in which we live. As clergy, let us respond to the real needs of our faithful whose lives are integrated in society and who need our guidance in living authentic Orthodox Christian lives.

This letter accompanies our annual Pastoral Letter on the Nativity of our Lord. The Letter is to be read <u>in every parish and mission</u>. This is the tradition of the universal Church - the teaching from the hierarch to his flock. There should be no exception to reading this pastoral letter at the conclusion of the Nativity Divine Liturgy. Even though you may print it in your parish bulletin, or put it on your website or see it in some other form, the Nativity Pastoral letter must be read in the parish/mission. Please do give us this courtesy.

We close this letter as we began it, with thanks to you for your service to our Lord; with recognition of the sacrifices of your family; with a call to patience and love for the flock entrusted to you, for this service is your crown as a priest in the kingdom which is to come; and, with thanks to the Lord for the good and dedicated faithful parishioners who also love and serve the Lord in "fear and trembling" for their eternal salvation. Let us remind ourselves that we are shepherds in the name of Christ and not in his stead.

Please remember that His Grace Irineu, and we do pray for you and for your loved ones, for the faithful and for the good of the holy Orthodox Church in the United States and Canada. Let us be sincere in our services toward him and toward one another so that "with one voice and one heart we may praise the Father, the Son and the Holy Spirit."

With paternal blessings,
+*NATHANIEL, Archbishop*

Youth

21

"Often during teen years, tears will flow; misunderstandings, accusations and indifference towards us will come. The Holy Spirit is the comforter who really knows about injustices. He also knows you and when you are negligent and how to guide you without forcing you or threatening you. What a great friend . . . a true friend who can and does understand and comfort.
"On the bus, as you walk, in school and everywhere pray to the Holy Spirit and make sure that you are receptive to Him. Let the Spirit work in you and with you to bring you to maturity and a full and total YOU."

(June 1989)

In these words to teenagers, Archbishop Nathaniel reveals his love for young people, and his deep desire to reach them directly. The simplicity of style belies the depth of His Eminence's message. His Eminence begins by demonstrating his sensitivity to the difficulties of this crucial period in every person's life, and ends by providing a specific, concrete recommendation for bolstering one's spiritual strength in the midst of a teenager's daily trials.

Teen Time and the Holy Spirit

If you are a teenager, you may be aware that many people take notice of you and your actions. You may feel that there are too many. "Why does everyone, everywhere constantly remark about how and why and what I do?"

One reason is that your teen-time is precious. You are no longer a child. You are not yet an independent adult. It is a time though, when you are very receptive to ideas and direction. As you grow older, more people will exert their influence on you: teachers, employers, and lovers. Teen-time is a very personal period when you can freely choose and make things your own, things that will reveal you in the future.

Since it is such an intensely personal time, it is precious to the Holy Spirit too. The Holy Spirit works in and with each one of us as we are: individuals, different from others and truly independent. Although the Spirit labors separately with each of us, He draws us together by His presence in others.

The following prayer is said at all church services. It is one that you can say. It is a prayer that can be a teenager's code of commitment.

Heavenly king, comforter and Spirit of truth, who are everywhere and fulfilling all things, treasury of blessings, giver of life: come and abide in us, cleanse us of every impurity and save our souls, O good one.

We all follow leaders. Some of us have a hero-leader, others have a gang-leader. As Christians, our leader is God. Jesus Christ sent the Holy Spirit to be with us, and we call Him our leader, our king. Since He is not elected nor is He a hereditary leader, He really belongs to everyone. He is not limited to nationalities by being a Greek or a Romanian or an American. He belongs to everyone, because He is from heaven.

Often during teen years, tears will flow; misunderstandings, accusations and indifference towards us will come. The Holy Spirit is the comforter who really knows about injustices. He also knows you and when you are negligent and how to guide you without forcing you or threatening you. What a great friend...a true friend who can and does understand and comfort.

Everyone has known someone who told him that he was telling the truth, but who led him astray. When troubles came because of it, he left him all alone. How alone then and how abandoned...not knowing what was true and what false. Truth is something that God alone knows about everything. Men may know some true things but depend upon God to reveal and guide to truth. When you are ever in doubt about someone or something, call upon the Spirit of truth to enlighten and guide you.

Even on the darkest, moonless night when you are in your room and the door is closed, when you are walking through the fields and see no one for miles around, God is present. He is likewise present in the largest, pushiest crowd of shoppers and among the noisiest spectators in every sports stadium. God is everywhere, because He created and keeps everything going. We must be careful not to ignore Him or not "see" Him and turn away from Him. Unless God is with us, we are not fully ourselves. An electrical appliance does not work and is not really anything until it is plugged into an electrical source. So we are not really totally ourselves unless we are connected with God. He is the beginning and the end for us. He fills us with those things that we lack and for which we pray.

If you wish to borrow something, you must go to the person who has what you want: to a bank for money, to a friend for a record album, to your parents for help and their experience. But all of these sources have just so much to give and that's all. The Holy Spirit has all blessings, earthly and heavenly, and gives them to all who ask. There is nothing which does not ultimately come from God: good health, love for others and even trials and crosses to bear. God is also called a treasury, because all blessings and every perfect gift, and all treasures come from Him.

In a chorus-line, the first person, the leader sets the step. He is the important one, because he begins the movement. Everyone who wants to dance follows his lead. God is called the "chorus-leader", or as we say, the giver of life. All existence and movement begins (and ends) with Him.

After having called upon the Holy Spirit and made an act of faith in Him as King, comforter and giver of life, we commit ourselves to Him and ask Him to come and stay with us, not to leave us to ourselves and to our selfish ways. If God is among us, we can be sure that all will go well. As a promise to him, as a kind of offering for His coming, we ask Him to purify us of our bad habits, our narrow way of thinking, from all forms of self-interest.

Finally, we ask Him to save our souls. This is another way of saying: "Save me, Lord; my body, my mind, my heart and all, that I may do your will and not be afraid to stand up and be counted among those who love and serve you."

And because we know that God will give us whatever is necessary and useful if we ask for it and sincerely try to fulfill His will, we call Him the good one.

Say this prayer daily, even hourly. On the bus, as you walk, in school and everywhere pray to the Holy Spirit and make sure that you are receptive to Him. Let the Spirit work in you and with you to bring you to maturity and a full and total you.

*A Moment with the Boys of St. Innocent
and Project Mexico Founder, Gregory Yova,
Tijuana, Mexico, 2001*

22

"Thank you, dear Lord, for your example to all of us to come and share the Good News and direct us on the path of salvation. You came to teach us and share your heart's concern for us. Teach us, O Lord, not to be mediocre, lazy, and indifferent but rather zealous, energized and interested."
(September 1990)

Teaching is the second ministry of the Church, after prayer. The Archbishop takes a moment to thank all those who make religious education possible in the parishes of the Episcopate.

Thanks, Church School Teachers!

Once again, our parishes are preparing to reconvene the church school for the purpose of "teaching our faith!" Most parishes do have some form of program; those who do not, ought to begin with whatever number of children is in the parish.

This issue of SOLIA carries a number of news items and some articles about education and scholarships, the youth conference ("AROY 41st") and the Camp Vatra for Seniors.

In Diane Farah's article, "You are My Church School Teacher – A Letter from a Child," she begins with the very important, but often over-looked definition of a teacher and a church-school teacher. Her thesis is that the church school teacher imparts knowledge on how to "live," not just on what facts to remember.

Our thanks to Church School Teachers in advance of the close of the term! Without your interest and concern, we could not share the teachings of our Holy Orthodox Church with our children; rather, you are part of that system of teaching.

Thanks to you, Parents! You are the beginning of the line, because your kids depend on you to drive them, to enroll them, to get them to the church on time! We hope you keep up your good habits! We hope that others change theirs from dropping kids off and going back home; from stopping off at McDonald's first and then, if time allows, getting them to the school.

Thanks to you, Parish Council and Auxiliaries, which support your education programs. I don't know of any parish going out of its way . . . we are kind of down the centerline. Most church budgets begrudgingly put in a "few bucks" for the "Sunday School." We hope there is more time spent in the councils on these programs and needs.

Thanks to you, Parish Priests and Preotese who are actively involved in the church school programs and do take an interest and role in the programs. Some of us "delegate it to others"; some are in with both feet; others find excuses for not having a program. There should be, however, a priority in the mind of every priest, and that is for the proper education of these youngsters in your care.

Thanks, kids! You try to learn . . . sometimes, we are lacking; sometimes, you are tired and appear to not be interested; but as the article reads: you are listening and watching!

Thank you, dear Lord, for your example to all of us to come and share the Good News and direct us on the path of salvation. You came to teach us and share your heart's concern for us. Teach us, O Lord, not to be mediocre, lazy, and indifferent but rather zealous, energized and interested.

We will know more and more, so that we can really LIVE AND HAVE LIFE IN ABUNDANCE!

23

"When we have come to act maturely, we no longer depend on others in the same way as before; we become responsible for ourselves and to others. We must answer for our own decisions. We do not and cannot live in isolation from others. We need them, and they need us in order for us to continue our 'star-quality' existence, that is, to continue our good works, words and qualities."

(October 1992)

Bishop Nathaniel gave this address to the 1992 AROY convention in Akron, Ohio. His Grace also represented the Episcopate at the Biennial Union & League Banquet in Cleveland, Sunday, September 5, 1992 and left this message to be read. At the request of a number of those who heard it, SOLIA reprinted the Address.

"With God, All Things are Possible"

Christ is Among Us!

We have stolen a few days from school to come together as young people of our Church in order to reaffirm who we are; and then, we will return to our routines of school, home, work and our parishes.

We know that we must be responsible young people, and we have taken a mature decision. We have decided that we will move the AROY Conference from the "stolen days" at the beginning of the school term to our "free" days in summer after the Vatra Camps. Next year the Conference will be on the weekend of August 21. Now no one needs to feel guilty about skipping school to attend an AROY Conference!

Last night, many of us became "A Star Tonight!" Imagine! In a few minutes, people actually applauded us and wanted our autographs! Stardom and recognition may come "in a single tonight," but there were "years of nights" in preparation, which passed by before last night, and "years of effort" in remaining at stardom in the future.

Recently, I read that Garth Brooks, the new Country Singer Star, wondered how he had become a star. After a short time, he was already exhausted from the demands made on him by his fans, his agents, his recording company and all of those who "grab hold" of a rising star. He felt that he was no longer himself and wanted **"O U T."** Garth was looking for some precious moments with his own family.

While we all want to be and need to be appreciated, recognized and loved for who we are and for what we do with our God-given talents, we need to remember that there are years of preparation before and years of efforts thereafter to maintain our "star-quality!"

Stardom for most of us can be said to be the "age of maturity," when we can responsibly do things and live as self-supporting individuals.

In the beginning, pre-stardom, pre-maturity stage, we depended on family, teachers and friends, who hopefully influenced us to do good. When we have come to act maturely, we no longer depend on others in the same way as before; we become responsible for ourselves and to others. We must answer for our own decisions.

We do not and cannot live in isolation from others. We need them, and they need us in order for us to continue our "star-quality" existence, that is, to continue our good works, words and qualities. They recognize them in us and help us to continue to polish them and use the good sense, mental gifts, physical beauty and free will with which we have been blessed by God.

As the stars of stage and sound, we, too, have an audience, which continues to like us or which we may alienate, and which drops us from its "charts." We can be good people, loving and concerned Christians, or we can become self-centered, unkind burdens on society that will "write us off."

As at our Karaoke sing-along last night, we have a variety of songs and words from which to choose. We need not only to choose the best of what we know, but must also learn and know more and make ourselves better if we want to be and remain a "star" in everyone's book, and first of all in God's.

The songs that are written by professional songwriters and lead-singers come from their own concerns and observations, from their personal problems or those they see. Our songs, that is, our choice of words and actions, come from the best songwriter, script editor, from God himself. He reminds us of love, not just of an "up and down" human emotion that causes "achey-breakey hearts," but of his own love which mends broken hearts and helps us heal wounds and doubts and anxieties. His is a steadfast love that is always waiting in the "wings of the state of life." "With God, all things are possible."

Young people, at maturity . . . stardom . . . frequently become aware and disappointed that adults, "grown-ups," "them," have faults and are often poor examples. They may physically and emotionally hurt us and cause our own personal "achey-breakey hearts." Sometimes, we label them "hypocrites."

Older "stars," ones who have been in the business of life for a while, would not be too quick to write off another. They have gone through more days in the public light and know what it is to be under the pressure of family, work, and society. They have experienced having made some "bad" selections, which might have taken them down on the chart of esteem.

As young people, it is good to keep your eyes looking up to Christ, THE STAR, and to avoid following poor examples of too much drink, gossiping, sleeping-around, unkindnesses . . . you fill in the blanks. Everyone needs to be a star for him or her self, because God creates us to be stars for him and for others, for parents, sisters and brothers, teachers, friends, family.

A "star," being a mature person, comes through good relationships; and, AROY's prime time relationship is in the Church and as AROY. If there are good things in your chapter, make them shine even more brightly! If there are dim and dull ones, make an effort to polish them up! "With God, all things are possible!"

God gives us a wonderful gift called "memory." You have memories and constantly input more into the recesses of your personal computer, your heart. This AROY Conference will mean something both the same and different to each of us. We will all carry memories of this weekend in our hearts. We were at the same meetings, ate the same meals, prayed together at the same services, and were at the same social events. Whether we responded as "stars" and mature people or as "falling stars" and "geeks" were choices we made. Were we responsible and mature or are we taking our first steps on the road to "hypocrisy? With God, all things are possible.

Let's support one another's search for Christian "stardom," which is living a good life both here and now and crossing over onto the "stage of eternal life" to come. Let's show to our family, our friends, our parishes that we are not only "stuff for stars," but are already "star-quality!" We are AROY! We are mature and responsible young Christians.

May Christ the true light of the world shine in us and through our AROY lives!

24

"If there is a form of competition in this tournament, it is an individual and collective challenge to each to consciously strive to fulfill oneself and to acknowledge that there is only one correct answer to life, just as there is only One Truth, and that is the All Holy Trinity, Father, Son and Holy Spirit."
(January 1998)

Taking time from his busy schedule to address a small group of students as they prepare to enter a scholastic competition, Archbishop Nathaniel shows the personal care for every member of his flock that endeared him to the faithful across the North American continent. As always, His Eminence writes in a manner that is understood by the least member of his audience.

To the Participants of the Bible Bowl Tournament

Congratulations on your participation in the "Bible Bowl Tournament" today. Your presence at this event signifies the importance you give to the major efforts you, your teachers and your Parish Priest have expended in preparing for this challenge.

St. Paul says that for one to win a race, one must train. The Church today reminds Orthodox Christians that all of us are, in fact, athletes of Christ who are running the race of life, hopeful of receiving a heavenly and unfading crown in eternity. In the Second Prayer of the Divine Liturgy, we say: "Give us in this present age the knowledge of your truth and bestow on us in the future age, everlasting life."

Your study efforts were not solely directed at acquiring knowledge but in living this knowledge so as to shape your life to reflect the presence in you of Him Who is The Way, The Truth and The Life.

If we dread an exam, it's usually because we haven't prepared ourselves for it, and we just want to get through it, to pass with acceptable grades. Today's tournament is not that kind of examination. It is not merely a test for knowledge of subject matter memorized but is a "user-friendly" occasion to express oneself among fellow believers.

The information learned, this knowledge gained is the real stuff that shapes our very life. The subjects taught and learned in public school are to train us to get along in the physical world in which we live, to prepare us to "make a living," as we say. The subjects that will be discussed today, the theology or the study of God, transfigure our mental, spiritual and physical being and give true meaning to "living." A computer can output only what is fed into it, the input. Human beings, on the other hand, are their own "in-putters" and can only output or live according to that knowledge and experience about God that they input into their hearts. We make decisions and choose to act based on what we believe about ourselves, about others and primarily about our faith in the All Holy Trinity.

In the prayer before reading the Holy Gospel, we say: "Enkindle in our hearts the pure light of your divine knowledge O Master, lover of mankind, and open the eyes of our mind to the understanding of your evangelical proclamations. Instill the fear of your blessed commandments in us, so that trampling down all bodily desires, we may practice a spiritual life, thinking and doing all which pleases you. For you are the illumination of our souls and bodies, Christ God, and we offer glory to you, together with your Father who is without beginning and your all-holy, good and life-creating Spirit, now and ever and unto ages of ages. Amen."

In today's event, there is really no competition in the worldly sense but rather an orderly possibility to demonstrate one's "knowledge of the Truth." If someone is not knowledgeable and misses the mark and another responds, the first person is still a winner, because that person can learn the correct response right then and there.

If there is a form of competition in this tournament, it is an individual and collective challenge to each to consciously strive to fulfill oneself and to acknowledge that there is only one correct answer to life, just as there is only One Truth; and, that is the All

Holy Trinity, Father, Son and Holy Spirit. This kind of competition is beneficial, for in knowing an answer, we are stating that it is a part of our lives. In not knowing an answer, it means that there is room to grow by finding the proper response and making it our own.

We do know that there are many demands made on your time and many pressures placed on you to choose one activity over another. We are honestly glad that you have made this tournament your personal priority for this Saturday, the feast of St. Nicholas.

This early hierarch of the Church is considered to be a patron for young people. He was understanding of the needs of teens; he knew the many pressures placed on them by their peers. Yes, in those days no less than ours, the young faithful were put to the test by their non-believing friends and by society at large. Under his holy patronage, we are certain that the competitive aspect of the tournament will be a Christian one based on respect, love and mutual support and informative, and that you will bring honor to your parish and yourself.

With blessings and all good wishes for the holy season of the birth of our Lord and God and Savior, Jesus Christ.

25

"The context in which we live demands action for the good of our salvation. We need to be unified so that the great talents of our teachers and the many assets of our communities can be put to better use. If our faith is dynamic, we can say to the mountain, "Come here!" If our faith is dynamic, we can say to ourselves, "We can do it!" Let us join together and establish the best educational facilities for our needs as we are able, and let us do it under the watchful eye of our own Patriarch of the United States."
(September 2000)

A truly effective program of Orthodox Christian education is only possible when the Church has schools in which to raise up the new generation of believers. Those schools will only become reality under a united, local Church. Archbishop Nathaniel returns to two of his most urgent themes in this article from September 2000.

School Days, School Days and the Bell Tolls

"An important quality of dynamic, working faith is the ability to relate in a meaningful way to the context in which one lives."

--- Archbishop Demetrios
Greek Orthodox Archdiocese

The end of summer and the beginning of the school year -- our children and many of our adult faithful have returned to school either as pupils or teachers. The Orthodox school-age population may not be a large percentage of American students, but it is significant to us as a Church. It is important to us, pastors and parents, that our children be well-educated, but also that they live as Orthodox Christians; because, they are living in a secular society and are attending schools based on secular standards.

His Eminence, Archbishop Demetrios, noted in "Praxis," a new publication of the Department of Religious Education of the Greek Archdiocese of the United States, that the ability to relate in a meaningful way to the context in which one lives is an important quality of a dynamic working faith.

In the Church in North America, we do not have the benefit of operating our own parochial schools, schools as a pleroma, or a fulfilling of that which is lacking in the secular, common-denominated public education system. Those of us who were educated in this system in previous decades may think that the public school system is still the same system with the same values as when we attended classes in the 40's, 50's, and 60's. Not so, not so.

What great benefits could be had from a single, well-staffed Department of Religious Education for all our educational needs, adult and children? But we do not have this, as a direct result of not being unified. It is possible to have parochial schools in those cities where there are numerous Orthodox parishes of various jurisdictions. At the present, we isolate our children from one another instead of strengthening them by creating educational opportunities in which they can worship, learn and grow together in the faith. Such unified educational programs would benefit the clergy, laity and communities as well.

One has to admire the Moslem community, which, after arriving in great numbers to these shores, immediately established Islamic schools. They are determined not to surrender their children to secular America, and they gladly finance a separate educational system. Why? They are not concerned that their children will not find professional jobs nor financial successes, but they are concerned that the basis for life is placed on their faith in Islam and not on capitalistic economic consumerism.

Almost every American Christian, Jewish and Moslem community has a history of parochial, high school and college/university institutions. This may be because they knew that education through a faith institution was most productive vis-à-vis the secular public school system, and they sacrificed for the end result: adherence to their creedal communities.

The church continues to multiply her efforts to produce works in English, duplicating curricula, training teachers, and all this at a tremendous effort, abuse of talents and squandering of precious funds. But we do not have any educational institutions for the general Orthodox public. We stumble over each other instead of working with each other. We are always surprised that the work "our department has done" is or has been done by "someone else, too."

Reflecting on the recent activities of the Mother Churches in the field of education, we find that in most Orthodox countries the Church has re-entered into the public school system to teach the faith; new seminaries have sprung up in grand numbers; theological courses for men and women have numerous students; radio programs and multiplication of learning texts. The Church is reaching out in a meaningful way, because she knows and responds to the context in which her faithful are living. Each Mother Church cares for a given territory, and her response bears fruit because she is familiar with her own. Do we not also have a given territory, a history, a context with which we are most familiar? Should we not be working as one?

In the United States, which territory is a large part of the North American Continent, the Church is ineffective, because her power and her talents are in disarray through the reality of disunity. This disarray has become so much of an accepted state of being, that there is a horrendous lethargy to make an effort to leap out of it; and so, we continue to plod along as we have from decade to decade, losing ground as the decades slip by. Which "jurisdiction" does not confess that we lose our faithful in the college years?

The belated effort to create "Sunday Schools" or "Church Schools," to parrot what others have already tried (and found wanting), has done little to bolster the spiritual growth of adults and children. With Archbishop Demetrios, we recognize the presence of the "era of the Internet and the dawn of the Information Age." These tools should be utilized by the entire Church as one. Without Orthodox unity, the sound of the school bell is more of a knell of warning that our children are not being educated to live Orthodox Christian lives, neither in the secular public schools nor in our own time-consuming church schools. We need our own school system.

SCOBA has shown no interest in the welfare of our children; the various local synods have little if anything on their agendas; parish councils are worried more about the roof and the increase in the cost of health insurance for the priest than in their children's growth in spiritual knowledge. This breakdown in responsibilities spells personal and communal judgments on us before the Lord. But most of all, we are failing as pastors and parents, as responsible faithful to pass on to the next generation the wonders which the Lord has done for us and for them.

School days and most of our parishes will struggle to find teachers, argue with parents to bring their offspring on a regular basis and count the days until summer when there will be no "Sunday School" or "Church School." School days, and we will pretend that our children are being "educated in the faith." Surely, one hour a week is not sufficient! It is time for the school bell to ring out to our students on a regular, daily basis. Will the cost be great? "What will a man gain if he wins the whole world but loses his own soul?" (Mt. 16:26).

The context in which we live demands action for the good of our salvation. We need to be unified so that the great talents of our teachers and the many assets of our communities can be put to better use. If our faith is dynamic, we can say to the mountain, "Come here!" If our faith is dynamic, we can say to ourselves, "We can do it!" Let us join together and establish the best educational facilities for our needs as we are able, and let us do it under the watchful eye of our own Patriarch of the United States.

26

"The CEOYLA struggled for years to please the hierarchs and the clergy, to be understood, to be accepted, to be messengers of a unified Church in North America, but to no avail. They didn't know what they were doing 'wrong' or what was considered 'acceptable.' The Church withdrew or let languish its support of the CEOYLA and the young of the various 'jurisdictions' stood apart, as though some form of invisible 'ecclesiastical Berlin Walls' had been erected between them."
(April 2000)

The history of the rise and fall of the Council of Eastern Orthodox Youth Leaders of America (CEOYLA) offers a lesson as we contemplate the history of Orthodox disunity in North America. His Eminence laments the failure of the Church's leadership to nurture the dreams of her youth, and calls for a renewed commitment to the dream of a united American Church.

Where Have All the Flowers Gone? Or, Where Lies CEOYLA?

As everyone knows, a flower has the potential to become fruit, which, in turn, bears seed that is a source of new life. An old German song entitled "Where have all the flowers gone?" referred to the young men who had been sent off to war. It was a verifiable assumption that many would not return to initiate new life in society. What a dismal future this foretold, youth nipped in the bud!

Do we have a similar situation in the Church today, not in context of political warfare but in the context of youth losing the warfare for their eternal salvation? No one knows the true number of those who have left or leave the Church in search of spiritual nourishment elsewhere or who abandon faith in the Divine. The attendance of young people at divine services and educational programs brings us to the real assumption that they do not hold Church worship as a priority. We all acknowledge that once they are out of the parish and family situations, they are not as involved with the Church as they ought to be. Does the Church recognize this, and is she also doing something about it?

A glance at the history of the Church in North America shows us that youth has fared poorly at our hands. Because of the unintelligibility of liturgical languages, a tendency to "Americanize" to accept that all beliefs are "the same" which caused a crisis of indifference and confusion in their minds, and because of other reasons, the Church has lost generations of young people.

Where is that tender flower, the "CEOYLA?" The Council of Eastern Orthodox Youth Leaders of America once represented most young Orthodox of various ethnic jurisdictions. The CEOYLA began from a desire of the young people to be together; it was not the creation of an external authority but of a recognition of oneness of faith. The CEOYLA was strong, as strong as the groups of which it was composed, but this fertile ground was neglected. Instead of being filled with guidance, it went unattended by parish clergy and lay leaders, and the hierarchy.

What titanic measures these young leaders had to undertake to receive a modicum of permission (a blessing) to meet together, socialize together, pray together, witness together to their common Orthodox faith! Their good intentions, their innocent programs to know one another, to serve the Church in America, to create a working basis for the future, were overcome by the weeds of leadership-indifference.

The CEOYLA struggled for years to please the hierarchs and the clergy, to be understood, to be accepted, to be messengers of a unified Church in North America but to no avail. They didn't know what they were doing "wrong" or what was considered "acceptable." The Church withdrew or let languish its support of the CEOYLA and the young of various "jurisdictions" stood apart, as though some form of invisible "ecclesiastical Berlin Walls" had been erected between them.

Today, the Church in North America is reaping the fruit of the death of the CEOYLA. Much of that "future" left the Church, frustrated, disappointed, angered, "turned-off", sidelined. Judging from the number of mixed marriages, indifference by local parishes to spouses who had converted to Orthodoxy was a major factor, and many of these good-intentioned neo-converts, and their Orthodox spouses, in frustration, left the Church for a church which embraced them and in which they felt their spiritual needs fulfilled. Instead of being fertilized with love and concern, respect and support, the CEOYLA was judged insignificant, brash, ill-timed, even "disobedient."

There are some CEOYLA people who reminisce about the programs and dreams they had formulated and who nourish the hope that "something" similar to the CEOYLA can still be created. They did not all leave the Church, although their hearts still ache and bear the scars of the indifference of the Church's leadership. They consider hierarchal withdrawal of support as the death blow dealt to the CEOYLA.

What concrete actions did the Church take for the youth? Which are examples over the decades of any united effort to guide the youth in its witness to the Lord? In the meanwhile, the new youth watch and wait; wait and are placated; placated and drift; drift and abandon, because the Church does not work together with the youth.

Christ never said that the "ethnic" planting of the Church in America would bear future fruit. He said that the powers of darkness would not prevail over the Church through the eons. A two hundred year old vine does not assure a fruitful plant; the leaders of the Church must tend the young people and cultivate them to produce the fruit of the Church today, let alone tomorrow. Indifference to youth is indifference to Christ.

In recent times, general support has come forth from all jurisdictions for the International Orthodox Christian Charities (IOCC) and the Orthodox Christian Mission Center (OCMC), two activities which sprang up in response to pan-jurisdictional needs. Credit must be given to those who initiated the IOCC, which was then adopted by the Standing Conference of Canonical Orthodox Bishops in the Americas (SCOBA), and to the Greek Archdiocese as the foundation for the OCMC, which was also adopted by the SCOBA.

Is it not equally important to have all-out "jurisdictional" support for the youth in as "united" an effort as has been given for charity and mission? Admittedly, each "jurisdiction" may be doing its "own thing," but is this not a terrible judgment on the entire Church? The Church is One Body, and no one can assume the luxury of not being concerned for the entire youth. "We're doing our thing for our kids," is not an acceptable, mature and Christian refrain. All kids, all young people, are members of the One Church and not of temporary "jurisdictions." Does the hierarchy have a national youth organization on its docket?

Most Orthodox peoples around the globe have their own national Orthodox youth organizations. Not so, the Church in North America. We, this great nation, have no Orthodox youth representation neither as a witness here nor a witness abroad (Just as we have no representation in the plans for the "Great Synod" which is yet to come.). After the skeleton CEOYLA was brought down, nothing else was erected in its place. How we laud and praise "Syndesmos," but create no Orthodox American Youth Organization! Is it not unusual to praise what others have and neglect to do the same for oneself? To admire "Syndesmos" and to not be concerned for our own youth is unacceptable. It is time for the hierarchs to act! It is time for unity of action with all diocesan and parish leaders! There needs to be a National Orthodox Youth Organization.

Where have all the flowers gone? Look around and see. Where have all the flowers gone? Pressed dry between the pages of the empty catalogues of our materialistic, consumer-based society, syncretism of belief, the screen of internet claims to "truth" and our own weak, inexcusable indifference. "Now is the time, says the Lord; I will grant them the safety they sigh for."

Feasts and Fasts

27

"Dearly Beloved in Christ, let us rejoice in the love of God for us, who has moved our holy fathers to establish this blessed season as the 'spring of the soul.' Let us take every opportunity of services and communal prayer, charitable activities, confession based on true repentance and the participation in singing the hymns of praise to God and change of heart."

(February 1985)

Likening Great Lent to a spiritual spring-cleaning, His Eminence instructs his flock about the necessity of putting our spiritual houses in order each year. He covers a range of topics, including prayer, fasting and repentance. As always, His Eminence displays a fatherly concern for the weaknesses of each person in his care, praying that each will be strengthened and guided by his own guardian angel.

Housecleaning of Our Soul

Spring housecleaning is a part of the good order of every home: once a year, at the change of seasons from inclement weather to seasonable, the householder stands back from the routine and makes a survey of what must be done to have "taken everything apart and put together again" for the sake of wholesomeness.

Business takes an inventory of goods to know what stock is available, what is in surplus, what is lacking. The factory or store is closed for a period to enable the owner to systematically, so to speak, bring everything under his control by counting, evaluating, rejecting and discarding what is no longer useful.

Even nature has its cycle of cleansing. Scientists say that the spring rains are necessary to wash away the residue of the winter month's accumulation of unnecessary chemicals, etc. Trees shuck the husks off the sprouting new leaves; flowers break through the soil, pushing aside whatever is in the way so as to bear their blossoms; animals change their heavy winter coats for the warmer climate arriving.

The period preceding the holy Pascha is known by a variety of names: "Great Lent", "Great Fast", "The Forty-days", "The Paschal Preparation." Perhaps, the "Spring-housecleaning of the Soul", an "Inventory of the Interior Life", a "Pruning of Non-productive Habits" would also be likely titles to define this annual review of our Christian life.

Whether we are concerned with the house, business, nature, or the state of our soul, we are speaking of taking time off to reflect on "where we stand". It is an effort to make better the present status of existence. Even though the good order of work and home are beneficial, the most important aspect of our human life is our spiritual pilgrimage and our place along the path of salvation.

In his first letter to the Corinthians, St. Paul reminds us that *"You know that your bodies are parts of the body of Christ...You know that your body is the temple of the Holy Spirit, who lives in you and who was given to you by God. You do not belong to yourselves but to God; he bought you for a price." (6, ff)*

It goes without saying that we know that we are concerned for our homes and possessions. We spend much time in energy and thought to make our livelihood, but how much more concerned must we be for our spiritual status; because, the Holy Spirit dwells within us, individually and in the Church, collectively.

We wash the windows of our home to let in light and see out clearly; how much attention do we give to our eyes as the window of the soul, and what we seek through them in pleasure or in darkness, to good or evil? Dusting, moving furniture, returning tools to their places, scrubbing down to allow each article a proper place; do we review our way of prayer, of charity, of compassion, of repentance, allowing each its rightful place in our life?

There is, however, a major difference between our motive for putting good order in our earthly affairs and for reviewing our spiritual life. St. John the Evangelist states, "Every man is a sinner." This being so, we are in need of spiritual renewal and this, in the form of repentance. Christ died for us on the cross, carrying our sins, and as our true benefactor nailed them to the wood. In our everyday life, we fail to always respond to his sacrifice for us. Little by little, by our inattention or weakness, we give in to small points and find ourselves not as good Christians as we ought to be.

Our hearts grow cold to the suffering of the Lord; our eyes see only our personal needs and not those of our family and others; instead of reaching our hands out in spiritual guidance to others, we fold them in front of us, afraid that someone may, indeed, call on us to help him from the depths of his soul.

This holy time of preparation is a necessary time for us. It is a period of renewal, or revival, or re-vitalization in Christ. Being a part of his body, we must function to the best of our ability, by his grace. Just as a well-tuned machine needs a "tune-up," so we also need a spiritual check-up to serve the Lord with concentrated and purified effort.

There are steps to be taken in every human action: a problem is raised, its points reviewed and a solution devised and put into action, resulting in success. St. John, author of "The Ladder," gives steps toward spiritual growth. Our problem is that we are in need of constant vigilance, for St. Peter warns, *"Satan goes about roaring like a lion to devour us"*.

We do need to reflect on our pilgrimage to heaven; we do need to cleanse ourselves of bad faults, habits and, yes, sin itself.

The Household of believers, the Church, sets aside this time of the year as a "housecleaning" of the soul. Every Sunday has a theme: the Publican and the Pharisee heralds the time of preparation; the Prodigal Son instructs us to return to our heavenly Father; Farewell to Meat reminds us that there is a last judgment for all mankind; Farewell to Dairy recalls the fall of our father, Adam and our invitation to return to Paradise.

The Sundays of Orthodoxy, St. Gregory Palamas, The Holy Cross, St. John of "The Ladder", St. Mary of Egypt, prepare us for the Great and Holy Week of the Lord's own suffering for us. Finally, prepared in body and soul, we reach out to the resplendent hand of the resurrected Christ, embracing one another and crying out, *"Let us forgive all things because of the resurrection and cry out that 'Christ is risen'!"*

The preparation is called a "journey," for we begin at one point of distance from the great feast; and daily, almost before we know it, we come to our destination, the receiving of the holy Eucharist on Pascha!

As maps and guides along the way, we have the holy services of Vigils, Great Compline, Canons, and blessed Presanctified Holy Liturgy. The tools we use to assist us on our way are: fasting from certain foods and actions, works of charity and compassion, abstention from words, thoughts and deeds which are detrimental and poisonous to our souls.

To fast is prescribed by the Lord himself when he replied to those who asked, "Why don't your followers fast?" *"I am still with them, and they will fast when I return to the Father,"* he said through the parable of the guests at a wedding rejoicing in the presence of the groom. At his departure, the party ends, and those who reveled in the goodness of their friend settle down to a life of restraint and longing to see their companion again.

Fasting from goods is not easy: we are usually tempted to say that it doesn't matter if we eat one thing or another. However, it takes will power to not eat chosen foods; and in strengthening ourselves in this, we strengthen ourselves in other spiritual feats such as prayer and reading of the Scripture. If we cannot refrain from simple actions such as what foods we eat to please our taste buds, how can we be aware to refrain from other actions which harm our souls? If we cannot say "no" to a Big Mac, how can we say "no" in being tempted to speak badly about another? Step by step, we are strengthened to "try just a little bit harder" to weed-out the faulty ways into which we can fall.

Recalling the story of the man possessed who ceased doing bad but failed to replace those habits with good ones, and in time, the bad habits return and more were added; we, too, must be careful not only to put aside bad habits but to cultivate good ones pleasing to our Lord.

The marvelous thing about this time of preparation is that the entire Church, all of us, is deeply involved in the same soul-searching. We have one another as supporters on the way; we have all forgiven one another at Forgiveness Vespers; and led by the Holy Spirit, we spring forward in a spiritual dance of renewal as the dwelling place of our Creator.

Dearly Beloved in Christ, let us rejoice in the love of God for us who has moved our holy fathers to establish this blessed season as the "springtime of the soul". Let us take every opportunity of services and communal prayer, charitable activities, confession based on true repentance and participation in singing the hymns of praise to God and change of heart.

The cleansing of our lives is the most pleasing gift to God and most beneficial activity for others as well as for ourselves. We must be prepared to be filled with joy and gladness, walking with the Lord on the way to Emmaus; we must be purified of ourselves so that with Thomas we can shout out, *"My Lord and my God!"* We must remember that to us was given the angelic directive: *"What are you standing about for, looking up...Go out and preach to all nations...for the Lord is coming soon!"*

May our guardian angels assist us in our Lenten journey.

28

> *"The Church is in great need of assisting others to come to know the truth of God, to bring others the message of forgiveness and the invitation to salvation. This is done in a practical manner: through efforts supported by the financial gifts and offerings of the faithful."*
>
> *"The simple offering of two turtle doves reminds us of the greatest sacrifice of all time; certainly at this time of the year when we celebrate this feast of the presentation of our Lord, we should take time to review our own habits of dedication, sacrifice and giving in return."*
>
> (February 1985)

One of many straightforward, practical appeals to the faithful, this article was written for the feast of the Presentation of Our Lord. His Eminence notes that the sacrifice of Joseph is an exhortation to each of us to give sacrificially for the work of the Church. The Church is the Body of Christ, yet she works in the world and must use the resources of this world to accomplish that work. This cooperation between the mundane and the divine is central to the Church's identity. Salvation and material stewardship are inseparable. In this letter, we see a foreshadowing of His Eminence's well-known and continuing insistence that the financial affairs of the Church always be conducted openly and in good order.

The Presentation of Christ: Cooperation with God

Throughout the history of mankind, there has been a constant theme of cooperation between God and his creation: Adam and Eve were the caretakers of Eden; Moses was the appointed leader to bring the people out of bondage and into a national unity to witness to the one true God; Elijah the prophet, Jeremiah and others were the "Spokesmen" of God to their followers; John, the pioneer before Jesus, prepared the people for the arrival of the Savior.

With the birth of the Lord Christ, the unique value of mankind was re-emphasized and with his death, resurrection and ascension, it was restored to its rightful place near the throne of God. No less than previously, man was called on to not only cooperate with the Almighty, but, by being baptized in water, receiving the Holy Spirit and partaking of the holy Mysteries, he too called on the name of Christ and became, through incorporation into the Body of Believers, a new being, a Christian. No longer living for himself, having "cast off the old man", the believer lives "for Christ alone."

In the universe created by God, his hand is on everything. He alone sustains it by his loving will. He gave to man the direction to use well both his own God-bestowed talents and the material world around him; to use all to glorify and praise the only true Creator and Lover of Mankind.

At the end of the forty-day period after his birth, Jesus Christ, God Incarnate was carried in the arms of his blessed mother and presented at the Temple in Jerusalem. From among the crowd, an old man, Simeon, moved to cooperate with God, spoke to all about the Child as being the savior of Israel and cause for many to rise and many to fall. Those who would rise are those who accepted the child as the Christ and all who do likewise. Those who fall are those who reject him and fight against his message of reconciliation, peace and eternal life.

As a seal of the dedication of the child to God, an offering, most probably two pigeons or doves, was left at the altar. In this simple gesture of sacrifice, the entire life of the cross was foreshadowed. It was not in the value of the gift, but in the fact of dedication sealed with an offering that the Virgin understood the special calling of her only child. Standing back from the scene of the holy prophet Simeon exalting in the presence of the infant, she comprehended that her act of parental obedience to God's law would, in fact, call forth future dedication and sacrifice.

Today, it is also a privilege for us to be cooperators with the Lord, using our talents, exploring the reaches of the Universe; making scientific progress to care for others; advancing in medical knowledge to relieve suffering and illness.

There is, however, precaution to be taken: that we remember, indeed, earth is but a place of pilgrimage and passage; that the ends of the universe will reveal the presence of God but not any more than does the innermost part of the human heart; that scientific advancements help us understand the world we live in, but that grace alone can reshape our society; that medicines and the physician's art may relieve but cannot overcome the reality of man's mortality and longing for eternal life which is, in fact, freely offered by him who is "ineffable, inconceivable, invisible, incomprehensible, ever-existing and existing ever the same."

In the Divine Liturgy, after the sanctification of our gifts of bread and wine by the Lord's words and before the calling of the Holy Spirit to change them to the life-giving Body and Blood of the Lord, the priest, in our name, sings: "We offer to you your own of your own, in behalf of all and for all." With these few syllables, the universe is restored to God, and man dedicates himself to cooperate with the ongoing sanctification of the world.

In place of the animal sacrifices of old, we offer to the Lord gifts from the work of our hands, the sweat of our brow, and mind. Material gifts of money are as necessary for us to give to God as were those prescribed offerings of the past. God, indeed, says that he has no need of animal sacrifices nor even of gold or silver to accomplish what he wishes. But we humans do need to show our dedication and cooperation through every human possibility open to us; to share the Gospel with others and through the use of all the means of communication, written, oral, and visual, as can be employed.

The Church is in great need of assisting others to come to know the truth of God, to bring others the message of forgiveness and the invitation to salvation. This is done in a practical manner through efforts supported by financial gifts and offerings of the faithful.

There is a great movement in the Church to reach out to others; to add voices to voices in praise of God; to bring the life-giving mysteries to new brothers and sisters in Christ. All of these efforts, however, await financing through the combination of giving thanks to God with using our talents and our money. We give so much to "worthwhile" causes: Cancer Society, Community Chest, United Appeal, etc., etc., etc. How much more ought we to give to the appeal of the Lord's voice to go out and preach to all nations and make them followers of the good Shepherd!

We all anticipate the April 15th income tax deadline; how much more concerned we should be of the last breath of our life when God will ask us: "What did you do with your talents? Did **you** announce my name to others?"

The simple offering of two turtle doves reminds us of the greatest sacrifice of all time: certainly at this time of year when we celebrate this feast of the presentation of our Lord, we should take time to review our own habits of dedication, sacrifice and giving in return.

*Serving the Homeless,
Phoenix, 2009*

29

"This spark, the fire, the light which bursts forth on this day and is passed from person to person, lighting not just the candle of wax in our hand but the candle of the soul, is the only truth which has created civilization, inspired humanity, and overcome the devil."

"Let us be glad in the power which has been given to herald the Good News, Christ is risen! And with Him, all mankind!"
(April 1985)

"The reality of the resurrection which is so difficult for some modern men to accept, nevertheless abundantly confirms those who in faith seek to come close to God and to do his will."

"Crucifixion leads to the resurrection; death leads to life, a stumbling stone for those who follow other philosophies both yesterday and today."
(May 1986)

The following Pastoral Letters were written in the earliest years of Archbishop Nathaniel's tenure as ruling hierarch of the Romanian Orthodox Episcopate of America. Short and simple, they are alive with the joy of the Resurrection. The words convey a deep desire to share that joy with us, to charge us with the energy that comes from knowing the Good News of Christ's victory over death. As always, His Eminence is mindful that he writes, not for an elect group of theologians and intellectuals, but for every person entrusted to his care.

Christ is Risen!

"Yesterday, I was buried with you, O Christ. Today, I rise with you in your arising. Yesterday, I was crucified with you, O Savior, therefore, glorify me together with you in your Kingdom."

Dearly Beloved:
Christ is risen!
On this great day of rejoicing, our hearts reflect on the goodness of God and the depths of his love for us. On this holiest of holy days, we are reminded of the continuous concern and the marvelous plan that the Creator has established for all mankind and forever.

What was created "good" was abused, and man and all nature suffered from the fall. The Spirit of God which hovered over the waters of creation did not abandon the handiwork done out of love but remained protective, guiding and restoring. Through prophets and holy, dedicated souls, the fact of God's love and concern for man was kept alive. Through the mouths of men and angels, humanity was reminded of its dependence on the one, the only and true God.

In time, that love burst into flower by the presence of the King of kings, the Lord of lords, among us. He came as an infant, born from a woman and lived the years of human existence among us and lighted an eternal flame, the true and only worthwhile light by which man could find his singular way through the dark, unknown days of his earthly life.

This Jesus of Nazareth, true God of true God, is whom we celebrate today. Our songs are about victory over evil, the triumph of life over death, of truth over falsehood, of light over darkness, of hope over despair. Jesus is over all of these things. He is our "eternal," our unending joy. How is that to be understood? Jesus Christ is the answer to every question that rises in the depths of man's troubled heart.

During his sojourn on earth, the Lord healed people of their many physical ailments; he raised the dead from the clutches of annihilation. Rejoicing in this, men drew closer to him and heard not only the words of healing of the body's woes, but learned of reconciliation with God through the forgiveness of sin. This is what makes our hearts start and leap for joy: our sins are taken away, our transgressions erased!

When the followers of the Lord stood hidden from his crucified agony, while those who rejected his Sonship and ignored his voice scoffed, the power of the Almighty wiped away the sins of all mankind and this forever, by the outpouring of blood and water which gushed from the side of the Lamb of God - Jesus, Word of God.

His precious body was laid to rest and stillness crept into the hearts of his followers. A silence covered the land and hope stood at a threshold. But out of that quiet, the Lord appeared to Mary, to Peter, to John and the others and enkindled the spark of joy which spread like wildfire from mouth to mouth, from heart to heart, from troubled soul to troubled soul: *"The Lord is risen, granting great mercy to our souls!"*

This spark, the fire, the light which bursts forth on this day and is passed from person to person, lighting not just the candle of wax in our hand but the candle of the soul, is the only truth which has created civilization, inspired humanity, and overcome the devil.

There are those who wish to make Christianity one of many religions. Others struggle mightily, but vainly, to eradicate the message of hope and eternal life. By destroying the icons on the walls of the churches, they think they can silence the lips of God! Still others attempt to knead the uniqueness of Christianity into an all-embracing society based on the invention of men's minds and rituals, to erase what they feel "divides" men one from another.

What divides men is sin. Who would silence the Word of God is spiritually dead. Which man-made philosophy is not folly?

Dearly Beloved,

Let us rush forward to meet Christ our Savior on this day and fall at his feet and embrace them. Let us say, "Brother" to those who hate us. Let us kneel before our confessor and pour out our sins for the Lord to forgive. Let us make bold our hearts, for he is with us and the powers of hell will not prevail.

Christ is risen! And the universe trembles! Christ is risen! And mankind weeps for joy! Christ is risen! And unending life is announced.

Let us not keep secret that which the Lord tells us to proclaim.

Let us not be judged for being lazy or indifferent.

Let us be glad in the power that has been given to us to herald the Good News. Christ is risen! And with him all mankind!

"Having beheld the resurrection of Christ, let us worship the holy Lord Jesus, the only sinless One. We venerate your Cross, O Christ, and we praise and glorify your holy resurrection; for you are our God, and we know no other than you; we call on your name. Come, all you faithful, let us venerate Christ's holy resurrection. For, behold, through the Cross joy has come into all the world. Let us ever bless the Lord, praising His resurrection, for by enduring the Cross for us, he has destroyed death by death.

Jesus has risen from the tomb, as He foretold granting us eternal life, and great mercy."

Pascha

To our beloved clergy, monastics and all Orthodox Christians of our holy and God-protected Diocese, grace and peace from Christ risen from the Dead, and the hierarchal blessing from me, His unworthy servant.

Dearly beloved,
Spiritual children and beloved brothers in the Lord,

According to the Gospel of Saint Matthew, we find that after Saturday, before the light was dawning, on the first day of the week, that is, on Sunday, three days after the crucifixion, our Lord Jesus Christ rose from the dead.

When the ointment-bearing women had left the tomb to go and announce the wonderful news to the disciples, Jesus himself appeared to them, and said: "Rejoice!"

This is the same message which the Holy Church has heralded throughout the turmoil of the ages, and it is the same message of victory and joy, which I as your archpastor in these blessed nations of Canada and the United States, announce to you this day.

This is the exact message of joy and brotherly love, of the victory of life over death, of the triumph of light over darkness.

Indeed, as the hymn, which resounds in all Christian churches on this day of resurrection, as the words, which echo in the hearts of millions of faithful, *"Christ is risen from the dead, trampling death by death, and bestowing life on those in the graves."*

Indeed, this is also what we hear from our holy father among the saints, John Chrysostom, in his writing on the holy radiant day of the glorious resurrection of Christ, our God: *"Christ is risen, and life is revived: Christ is risen and there are no more dead in the graves; for Christ in rising from the dead, has become the first fruit, the first of those fallen asleep. To him be glory and might unto the ages. Amen."*

In fact, beloved faithful, we rightly call the resurrection of the Lord the "feast of feasts and festival of festivals".

The resurrection from the dead is, in fact, the cornerstone for the Church of Christ, the foundation of Christian teaching. This is just what the holy apostle Paul tells us: *"If Christ has not been raised then our preaching is useless and your believing it is useless." (1 Cor.15:14)*

Only through the resurrection *"was Christ proclaimed Son of God in all his power through the resurrection from the dead"* (Rom. 1:4). *"God raised this man Jesus to life, and all of us are witnesses to that,"* (Acts 2:3), we find in the actions and witnessing of the apostles.

But the most powerful argument of his resurrection is the existence on this earth of his holy Church, an argument convincing through the actions, words and deeds of hosts of martyrs and saints who proclaimed and continue to proclaim this unique truth, hope and love based on the reality that *"Christ is risen from the dead, the first born of the resurrected of those fallen asleep."*

Inasmuch as death came upon man, that is, through Adam, the resurrection from the dead has come through a man. Thus, as St. Paul says: *"Just as all men die in Adam, so all men will be brought to life in Christ"* (1 Cor. 15:42-43).

This is also our hope; this is our faith, too; and this is the reason why we call ourselves "Christian" and are part of the Church of Christ.

The power of the resurrection gives us, through faith, the right to ask: *"Death where is your sting? Death where is your victory...so let us give thanks to God for giving us the victory through our Lord Jesus Christ"* (1 Cor. 15:55-57).

St. John Chrysostom advised the faithful of his time: *"Do not be afraid of death for the Savior has saved us from death."* And the Blessed Augustine tells us, *"The death of Christ destroyed death, for his life devoured it and shown forth the fullness of life."*

Dearly beloved:

The reality of the resurrection, which is so difficult for some modern men to accept, nevertheless abundantly confirms those who in faith seek to come close to God and to do his will.

Crucifixion leads to the resurrection; death leads to life, a stumbling stone for those who follow other philosophies both yesterday and today. We, however, proclaim now and ever through our unchangeable faith that "Christ is risen from the dead, trampling death by death, and bestowing life on those in the graves."

Therefore, as Orthodox Christians, we follow and will continue to implement here in the "new world", in this atomic age and era of constant information, the teaching of the Lord Jesus to his twelve disciples to whom he showed himself in Galilee after his resurrection:

"Go therefore, make disciples of all the nations; baptize them in the name of the Father and of the Son and of the Holy Spirit, and teach them to observe all the commands I gave you. And know that I am with you always; yes, even to the end of time" (Mt. 28:18-20).

This is, in fact, the theme of the forth-coming All American Council of the Orthodox Church in America this year in Washington, DC. This is also the goal, hope and faith of this God-protected Diocese, which through the mercy of God and in whose name I wish all of you good health and prosperity in the Lord.

Christ is risen! Truly he is risen!

With the ROEA delegation, All American Council of the Orthodox Church in America, Washington DC, 1986

30

"The Church in America is not cut off from the Church throughout the world: our faithful are one with the faithful of all lands; our message, the message preached throughout the world; our salvation is tied to the salvation of the entire Body of Christ. In Jesus, there are no land boundaries which separate, no languages more precious than others, no people more comely than others, no perfect political or economic systems; the Kingdom of God is not of this world, nor can believers be kept from one another in the Lord."

(May 1985)

Consistent in Archbishop Nathaniel's vision of the Church is the principle of her universality. In this article, as in so many of his writings, His Eminence begins by teaching us the "basics" before exhorting us to our higher calling and "zeal for the House of the Lord." His Eminence reminds us of the Spirit of Pentecost that brings men together today, just as on that fiftieth day so long ago. He urges us to become filled with that Spirit, so that we may earnestly fulfill the mission of the Church in America: "to refresh the world and bring all men to Christ the Savior."

Pentecost: Gift of Renewal

"Christ is risen! Christ is ascended! Christ is returning!" These phrases explain the Christian proclamation of the Lord Jesus' suffering for us; his lifting of our humanity to glory and the approaching return, when all things will be put into order to the glory of God: Father, Son and Holy Spirit.

There is a very definite constant movement in our beliefs, a real movement, which in fact is the promise of unending life. Our earthly existence obviously ends at the grave, and those who have not accepted Jesus Christ and his Gospel, remain without hope and without total dedication to God. Yes, they may have some very good points and live ethical lives, but in fact, they remain based on relative, earth-defined values and experience.

Those who have been baptized and have put on Christ share with him in his resurrection, glorification and eternal life. That experience, however, does not wait for the final resurrection, but is already lived, "in a shadow," now. The promise motivates us, and the hope sustains us that life continues, on and on.

The ascension of Jesus Christ, true God and true man, into heaven is our own human ascension to our rightful place at the right of God the Father. In his rising to glory, we are taken up with him: *"And he will send his angels with a loud trumpet to gather his chosen from the four winds, from one end of heaven to the other"* (Matthew 24:30).

Looking upward, the disciples were sad to see the Lord leave them; they remained gazing, longing for him not to go. They had just asked him if the "time had come? Would the kingdom be restored to Israel?" Instead of affirming their hopes of immediate fulfillment, he let them know clearly that they must also proclaim the good news, taking part in the preaching of the kingdom by sharing the news with others and bringing all nations to the Father. *"You will be my witnesses... to the ends of the earth"* (Acts 1:8).

Their melancholy was of short duration, however, for while they remained at the spot of the ascension, hesitant to leave, the angels of the Lord chided them, saying: *"Why are you men from Galilee standing here looking into the sky? Jesus who has been taken from you into heaven, this same Jesus will come back in the same way as you have seen him go there"* (Acts 1:11).

Galilee was the crossroads of the area; peoples of various nations passed through. The followers of Jesus had themselves been born amidst strange languages, commercial movement and familiarity with the unusual. It was "in their line" to go out and meet strangers, but it was the reminder from the messengers of God that woke them up to their calling. They were chosen for the preaching of the Gospel, because they were adept at working with others.

Human courage and zeal, however, are not strong enough to stop the mouths of lions, stand before tribunals and judgments; it needs the power of God himself to proclaim his message. This is why the Lord ascended into heaven: to send down the Comforter, the Spirit of truth, who fulfills all things, who is present everywhere. The Holy Spirit, who is everywhere, needs men everywhere to work with him in proclaiming and nourishing the good news.

Thus, ten days after the parting of the Lord Jesus, the Holy Spirit came down upon the assembled disciples, filling them with courage, with joy, with hope, with divine zeal, which moved them to go out into the world and make disciples of all nations. The feast of Pentecost, a Hebrew festival of first fruits of the earth, became a festival of fruits of a new harvest: souls of all nations for the God of Abraham, Isaac and Jacob.

It is that same indwelling of the Spirit which inspires men to overcome all difficulties, to reach out to others to draw all men in their "nets" to Jesus Christ. *"The Spirit of truth comes...will lead you to complete truth...will glorify me"* (John 16:14). It is only by the presence of the Comforter that men come to know and confess Jesus as Lord, come to knowledge of that truth, and keep their eyes on the kingdom of heaven.

In the Psalms, it says "zeal for your house devours me," and this was the same burning dedication that came into the followers of the Lord after the Holy Spirit flowed over them in the upper room. This is the zeal of missionaries, true hierarchs and clergy, pious faithful, and the crowned martyrs. The power of the Most High cannot be contained, but it is poured out upon those who turn to him: *"I will pour out my spirit on all mankind"* (Joel 3:1).

In America, we must test the spirit within us to be sure that it is THE SPIRIT. Sometimes, it appears that we are too ready to become "the accepted religion" instead of THE WAY. In our eagerness to bear witness to Orthodoxy, we must be certain that it is, indeed, the zeal for the House of the Lord, and not for the sake of statistics, acceptability and worldly acknowledgement and recognition.

"I will give you a new heart, and put a new spirit in you" (Ezekiel 36:26). The yeast must be active and fresh to produce movement: we must be filled with the true Spirit who will work through us. If our heart is that of this earth, our bread will not rise but remain an inert mass of tastelessness. The "old man" must

truly have died and not be allowed to rise up, lest the spirit not be new and renewing, but old and destroying.

The Church in America is not cut off from the Church throughout the world: our faithful are one with the faithful of all lands; our message, the message preached throughout the world; our salvation is tied to the salvation of the entire Body of Christ. In Jesus, there are no land boundaries that separate, no languages more precious than others, no people more comely than others, no perfect political or economic systems; the Kingdom of God is not of this world, nor can believers be kept from one another in the Lord.

As a spring must flow constantly to bring forth sweet, fresh water, so the Church must be filled with the Spirit in all of her members to refresh the world and bring all men to Christ the Savior. Pentecost is a day of great moaning, for what we wish to do in the Lord we must be open to do: it is a day of great longing, for we wish to be united with Jesus and call on him to come; it is a day of celebration, for the separation of men from men, nations from nations, people from people is overcome by the one Spirit in the one Lord from the Father.

Pentecost is the beginning of a new era -- indeed, the "common era" when all are called to salvation, all are one in Christ. It is also the "year of the Lord," for it is the proper time, the fitting time, the "now" in which God, who is ever present to move us, would act in us. Let us look into our heart and see if it is "renewed" in the Spirit; let us test our spirit to see if it is one with the Comforter.

31

"Today is to be another Pentecost. We are to be moved by the Spirit. Let us not pretend any longer that God is not everywhere. Let us not continue to relegate His presence to the "church." Christ is among us and everywhere, whether we consciously affirm this or tacitly ignore the fact."

"Let us be the salt of the earth, for we have no excuses that we are hindered by government or politics. Let us be the light on the mountain, for we have the strength and the calling to turn things around. Let us come out of our comfortable ghettoes we have created and bear witness."

(May 1985)

On the Sunday of Orthodoxy, 1985, then Bishop Nathaniel offered the following words to his listeners. Beginning with the history of the feast, His Eminence ends with a clarion call to every person and a joyful exhortation to repentance and love in the spirit of Great Lent.

Excerpts from the Sunday of Orthodoxy

The celebration of the Sunday of Orthodoxy in America is like our own Orthodox "Thanksgiving Day". The manners in which we gather in numbers with combined choirs, a fraternity of clergy, a unity of believers, is very "American." It has become a festival, a gathering in the Holy Spirit, a rally, a "pep-talk", a demonstration of unity in faith and an outreaching in love.

Originally, this event commemorates the reinstallation, in 843, of holy icons in the churches, and primarily so, in the capital of the empire, Constantinople, the very city named of Saint

Constantine. It testifies to us today that the reality of the politics of this world and its leaders are usually contrary to the way of God. **There is a tension that exists between this world and the kingdom of God.** There is, therefore, a tension in our own day and lives. "Render to Caesar the things that are Caesar's and to God the things that are God's."

From the year 813 until 842, the icons were banned from the churches; they were torn down, covered over, hidden or protected, depending on the faith of the individual. The time span is about 29 years, that of a generation. Those born during those years and who were not so familiar with holy icons knew of the struggle which continued to be waged, sometimes in the open, sometimes in private. But the issues continued because of the deep belief of those who revered icons, holy pictures, that it was, in fact, a matter of "right believing and right worshipping" that the icons be restored.

There are some today who are not totally aware of the struggle their elders and others have in keeping the faith. They know something is straining, some great pressure prevails against believers, but not being totally aware and not living in Christ, they are not affected by the Truth of the Orthodox faith.

Certainly, the Gospel was preached in the churches in those decades of persecution. **The word of God was heard.** But this was the real issue, that just as the will of God had been made known through the centuries through the mouth of the prophets and holy messengers, the angels, bodiless powers, in the "fullness of time," **not only was it heard, but seen!** *"Something which has existed since the beginning, that which we have heard,* **and we have seen with our own eyes; that which we have watched and touched with our own hands: the Word, who is life - this is our subject. That life was made visible; we saw it and we are giving our testimony,** *telling you of the eternal life which was with the Father and has been made visible to us. What we are telling you is so that you too may have union with us, as we are in union with the Father and with his Son Jesus Christ"* (1 John 1:1-3).

This is the subject: the icon of Jesus Christ, depicted here in this holy temple is, as St. John of Damascus states, a distinct affirmation and a reminder of the fact of his incarnation which has a vital significance for the salvation of the faithful, an affirmation which is guarded in the Orthodox Church to this day.

Those of you who were privileged to carry his icon into the church this evening please rise. No one should remain seated! All of us bear the image of God in us and carry it before us constantly. The image of Christ painted on wood or other substance portrays the Lord as he was seen in the flesh, but we continue to carry his image whether we are in the church, home, school, work or recreation. We are, indeed, "little Christs," or Christians. We are the temple of the Holy Spirit and testify to God's word by our lives.

Many today would have us believe that **man is a beast** and ugly; that we are not created in the image of God and that we ought to "let go" of all sense of dignity and honor. There are those who say that the "dark side" of man is his "natural" side, and there are no restrictions on man.

As Orthodox Christians, we reject this false idea, not even worthy to be called a "philosophy," and stand up for the pure image of man as seen in the Lord Jesus who let himself be seen in his glory before his suffering. Jesus Christ revealed himself to those three followers, "as much as they were able to bear, so that when they saw him crucified, they would know it voluntary." The transfiguration of Christ was not a change in him, but an unveiling. Like Moses whose face shone and radiated from the conversation he had had with God on the mountain, so moreso, Christ who is the reflection of the Father, took off, momentarily, so to speak, the veil of his humanity in order to strengthen his disciples for his upcoming suffering.

It is like this for us. We, too, are made in the image of God and bear his divinity in us. *"By his divine power, he has given us all the things we need for life and for true devotion, bringing us to know God himself who has called us by his own glory and goodness. In making these gifts, he has given us the guarantee of something very great and wonderful to come. Through them, you will be able to share the divine nature and to escape corruption in a world that is sunk in vice"* (2 Peter 3).

With the divine spark in us, we cannot deny the dignity of man and his rightful place at the right of the Father, already fulfilled by our Lord Jesus Christ. We must strongly resist and reject those false statements, which reduce man to a beast and raise matter to be idolized.

Orthodox witness must be stronger against abortion which snuffs out human life. What blood is already on our nation and, woefully, on some of us by choice! "Their voice goes out to the ends of the earth," but these small voices were not given the right to praise the Lord with their own lips. Yet, their witness is there. We know from Sacred Scripture that **the only reason for being born is to praise the Lord God** and by murdering those millions, **we are guilty of blasphemy, for we have stopped the mouths of those who were also called on to laud the Creator of all.**

There are other areas where our witness, personally and collectively, is weak: we abuse one another with arguments and gossip; we drink too much and in drunkenness cast a slur on the image of God in us; we are guilty of physically beating our wives, husbands and children, thereby abusing the icon of God; we too, of all ages, are hooked on drugs which distort reality and rob us of our powers, not unlike the Samaritan who was beaten and robbed and left for dead.

Students! Be honest and remember that the knowledge of this earth does indeed bring in the bread, but man does not live by bread alone but by every word that comes from the mouth of the living God. Do not starve yourself at the free banquet of the true knowledge, that about God. Do not neglect to worship and praise him and trust in him.

Those who are employed...do not be so tired that you neglect to come to the church to thank God for your health, the possibility to work.

Those who employ...be mindful that the Lord watches over all; and he, at the end, will distribute true justice to those denied it. Share of the benefits you receive: remember the story of the rich man who lost his soul while overly concerned with his pocket!

Retired people...do not sit back on your laurels. Do not let the abundance of your time be frittered away with the things of this world. You will say, "I have as much if not more to do now than before!" Yes, but have you given more time to God and to reflect on the end which will come shortly?

Let us celebrate the day, not as a triumph of what we do have and others do not...for we are at fault that the entire nation and world is not celebrating with us. Let us not celebrate in a spirit of false triumphalism, but **let us celebrate with truth and the recognition of it and its place among us.** Let us work to bring others to Christ.

We are used to "having it our way," to instant happiness. Commercials, songs, credit, lay-a-way allow us to be satisfied immediately and balk at dedication and life-long commitment to others, to the Lord.

Today is to be another Pentecost. We are to be moved by the Spirit. Let us not pretend any longer that God is not everywhere. Let us not continue to relegate His presence to the "church". Christ is among us and everywhere, whether we consciously affirm this or tacitly ignore the fact.

Let us be the salt of the earth, for we have no excuses that we are hindered by government or politics. **Let us be the light on the mountain,** for we have the strength and the calling to turn things around. **Let us come out of our comfortable ghettoes we have created and bear witness.**

The Lord Jesus came and opened his mouth and spoke! *"The time has come. The kingdom of God is close at hand. Repent and believe the good news"* (Mark 1:14). Metanoia means a turn around, a change back. It is an act of the will...not by force but by choice and desire, and this desire should be based on love. **We love the Lord, and therefore we repent.** We love the Lord for what he has done for us and what promises are in store for those who recognize him as Lord of their lives.

The feast of the restoration of holy icons is a reminder that the word of God is not only heard but seen, is not only listened to but lived. Do not be ashamed of holy icons in your home. You are not ashamed of having the Bible in your home. You are not ashamed to be able to quote from the scriptures as during the Liturgy. Then be sure that you **place icons in your homes and with one glance, you will remember all of the Bible** and all of God's wonderful acts of mercy and compassion you have heard and read. By seeing the icon of Christ, you will be flooded with thoughts about his power and mighty acts, and moved to praise him.

A thought of conclusion: by restoring the icons in this celebration, we herald the second coming of Jesus, his restoration among us.

With Missions Department Director, +Archpriest Constantin Tofan and "Sue."

32

"Who today is an apostle? Certainly, everyone is."

"Pentecost has showered on us the grace of the Holy Spirit; our churches are moved to bear authentic Christian truth; each of us is called upon to be an apostle of Jesus Christ."
(June 1985)

Pentecost, linked by the Apostles' Fast to the Feast of Saints Peter and Paul, gives His Eminence the occasion to return to a well-loved theme: the call of Jesus Christ to every person and the apostleship of every believer. Again, His Eminence begins by teaching some basic facts about these first ones among the apostles, and ends by calling us all to something greater than ourselves.

Apostles of Christ

"All of you who are holy brothers and have had the same heavenly call should turn your minds to Jesus, the apostle and the high priest" (Hebrews 3:1).

Jesus Christ our Lord was sent from heaven by the Father to call humankind to return to God. The Lord is the faithful Son who reveals to us, his brethren, the heart of our Father in Heaven. He is thus described in Hebrews as an apostle.

In turn, Jesus the Messiah, chose individuals to be his companions on earth, his witnesses to his ministry so that, in time, they would be sent out as apostles to continue the work he had begun.

There are lists of these followers, apostles, in each of the four Gospels: Luke 6:13; Matthew 10:1-4; Mark 3:14-19; Luke 6:13-16 and Acts of the Apostles 1:13. Twelve names are given, corresponding to the twelve tribes of Israel. Later, however, when

Judas denies his witness and thus, his apostleship, his place was given to another, Matthias (Acts 1:26).

Of the twelve, Peter was given the honor of being witness to events shared not by all of the rest: among them, the Transfiguration. It was also Peter who ran to the tomb and looked in, discovering that the body of the Lord was not where he had laid it. The others looked up to Peter in view of the fact that the Lord Jesus had also addressed to him the triple question: *"Peter, do you love me? Feed my flock."*

Peter's importance is based, mostly, on his confession of Jesus as the Messiah, the Chosen One of Israel, the Son of God. It was on this "rock" or foundation of witness and confession that the Lord lifted Peter above the others, because *"it was not flesh and blood that revealed this to you but my Father in heaven"* (Mt. 16:13-20). Peter has the mark of a true apostle, one to be sent out…he knows and bears witness to the Father who has sent the Son.

Although each of the other apostles of the twelve has certain particular stories connected with his witnessing, their efforts and final death for the Gospel, it is Paul who also uniquely claims to have the name of apostle, even though not chosen by the Lord himself while he was on earth. Paul was chosen *"by God to be an apostle"* (1 Cor. 1:1). He is part of the first fruits resulting after the Pentecost. It is he that also bears witness to the Lord Jesus because he too is sent from God by the divine call, *"by a revelation that I was given the knowledge of the mystery…of Christ. This mystery that has now been revealed through the Spirit to his holy apostles and prophets"* (Eph. 3:1-5).

Paul later refers to others, in addition to the twelve, as apostles: *"Those outstanding apostles Andronicus and Junias, my compatriots and fellow prisoners who became Christians before me"* (Romans 16:6-8).

The tradition of the Orthodox Church is that there are the twelve and the seventy, and, in time those who are "equal to the apostles", such being, generally speaking, great witnesses to specific peoples such as Nicetas of Remesiana is to the Romanians, Cyril and Methodius to the Slavs, Innocent of Alaska to the Americans.

The Orthodox Church keeps the feast of the Two Pillars of the Church, Peter and Paul, on June 29th and, the following day, the 30th, is a remembrance of all the apostles.

To be true to the calling, an apostle, every apostle, must repeat what was already stated in authentic witness. Like the "town-crier" of old, the apostle cries out to the world, proclaiming the good news of salvation as he has himself heard it. On the contrary, those who distort the truth, who by individual reinterpretation go far from the faith held by the entire body of the Church, become heretics or proclaimers of falsehood.

"Peter, rock and foundation; Paul, chosen vessel, drew all to the knowledge of God. Peter, leader of the apostles, rock of faith, and Paul, orator, light of the holy Churches, mouthpiece of Christ, founder of doctrines, you have now filled the first throne of the apostles...", such are the words of hymns of praise to the two pillars.

What led these two, the twelve, the seventy, and the myriad to be "apostles"? It was first of all the calling from God to be his witness, and this call, nourished by grace, filled each and all to undergo every physical and spiritual battle for the truth, put so very clearly and powerfully by Peter: *"That God the Father of our Lord Jesus Christ, who in his great mercy has given us a new birth as his sons, by raising Jesus Christ from the dead, so that we have a sure hope and the promise of an inheritance that can never be spoiled or soiled and never fade away, because it is being kept for you in heaven"* (1 Pet. 1:3-5).

It is in accepting the promise that the apostle became just that, someone sent out in the name of the donor, God in heaven. It was by explaining the truth, sharing the good news, living in grace, that they received the power and courage to continue in the face of adversity and persecution.

Who today is an apostle? Certainly, everyone is. Not all will fall into the category of the twelve, the seventy, and others, because they were for a certain time, a certain need. The Gospel, however, which they preached, the message they proclaimed, the witness they bore is for every time and eternity; and therefore, all people of every age must be a witness, an apostle to the world. *"Go forth and make disciples of all nations."*

In commemorating the holy apostles, we are put to the test as to our own witnessing to the Gospel. The Orthodox Church in America will meet in 1986, in Washington DC, to bear witness to the good news, having given the theme to that great council, "Evangelism".

Our own diocese has also given much consideration to the theme in the 1985 issue of the SOLIA CALENDAR. Articles in Romanian and English review the past, look at the present, and prepare for the future; but all of these things, the themes, articles, celebrations only bear the fruit of what is in our own hearts and lives: we bear witness to what we know. If we know the Lord Jesus, we must bear witness; if we are uncertain of him in our lives, we cannot bear true witness.

Pentecost has showered on us the grace of the Holy Spirit; our churches are moved to bear authentic Christian truth, each of us is called upon to be an apostle of Jesus Christ.

The Early Years: Chancery Staff Relaxing

33

"Let us celebrate the feast of Christ's birth not as a 'winter festival' nor a religious holiday among the pantheon of holidays of the world. The coming of the Savior was in humility, but He is not on His way to come in glory and power, to call and recognize those who bear witness to his love. The star which shone over the roofs of the city of David must enkindle in our hearts to radiate with fervor and faith to bring others to rejoice in God, to take delight in the Savior, to shout out, like the stones of Jerusalem: 'Glory to God in heaven and peace to men of good will on Earth'."

(December 1985)

In his first Pastoral Letter, the new Romanian American bishop exudes the joy and optimism of a burning zeal and faith in Christ. The mystery of Christmas is contrasted with the superficial knowledge of worldly learning, and we are all incited to cry out with gratitude and fervor, "Christ is born! Glorify Him!"

The Stones and Stars Speak Out

"Glory to God in the highest heaven, and peace to men who enjoy his favor," sang out the great throng of the heavenly host in the city of Bethlehem at the birth of Jesus the Messiah (Luke 2:14).

This exultant praise of God motivated the shepherds to hurry to seek out the child lying in the manger. The message from the heavenly angel, the news that had been told to them, showed to be true. Filled with the Spirit, rejoicing in God's mercy, the keepers of the flocks themselves picked up the song of the angels and glorified and praised God.

Others were also led to the infant, to *"the son given to us and dominion laid on his shoulders"* (Isaiah 9:5). *"The people that walked in darkness have seen a great light; on those who live in a land of deep shadow a light has shone"* (Isaiah 9:1). These magi or wise men came in search of the "king of the Jews," for they *"saw his star as it rose and came to do him homage"* (Mt. 2:2). As the song of the angels had filled the hearts of the shepherds with joy, so the sight of the star *"filled them with delight and going into the house they saw the child with his mother, Mary, and falling to their knees they did him homage"* (Mt. 2:10).

The shepherds, like David of old, meditated at length in the fields on the prophecies about the Messiah; and the song of the heavenly powers although startling, nevertheless was not strange to them. The announcement by the angels of the Good News brought faith to the shepherds. *"So faith comes from what is preached, and what is preached comes from the word of Christ"* (Romans 10:17).

The wise men, intellectuals of this world, servants of the wisdom of men, were *"taught by a star to adore you, Christ, the sun of righteousness"*; and thus, perhaps unaware of the prophets, nevertheless, they too came to know the Good News of the Kingdom of God whose "Prince of Peace" was heralded by the star of "great delight."

That wondrous Prince, Son of God, the servant of God, who later in his sojourn on earth was "lifted up" on the cross, was "disfigured", "despised", who bore our sufferings, who "was pierced through for our faults, crushed for our sins", on whom "lies a punishment that brings us peace and through his wounds we are healed"; that servant, the Lord Jesus Christ was the "preacher sent" whose footsteps are blessed and are the welcome sound, because he proclaimed the Good News (Romans 10:15) and lifted men up to heaven.

"Shout for joy, break into cries of joy and gladness, do not be afraid, do not be dismayed...for now your creator, his name is Lord of the Powers, your redeemer will be the Holy One of Israel, he is called the God of the whole earth" (Isaiah 54).

Throughout the public ministry of Jesus, men lifted their voices in praise and thanksgiving for the mercies of healing and power, for the forgiving of sin. While some challenged, others accepted his word. Many sought him, but some, like the rich man seeking the Kingdom of God, would not take up the cross and "follow him."

Praising God, revealed by Ezekiel (2:12) as a *"tumultuous shouting, 'Blessed be the glory of the Lord in his dwelling place',"* voiced by the heavenly powers and repeated at the birth of the Savior Jesus, is also the duty of man who is made in the image and likeness of the *"God of heaven and earth"* (Jonah 1:9). Thus, at the entrance of the Messiah into the earthly Jerusalem, *"the whole group of disciples joyfully began to praise God at the top of their voices for all the miracles they had seen. They cried out: 'Blessings on the King who comes, in the name of the Lord! Peace in heaven and glory in the highest heavens!"* (Luke 19:38).

Again, there were those who had listened but did not hear, whose eyes were open but did not see, and they criticized the disciples to Jesus saying: *"Master, check your disciples"* and *"Do you hear what they are saying?"* to which Christ replied: *"I tell you, if these keep silence, the stones will cry out"* (Luke 19:40).

Man is taken from the soil and shall return to dust (Gen. 3:19), but he is also *"little less than a god, crowned with glory and splendor, made lord over the work of God's hands"* (Ps. 8.5), and it was to this earth-formed, heaven-bent creature that God himself came down from heaven to lift back to his place at the right hand of God in glory. So great, in fact, is God's love for man, that he became like us in every way except for sin, and dwelt among us so that *"he that believes in him will not perish but will have everlasting life!"* Eternal life, however, cannot be measured, not even by trillions of years.

This year, the world again watches the skies, not for the star of Bethlehem but for the cyclical return of a comet, Halley's. Like clockwork, this celestial phenomenon returns to pique man's curiosity to look upward and wonder about the depths and workings of the universe and man's place therein.

Through the centuries, the wise men of science have been able to ascertain certain measurements of the universe, and man cannot but marvel at these statements. It is said that the universe is between 12-25 billion years old and our solar system is about 7.5 billion years. That one star in 1000 has developed planets, and one of 1000 of these has life-bearing conditions. One star in one trillion has earthlike planets, and there are 100 billion billion stars; and thus, about 100,000,000 earths exist.

Once every 75 years, however, around comes Halley's comet, and once in time, came the star over Bethlehem. Halley's Comet is a part of the cosmic time clock, but the star over the manger is eternal; it stands outside of time, for it is once that the King of the universe was born of the Virgin and took his place among us to give the Good News and to call man, earth-made and heaven-bent, to be in union with the creator of all.

"Where were you when I laid the earth's foundations?" asked the Lord Almighty of Job (Job 38:4); and in confessing his limitations, the troubled searcher said: *"I have been holding forth on matters I cannot understand, on marvels beyond me and my knowledge. I knew you, God, then only by hearsay; but now, having seen you with my own eyes (of the soul), I retract all I have said and in dust and ashes I repent"* (Job 42:4-6).

When the wise men came to the infant Jesus, they bowed down to something, someone who stood outside their human calculations. There before them was present the immeasurable but understandable sign of the power of the Creator to take on flesh and bathe man in the aura of his immeasurable love and mercy. God himself bridged the problem between the earthly man who seeks to control and fathom, and the spiritual new man who lives by faith and outside of time and the ravages of change.

Indeed, the stones and stars speak out and bear witness to the power and wisdom of the Maker of the universe, and we, sons of the earth and sons of light, reborn in the waters of baptism, must also speak out to a world which bears the imprint of our Creator and which follows along a path established by his wisdom and according to goals he has established.

Those who have been baptized and put on Christ, filled with the Holy Spirit, must bear witness in three ways: to those who do not know of the Son of God and the Holy Trinity; to them standing yet in darkness; to those who have gone astray like sheep from the fold and while confessing some truth, like the wise men and basking in their limited warmth, do not enjoy the full radiance of the Son; to those who indeed bear the name of right-believing but who have grown weary and whose lives have become a cyclic, repetitive routine instead of witness "raised at the top of the voice" to the miracles revealed to us.

The celebration of the birth of the Savior is a time when we reflect on the humility of the Father who sent his Word to dwell among us and then poured out his Holy Spirit upon the earth. The universe may indeed be billions of years old, but *"man lasts no longer than grass, no longer than a wild flower he lives"* (Ps. 103:15); and thus, time for us is sacred, is essential, is the liquid of life leading us to eternity. The words of Paul must not be applied to us: *"What has become of this enthusiasm you had?"* (Gal. 4:15). We are the salt of the earth and are cast aside if we lose our dedication; we are the light of the hilltop unless we hide in the caves of indifference, spurning the love of God.

Let us celebrate the feast of Christ's birth not as a "winter festival" or a religious holiday among the pantheon of holidays of the world. The coming of the Savior was in humility, but he is now on his way to come in glory and power, to call and recognize those who bear witness to his love. The star which shone over the roofs of the city of David must be enkindled in our hearts to radiate with fervor and faith to bring others to rejoice in God, to take delight in the Savior, to shout out, like the stones of Jerusalem: *"Glory to God in heaven and peace to men of good will on earth."*
Christ is born! Glorify Him!

34

"How very important, then, is the blessing of water in our parish churches and cathedrals. By blessing the water and sprinkling ourselves, our churches, our homes, our food, plants and all things with it, we are reaffirming the dominion of God over them. Our actions acclaim his lordship over the universe, and we affirm and state that man is no longer a slave to cosmic forces, for by the coming of Jesus into the waters of the Jordan, his divinity has restored all things to God."
(January 1987)

Ever mindful of the teaching ministry of the episcopacy, Archbishop Nathaniel has produced a vast number of instructional articles over the years. Here, His Eminence explicates the symbols and message of the icon of the Baptism of Our Lord. He elevates the lesson from a mere explanation of the image, finally showing us "the Hand of God Himself" leading us back to Heaven.

Christ's Baptism: Our Renewal

The actual ministry of the Lord Jesus Christ began after his personal encounter with St. John the Baptizer at the Jordan River. From his birth to the one event of the pilgrimage to the Temple in Jerusalem, the Gospels are quiet about the child. It is certain that it was only after the baptism, with his public ministry, that the doctrine and teaching of Christ was made known, and this is what is important for our salvation.

St. John Chrysostom says: "It is not the day on which Christ was born that should be called the Epiphany (manifestation) but the day on which he was baptized. It wasn't through his birth that he became known but through his baptism. Before his baptism he wasn't known by the people."

For most Orthodox Christians, the feast of the baptism is known to be closely tied to that of "Christmas". We are all aware that on the second day we celebrate the "Epiphany," and we participate in a special service of blessing water, the "Jordan Water."

Epiphany means the manifestation or showing-forth. It was at his baptism in the Jordan River that God the Father and God the Holy Spirit bore witness to the divinity of Jesus, the Only-begotten Son. *"As soon as Jesus was baptized, he came up from the water and suddenly the heavens opened and he saw the Spirit of God descending like a dove and coming down on him; and a voice spoke from heaven, 'This is my son, the beloved; my favor rests on him'."* (Mt. 3:17).

The manifestation was not a "spiritual" or invisible event but a visual, audible witnessing. The voice, like that which Moses had heard at the burning bush, was heard; the Holy Spirit, who had also been witnessed as a pillar of fire and a cloud of covering, was seen as the dove.

In our SOLIA cover, the voice is represented by the fine lines and rays of light coming from above and resting on Jesus' head. This ray is also evident from the icon of the birth of Christ, bearing witness to the will of God the Father over the birth of his beloved Son.

In line with the light-ray is the figure of the dove. The Holy Spirit is spirit, not a real dove, but the figure is made visible to be a witness, to bear testimony to our human frailty. He rests directly over the head of the Lord.

The appearance of the Holy Spirit in the form of a dove is by analogy with the flood in the days of Noah. The world was purified by the waters of the flood, and the dove brought an olive branch into the ark to announce both the end of the flood and peace and reconciliation with God. At the Lord's baptism, the Holy Spirit comes down in the form of a dove to announce the remission of sins and God's mercy to the world. St. John of Damascus says: "At the time of Noah, the olive branch was given; at the baptism in the Jordan, the mercy of our God."

At the feet of the Lord are two small figures in the water: a man holding a gushing vase turning away from Christ, and a woman seated on the back of a fish. These two figures remind us that all nature responded to the manifestation of Christ as true God and true man.

The prophecy of Psalm 113:3-5 is fulfilled and shown by these figures. The man is the Jordan River pouring out the stream from his vase, and he is apparently turning from Christ: *"1The Jordan was turned back!"* The woman represents the sea and fleeing from the Lord: *"The sea saw you and fled!"* From whom did the Jordan turn its water path and from whom did the sea run away? From the Lord who is the creator of heaven and earth and the sea and streams.

Nature did not fail to recognize its Creator, even after he had taken on our human nature. It could not help but bear witness. Just as the Sea of Reeds (Red Sea) parted to let the children of Israel through, and the Jordan parted its watercourse when the Ark was carried through it and when Elijah struck it with his cloak, so it also responded at the coming of the "Mighty One," God himself, Jesus Christ.

Looking closely, we see the "faces" in the rocks and mountains; indications that all nature responded to the presence of God. How often Scripture speaks of the "stones crying in witness" or the "mountains shouting for joy" at the coming of the Lord! Certainly, these are ways of speaking about the reality that nature also shares in the events that have to do with the salvation of man, the image and likeness of God.

On the other hand, St. John the Baptizer looks up in wonder at the heavens, overcome by the great love and compassion of God to descend from on high to our lowliness in order to lift us to the heights of heaven. His hand is over the head of the Lord, not resting on it; for he is terrified that he, the servant, should lay his hand on the Master's head.

Both the portrayed reactions of nature and man reveal the truth of our celebration: God-is-with-us, and in realizing this, we are overcome by the power of its meaning.

Let's go back to the need for God-is-with-us, for the birth of Christ and his death on the cross.

Although God had given man control and authority over nature (Genesis 1:28, 2:20), by his sin, man lost control and became subject to it, thus losing his freedom. All nature suffered from the turning from God of Adam and Eve.

Instead of using the potentialities of his nature to raise both himself and nature with him to God, man submitted himself to the desires and passions of the material world. In other words, man, who was **created good** and with the possibility to do good and make things around him respond in like manner, turned to himself; and, limited by his own self, brought everything down with him.

The world, **created good** by God, thus became a kind of "prison" for man and a constant temptation, pulling him away from God. What God gave us as a blessing became a curse. What God gives us, we still continue to abuse. Nature still fights us in our relationship with the Creator.

Another reviewing of our icon of the feast reminds us that there is an ideal side of creation: that in which the angels participate. Created to serve God and his image, man, they stand ready to serve the Almighty God. Their hands are covered with cloths in respect for the divine whom they dare not touch. They recognize the "King of kings" and "Lord of lords" and come in ministry of praise and service as we read in the Holy Prophet Isaiah (6:3) and St. Luke (2:13).

Angels are real; they are appointed as guardians to each of us, to nations, and to holy places. Like nature, they, too, are given to us for our assistance.

In the Divine Liturgy, we are called on to be like the angels: *"Let us who mystically portray the cherubim...Grant that with our entrance may also enter the holy angels, concelebrating and glorifying with us."* All creation, visible and invisible, awaits the return of Christ and the renewal of all things in him.

How very important, then, is the blessing of water in our parish churches and cathedrals. By blessing the water and sprinkling ourselves, our churches, our homes, our food, plant and all things with it, we are reaffirming the dominion of God over them. Our actions acclaim his lordship over the universe, and we affirm and state that man is no longer a slave to cosmic forces, for by the coming of Jesus into the waters of the Jordan, his divinity has restored all things to God.

The prayer of sanctification of the water states clearly that the "sun and moon, the stars and waters" all praise God; in other words, they are his servants, the works of his hands and subject to his voice of command. They worship Him! This means that the laws of the universe do not exist without the power, sustenance and direction of God.

By taking the lead, sprinkling, rededicating ourselves and "things" to God, by sanctifying them, we remove any "mystery" about them. We put everything, water, earth, food in the right perspective of being servants of God, created things which need to recognize the hand of the Master.

The feast of the Epiphany is for all year long. It is a rededication of the universe to God. All water is holy, because Christ stepped into it; and, by association, all things are blessed. The Epiphany is the turning point in which the Lord Jesus begins his ministry to reclaim all creation for his Father. It finds its triumph in the resurrection when Christ overcomes the law of death, of nature, and calls us to follow him, through baptism, to realize our destiny as lords over nature in God's name.

Finally, the presence of Jesus Christ in the Jordan water also indicates his presence at the creation, for "through him all things were made." This is a festival of light, for Christ is indeed, "Light of true light", and his coming has forever dispelled the darkness of sin and error. He is the Light whom no man can approach, and who, nevertheless, called all men to enlightenment and salvation.

By walking into the waters, Christ walked into the darkness to overcome it, and mankind's hope is renewed by this act of love and mercy. "Blessed is he that comes in the name of the Lord!"

Man, cast out by his own sin from paradise into darkness, has the doors of heaven opened to him and is led back by the hand of God himself.

"At your baptism in the Jordan River, O Lord, the worship due to the Holy Trinity was made manifest; for the voice of the Father bore witness to you by calling you his beloved Son. And the Spirit in the form of a dove confirmed the truth of his word. O Christ our God, who have revealed yourself and enlightened the world, glory to you!"

*Building a home for a homeless family.
Project Mexico, 2001*

35

> *"All of our life, our words, acts, and failures to act, are a preparation for our entering into the tomb. Like Jesus Christ, we too will be 'laid in a tomb' and like him all mankind will rise up, the good and the evil, the saved and the damned. The condition for eternal happiness though will depend on if we, like the Lord, were laid in humility in the tomb. Did we trust in God more than in ourselves? Did we always cry out to him and not just silently scream within, depending on our limited strength?"*
>
> *(March 1987)*

In this meditation of Great Lent, Archbishop Nathaniel brings us face to face with the problem of our own pride and the call of Jesus Christ to humility. As he so often does, His Eminence uses his words sparingly to drive home his point: that in order to be with Christ, we must become like Christ.

The Resurrection Fast or Great Lent

Most of us have experienced the outstretched hand of a friend on some occasion. Just when all seemed dark and no way evident and no light visible, there was someone who had the right word, the needed attitude to lift us out of a difficult situation or time.

How much truer it is that God himself is always present with us at all times and moments. His arms never grow weary of being outstretched, and his eyes never turn from our path nor his ears closed to our cry. David, in Psalm 140 of vespers, cries from the depth of his soul: *"Lord I am calling to you, hear me."* It is the cry of Adam and all his children to the only source of assistance. *"Do not put your trust in men of power or in any mortal man for he cannot save."*

During the weeks before the great celebration of Christ's victory of life over death, we are called to take stock of both how we reach out to others and how much God is part of our life. We call this the time of the "Resurrection Fast" or the Great Lent.

God is more than just that occasional friend; he is called "Guardian of my rights who answers when I call". The constancy of God's love and compassion, the depth of his humility, the length to which he endured all for us is so evident not only on the cross, but graphically when he is laid in the tomb. *"In a tomb they laid you, O my Christ and my God"* we sing on Great and Holy Friday. The next day we shout out, *"Christ is risen from the dead!"*

No human friend, no great philosopher or leader, not Moses, not Confucius, not Mohammed, not any king, president or any man or woman endured for mankind what God himself has: rejection, crucifixion and burial. Only by the cross of Jesus Christ are we saved and our sins taken away and death conquered. St. Paul rejoices, "Death, now where is your sting," your hold of fear over man?

Holy Iconography portrays that moment in sacred history, the only authentic history, as the entombing of the Son of God and the Son of man, Jesus of Nazareth. It is called "Extreme Humility".

"By Adam's fall, we sinned all," and pride is that which brought us low. Pride is a word which most of us reject today, just as in the time of Christ, beginning with Adam. On the contrary, God who is power and life shows that for us the way to peace and true meaning to life is in being humble.

We are happy to remind ourselves that we are made in the image and likeness of God, "Our Father in heaven," but we usually neglect to attend to this aspect of reality -- humility. God humbled himself by becoming like us to help us along the path of life. His children must be humble to rightly walk on the way to salvation. St. Athanasius says, *"He became like us so that he could lift us to become like him."*

All of our life, our words, acts, and failures to act, is a preparation for our entering into the tomb. Like Jesus Christ, we too will be "laid in a tomb," and like him, all mankind will rise up, the good and the evil, the saved and the damned. The condition for eternal happiness though will depend on if we, like the Lord, were laid in humility in the tomb. Did we trust in God more than in ourselves? Did we always cry out to him and not just silently scream within, depending on our limited strength?

Like the seed of the wheat, that small grain, so the Christian lives his life on earth and is thrown onto the dust from which he came. The plant, which grows -- eternal, unending life, sprouts from that. Now limitations, later fulfillment in God.

Do we call on the Lord? Do we reach out to our brother? This is the time of the year we are called on to reflect. Don't so much fear the IRS as fear the angel of judgment who will call us before the Lord's mighty throne on the real day of reckoning. Now we pay taxes for what we earn, but then Christ has paid the fee, and we shall enjoy the benefit...if on this earth, in this life, we do indeed "put our trust in God" who is of great humility for our sakes.

36

"The rejection of this crucial truth of the victory of the Savior over death is, in fact, the principal cause for the widespread skepticism which agitates the world today, and which is prevalent most of all where materialism and abuse of freedom dominate society and the souls of men."

(April 1987)

Written shortly after the falling asleep of His Eminence Archbishop Valerian and two years before the fall of the communist regime that hounded him to death, the 1987 Paschal Letter ties the concept of human freedom to the reality of the Resurrection. Only in Christ can true freedom be found – the paradox of freedom by obedience is at the heart of Christian life. We are freed to worship – so must we be fervent in carrying out our mission to evangelize our nation and even the world.

Dearly Beloved in Christ,

By the mercy of God and the will of the Orthodox faithful, Bishop of the Romanian Orthodox Church of America and Canada,

To our beloved clergy, monastics, faithful Orthodox Christians of the Romanian Orthodox Episcopate of America and Canada, and to the parishes under our hierarchal omophorion,

Grace, peace, and love of the Risen Christ and Episcopal blessings and intercessions from us for all which is good and useful for salvation.

Dearly Beloved in Christ,

Just as, almost two thousand years ago, the myrrh-bearing women proclaimed the wondrous Resurrection of Christ; and just as the apostles, disciples and every faithful soul heard of it and marveled; just as the Orthodox Church from the beginning as well as today preaches, so also do we, Orthodox Christians, joyfully proclaim as did the angel, the holy truth that *"Christ is risen from the dead, trampling down death by death and bestowed life on those in the tombs."*

This announcement, proclaimed in the services of the Church, at home, and wherever we gather in good will, is in itself a witnessing of faith, our most precious Christian confession; for truly, if Jesus is not risen from the dead, then our faith is in vain. More than that, if Jesus is not truly risen, then hope for our own resurrection, and for that of those departed from us, is also in vain.

The rejection of this crucial truth of the victory of the Savior over death is, in fact, the principal cause for the widespread skepticism which agitates the world today, and which is prevalent most of all where materialism and abuse of freedom dominate society and the souls of men.

The affirmation of those who historically saw and themselves came to believe in the reality of the resurrection and our own present spiritual confirmation in the light of the Lord's resurrection, penetrate deeply into the souls of believers, regardless of the material progress, scientific advancements and technological achievements of contemporary society.

The Savior's words concerning his holy resurrection and our resurrection are as real today as they have been in the past, living in the hearts of countless believers throughout history and according to God's plan of salvation for the world.

"The will of him who sent me is that I should lose nothing of all that he has given to me, and that I should raise it up on the last day..."; and, *"...whoever sees the Son and believes in him shall have eternal life, and I shall raise him up on the last day"* (Jn. 6:39-40).

For truly, through his death on the Cross, and especially through his third-day resurrection from the dead, Jesus has won for us the great victory of liberation from death and its consequences, freedom from sin and from the powers of darkness of this world. Jesus is thus both our hope of resurrection and *"the first fruit of all who have fallen asleep"* (Matt. 11:12).

Let us therefore rejoice in this victory of the Resurrection as well as in the feast of Pascha as established by our holy Orthodox Church. But let us not forget that the reality of the Resurrection is, first of all, a spiritual reality; and, that the grace which comes to us from the light of Christ's own resurrection must be embraced by our own will and personal decision as well as that of the entire Church to follow Christ in our struggle with ourselves, with the world, or whatever else can hinder us in our spiritual procession toward a spiritual truth and living a true existence.

Our struggle for justification and salvation, the Cross of Jesus' Resurrection and our own resurrection, comes about through "obedience even unto death" and in observance of God's commandments.

St. John Chrysostom reminds us that the cross is *"the will of the Father, the honor of the Son and the joy of the Holy Spirit."* Thus, in order for us to rejoice fully in all the gifts of the Resurrection, we must fulfill the Father's will, properly honor the Son and rejoice in the Holy Spirit.

Only if we "die together with Christ" can death no longer separate us from Christ, for we all *"believe that we shall return to life with him"* (Romans 6:8).

Beloved Spiritual Children,

Let us once again celebrate the great feast of the holy Pascha, *"the day which the Lord has made, and in which we rejoice and are glad."*

In blessed joy then, let us walk along the path of a new and upright life. Let us extol the One who has given us salvation, the Lord Jesus, but let us not forget that the gift of eternal life for which we have been redeemed by the sacrifice of the Blood of the Lord, produces also spiritual fruits, the fruits of the Spirit which are *"love, joy, peace, patience, kindness, goodness, trustfulness, gentleness and self-control"* (Gal. 5:22-23).

Only by living in Christ as new creatures, transfigured according to the image and likeness of God, shall we truly be *"children of the resurrection and heirs of the kingdom of God"* (Romans 7:17). Christ is risen and *"today all things are filled with light: heaven, and earth, and the places beneath the earth."*

May the great Feast of the Holy Resurrection, the Light of this Feast of feasts in which "salvation has come to the world, as

St. Gregory of Nazianzus heralds, embolden our faith, that we may be stronger in faith, in hope and in love for God and neighbor; for we are new creatures in the Spirit, and we ourselves are witnesses and beacons of the Resurrection of the Lord, fervent and responsible Christians sent out to evangelize our families, our nation and the world around us.

On the occasion of the holy Feast of Pascha, we extend to all the faithful of the God-protected Romanian Orthodox Episcopate of America and Canada, to all faithful Orthodox Christians in the "new world," to the clergy, the monastics, and to the faithful, our greetings for health and spiritual growth in the Lord.

CHRIST IS RISEN! TRULY HE IS RISEN!

37

"The history of Orthodoxy is mantled with the intercessions of the Blessed Virgin Mary who is one of us. It is splendid in icons, miracle-working icons, holy shrines and healings through intercessions of the Virgin. She herself put things into proper perspective at the first miracle of her divine Son when she said to those present: 'Do whatever HE tells you.' Certainly, she is not herself divine, is not God, is not 'taking' HIS place."

(August 1987)

Archbishop Nathaniel brings our attention to the important place of the Mother of God in true Orthodox worship and spirituality. He warns us against the 'slippery slope' of, little by little, abandoning our reverence for the saints in general, and the Blessed Virgin in particular, as we are ever more influenced by the attitudes and practices of our Protestant neighbors. In the lines below, His Eminence returns us to the basic truths about this maid of Nazareth who said 'Yes!' to the Lord's plan and so brought salvation into the world.

Veneration of the Mother of God

Can it be that Orthodox Christians in America have been influenced by our Protestant neighbors? It seems that we have acquired their attitude toward the Mother of God. While we still "call to remembrance our most-holy, most-pure, most-glorious Lady, The Birthgiver of God and ever-virgin Mary with all the saints" and are reminded to, like them, give our whole self and one another to Christ our God, our true devotion to them is in question.

Very few even know of the "Akathist Hymn" or the "Paraclis" service either to the Holy Virgin or the saints. Where are our shrines and holy places to their respect and honor? Who keeps even the one-day fast in honor of the "elect" of God?

The Reformers did not at first reject the fellowship of the saints. Only gradually did they see the intercession of the saints as "popish-roman nonsense". Today, it appears that even the Roman church has cooled in fervor toward recognizing the saints and the Mother of God in zeal to become "Christocentric".

Orthodoxy has always and only honored the Virgin Mary in her role as "Birthgiver of God", the maid of Nazareth who said "Yes!" to the Lord's invitation to cooperate with him in the plan of salvation through incarnation. The Gospel of St. Luke clearly reminds us that the Mother of God was filled with the Holy Spirit when she cried out her hymn of praise to "God my Savior!" She herself recognized her need for salvation, and the Orthodox Church, in her teaching, has reiterated that she too, a child of Eve, needed the redeeming blood of Christ for salvation.

The coming into the world in the flesh of Jesus, the second person of the All-holy Trinity, was through her "Yes!" The history of the world was altered by her "Yes!" Through the centuries, it was the courageous "Yes!" of that wonderful young woman who inspired and inspires the followers of the Lord to also "take up the cross and follow".

The iconography, the scriptures in writing of the Church, always show the Virgin Mary in relation to the Savior. She is shown holding him, being near him, among his followers and is never exalted above her son.

Little by little, however, it appears that our awareness of the communion of the saints and our fellowship with them has been influenced. While we sing, "O, Son of God, admired in your saints, save us who sing Alleluia to you!", we do not really praise those faithful servants of the Lord who also sang "alleluia" with their blood, their witness, their sanctification through him.

It is important for us to recall that the Gospel message is not for angels, and an abstraction but for you and me. It is for "flesh and blood" which is called to a higher plan of eternal existence. We are equally called to say "Yes!" to God; our witness must be as fervent as that of the saints before us. We take courage from them and their examples, true; but what is most important is that they are still alive in Christ and help us by their prayers. We are one Church unified in the Lord who is the only head. There is no Church in heaven, Church on earth, Church...wherever. There is one Church which exists in all time and space and is alive in Christ though asleep in the body.

To ignore the saints before us is to ignore those we love around us. To not praise them in their present state is to deny glory to their Savior. The saints and in particular the Mother of God do not "take the place of the Lord," nor are they some mechanical means of "attaining" heaven. We know that salvation is a gift from God, but we also know that we show our faith in actions of praise to the Lord who has saved them and who saves us.

The history of Orthodoxy is mantled with the intercessions of the Blessed Virgin Mary who is one of us. It is splendid in icons, miracle working icons, holy shrines and healings through the intercessions of the Virgin. She herself put things into proper perspective at the first miracle of her divine Son when she said to those present: "Do whatever HE tells you." Certainly, she is not herself divine, is not God, is not "taking" HIS place.

On the other hand, she is certainly "more honorable than the cherubim," for she is not merely the "throne" but the blood of which the Lord Jesus took flesh; she is "more glorious beyond compare than the seraphim," for she does not need to cover her eyes and face from fear as the angelic powers did, for she gazed into the face of the infant born in a manger, the preacher of reconciliation, the radiant, resurrected "Life of All." The Mother of God is not just one among equals; she is set apart being chosen by God and fulfilled by her response of "Yes!"

Unless we re-establish our praise of her, not worship, but authentic acknowledgement as the greatest person who has ever lived, we do not give honor to the Lord born of her.

The Weeping Icon of Our Lady of Chicago is a presence of God's power among us. Analyze the tears; pull apart the boards, scrape the paint! Her presence, her reality is part of that communion of saints and recalls us to reflect that we are sons and daughters of the Most High, called to inherit his Kingdom. Indeed, we are one in the household of the Lord, both those who have passed through this life and those traversing the way.

Our concern should be that we do not honor the saints, and thus, the Lord himself, as we ought. Our glory is, in fact, in the

Lord who made heaven and earth, but also in our call to become "like him" (2 Peter 1).

> *The devil comes and tempts all the servants of God. Those who are strong in the faith resist him and he goes away from them, because he cannot find entrance. So, he goes then to the empty and, finding an entrance, he goes into them. Thus he accomplishes in them whatever he pleases and makes them his slave.*
>
> *(Shepherd of Hermas)*

38

"Today, if we listen with our hearts, we can hear the beat of the angels' wings as they hover over the manger of the newborn Christ child and the mighty rush of their flight as they descend to the shepherds to announce the great tidings: The Christ is born! What joy was in the heart of the ever-virgin Mary, of Joseph the Protector, of the shepherds, magi; and, even the beasts of the field and cave and mountains rejoiced!"

(December 1987)

"From the Holy Scriptures, we know that man is a pilgrim, a traveler along the highway of this temporal life, journeying a certain length of days and years. Pope St. Gregory of Rome tells us that Christ was born, not in the house of his parents, but on a journey, that He might truly show that because of the humanity he has taken on himself, He was born as it were among strangers. Even strangers, however, take notice of a new presence in their sight."

(December 1988)

His Eminence tells the Christmas story in his own way, teaching us the essence of that story in just a few words. These Pastoral Letters, written in 1987 and 1988, bring the joy and hope of the Feast of the Nativity of Our Lord to the rank and file faithful of the diocese. Filled with deep theological truth, they communicate simply and directly in the style that will come to characterize the new bishop of the Romanian Orthodox Episcopate.

The Birth of Our Lord and God and Savior Jesus Christ

Dearly Beloved in Christ,

Once again, after a long year, we are today celebrating the birth of the Sun of Righteousness, Jesus Christ, the Light of the world! The burden of the weeks and months, the cares and decisions made, are laid aside on this great day of joy and feasting for the gladness in our hearts of the celebration of the birth of our Lord and God and Savior, Jesus Christ. In reflecting on his holy feast day, our spirits are renewed with the strength and courage that come from eternal hope.

Today, if we listen with our hearts, we can hear the beat of the angels' wings as they hover over the manger of the newborn Christ child and the mighty rush of their flight as they descend to the shepherds to announce the great tidings: the Christ is born! What joy was in the heart of the ever-virgin Mary, of Joseph the Protector, of the shepherds, magi and even the beasts of the field, the cave and mountains rejoiced!

Since the fall of Adam and Eve, all of creation, nature and man has striven to find its true and proper relationship with its creator. Man, in his search but in his pride fell farther and farther from heaven, growing more and more distant from the Almighty, and God saw that his image and likeness was darkened by sin and had become overwrought with despair.

"What was God to do in the face of this dehumanizing of mankind, this universal hiding of the knowledge of himself by the wiles of the evil spirits?" asks St. Athanasius the Great. *"What else could he possibly do, being God, but renew his image in mankind, so that through it man might once more come to know him?"*

God had sent prophets and even angels to call man back to him, but it was necessary for the Creator himself to stoop to earth to lift man to heaven. *"What wonderful progress,"* exclaims St. John Chrysostom - *"He first sends angels to men, then leads the men to heavenly things. A heaven is made on earth, since heaven must take to itself the things of the earth."* Jacob the Patriarch cried out: *"He is coming and the people will gather around him."*

The coming of the Savior was to wipe off the dust from the image of God in man and to restore him to his rightful place as heir of his Father's kingdom. St. Athanasius also tell us that, *"The Word of God comes in his own person, because it was he alone, the image of the Father, who could recreate man after the Image,"* quoting the words of our Lord: *"I came to seek and save that which was lost."* It was therefore necessary for God himself to come to us, announces St. Leo the Great: *For unless he were true God, he could bring us no aid; and were he not true man, he could offer us no example."*

The reason, therefore, for which Jesus was born of the Holy Spirit and the Virgin Mary, explains St. John Chrysostom, is: *"that coming among us he may teach us, and teaching us lead us by the hand to the things that men cannot see. For since men believe that the eyes are more trustworthy than the ears, they doubt of that which they do not see, and so he has deigned to show himself in bodily presence, that he may remove all doubt."*

In teaching us, Christ has opened our minds to the Scriptures and to the prophets; indeed, as David said, *"He shall come down welcome as a rain on thirsty soil!"* His birth is of cosmic importance. It has value not only for me personally, not merely for my family and nation but for the universe of which he is the Creator. Indeed he is welcome!

Coming to know him, we are called to worship him. *"For if Christ is God, as indeed he is, but took not human nature upon him, we are strangers to salvation. Let us then worship him as God,"* says St. Cyril of Jerusalem, *"but believe that he also was made man."*

Jesus the Savior, Christ the Anointed One, came as *"bread down from heaven that he might feed the hungry,"* invites St. Cyril; and men of every age have hungered and thirsted for the truth of his place in creation, and today's celebration of the birth of the Prince of Peace reminds the world that, indeed, man is the son of the King who calls all to eternal inheritance.

Do we rejoice today in his birth? Yes! We do! *"Acknowledge, O Christian, that dignity which is yours!"* exhorts St. Leo. Dignity, yes! For we are also *"the examples of the Holy*

Spirit" (1 Cor. 6:19) in whom God dwells and with whom he walks, calling each of us by name. Thus, we are never alone, not even in the darkest hour: not when satanic hands pull down our holiest shrines and churches; *"God is with us! Understand, O nations, and submit yourselves, for God is with us!"*

Wherever there is a true believer, there is the Church, and there is the temple of God. The steadfast worshipper holds fast to the cradle of the Christ Child and sings out with St. John Chrysostom: *"I rejoice bearing in my arms the cradle of Christ. For this is all my hope and this is my life, this is my salvation, this is my instrument of song, the harp of my soul!"*

At the birth of Christ, the angels cried out: *"Glory to God in the highest heavens and on earth peace to men who enjoy his favor!"* (Luke 2:14). *"This peace was made through Christ himself for he reconciled us with the Father and to God,"* St. Cyril exclaims. *"In persecution and in sorrow, in good times and in rejoicing, the peace of God knows no bounds"* (Isaiah 9:7). Thus, today, our own joy knows no bounds, and we rush forward to welcome the new babe, Christ, into our world, for he brings reconciliation and peace to all. He is welcome! Let us welcome him, for He is our God and we His people.

For today, *"to us a child is born, unto us a son is given"* (Isaiah 9:5); the rain has come onto our thirsty land, the sweet-smelling fragrance covered the earth, the gentle and protecting cloud come into our midst, the pillar of fire to lead us out of darkness into brilliant light and extends his infant hand to us preparing us for what is yet to come, for the promise yet to be fulfilled. *"For when Christ shall appear, who is your life, then you also shall appear with him in glory!"* (Col. 3:3-4).

Christ is born! Glorify him!

Christmas Pastoral Letter

Dearly Beloved in Christ:

God prepared for his great plan of salvation by sending his angel to teach the Holy Virgin in Nazareth and to the Righteous Joseph in a dream. He sent a host of them to the shepherds to guide them to the cave and the infant Messiah. Before the birth of Jesus Christ, St. John Chrysostom reminds us, the angels were sent to punish mankind but now, at his birth, they join the ranks with men in giving thanks to the Almighty, for he has revealed himself in his only-begotten Son.

According to the Holy Gospel of St. Luke, we hear that a song of praise came from both the angels and the shepherds, an harmonious ode of joy, says St. Athanasius the Great, pouring from the depths of the bodiless powers and from the inner heart of the simple pastors, because they rejoiced not just in the birth of a mere child but in the birth of the Savior, Christ, and because they were privileged to stand in the presence of the divine light!

The song was not a lullaby, not a soft, gentle crooning at a child's crib but a mighty hymn of power, of strength, of exaltation! The angels sang their heavenly hymn to God's glory, and while the birth was humble, even to the simple shepherds, it drew from them their words of hope and worship.

Not only to the Holy Virgin did the shepherds tell of what they had seen and heard, but they went out and told others, says St. Photios; and what is more, they impressed the others, for we read that after hearing the words of the shepherds, the others all "wondered." Here is the first sharing of the Good News, of the Gospel of righteousness. It came from having been in the presence of the Lord himself lying in the manger.

We recall that it was the same feeling of the presence of the true Messiah that motivated the woman at Jacob's well in Samaria to go and tell others what she had seen and heard, and brought her, also, to "wonder".

The infant Christ was placed in a manger, states St. Cyril of Jerusalem, because he found that man had become like a beast in his soul; and thus the Lord lay in the place of fodder, that we, changing our animal way of living, may be led back to the wisdom that fits mankind made in the image and likeness of God; that man stretches out his hand, himself not toward animal fodder but to the heavenly Bread and to wondering at the great love of God for man.

From the Holy Scriptures, we know that man is a pilgrim, a traveler along the highway of this temporal life, journeying a certain length of days and years. Pope St. Gregory of Rome tells us that Christ was born, not in the house of his parents, but on a journey, that he might truly show that because of the humanity he has taken on himself, he was born as it were among strangers. Even strangers, however, take notice of a new presence in their sight.

The last echoes of the angels' and shepherds' song had scarcely faded into the night when men began to decide for or against the newborn King of Peace. From a few days of rest nestled in his mother's arms, the Savior of our souls was carried off on a journey to Egypt, the land of safety for him, from those who rejected the prophets and who sought to take his new birth from him.

We, too, are called to wonder and to go out and tell others about the Lord. Him must we invite to travel with us on our personal journey from error and sin toward the light of the cave of Bethlehem. Ours must be that song of power and trust, of faith and hope, composed by the Holy Spirit in the angels and pastors. Indeed, God is the Lord and has revealed himself to us. Let us remember that we stand always by the cradle of Emmanuel and can bask in the divine light by crying out: "Jesus is Lord!" Alleluia!

Christ is born! Glorify him!

39

"If the Orthodox home is not blessed and dedicated with those who dwell in it, then it remains a house, not a home. If we are not sanctifying our homes through the Theophany blessing, we are not dedicating ourselves, and thus we cannot help society. On the contrary, we are part of its problem. Without the grace of God, we can do nothing; without the blessing of our home, it is indistinguishable from the rest of the fallen world."
(January 1989)

In another of his practical teaching articles, His Eminence reminds us that we are called to be holy and to sanctify our environment, from our home to our society. He writes simply, bringing the average reader to glimpse the profound meaning of a familiar ritual. He signs the article simply, "O.M.," that is, "an Orthodox Monk."

Theophany:
Baptism of the Faithful and of Homes

In the early centuries of the Church, the Mystery of Baptism was held only at certain times of the year and usually in conjunction with major feast days having to do with the life of our Lord and God and Savior, Jesus Christ: the Nativity of our Lord and Theophany; Resurrection; Pentecost.

Today, the Church baptizes, having a concern for infants, and the communal aspect of entrance into the Body of Christ, into the Church, has lost much of its impact. It has almost become a "family" happening instead of a parish celebration.

On the other hand, the service of blessing homes continues to be held with regularity on Theophany and, in some traditions, at the Exaltation of the Holy Cross. Perhaps the early baptized took some of the blessed water home with them to dedicate the house of stone in which they lived, just as they had dedicated the temple of their body of flesh and blood to the Lord.

An old adage says: "A man's home is his castle." The meaning is obvious that, although one cannot control the world outside the house, what takes place within is the responsibility and joy of the householder.

Certainly, society does influence the home and, in particular, today with the easy access into the inner sanctum of our walls of television, radio, newspapers and magazines. We are made aware that much of the ill within the home come from outside its walls.

On the other hand, we cannot deny that individuals make up the sum total of society; and therefore, individuals and households do carry their way of living to the world beyond. The house, in fact, is naturally the greater influence.

Orthodox Christians are knowledgeable that only through dedication of oneself and one's home to the Living God can that individual and house be blessed, let alone influence society.

If the Orthodox home is not blessed and dedicated with those who dwell in it, then it remains a house, not a home. If we are not sanctifying our homes through the Theophany blessing, we are not dedicating ourselves, and thus, we cannot help society. On the contrary, we are part of its problem. Without the grace of God, we can do nothing; without the blessing of our home, it is indistinguishable from the rest of the fallen world.

This blessing with holy water, "Jordan Water," is not a mere custom or a tradition; it is not a ritual or an occasion for a visit with the parish priest. The blessing of a home with its family is a willing and conscious act of an entire family to dedicate itself and its "castle" to service for God and to the nation.

An apple tree bears apples; an automobile transports; a baseball bat hits the ball; a home blessed is a source of power and strength for its inhabitants, a refuge, a dynamic well, an island of rest from which the faithful go out to their work and return for renewal.

How can our own lives be "blameless, painless and peaceful," if our homes are not blessed to be innocent, hope-filled and peace bearing?

Whereas once the blessing of the home was anticipated as a family dedication, as a NEEDED holy action in the house which is a reflection of the parish church, too often it has become something to be "endured" right after Christmas; a kind of secondary close to the Christmas festivities.

Man is a worshipping being; he works together with the Lord of Hosts to restore and renew society. We are called the co-workers of the Holy Spirit and co-operators in our salvation. No one would intentionally destroy one's house, but we are negligent to reinforce it with this wonderful annual renewal through water and the Spirit.

We repaint the outside and make repairs; the inside is scrubbed and vacuumed; leaks are repaired; wires are replaced; cracks filled, and we feel that the house is renewed. How much more should we consider and act for spiritual renewal of our house into a home; our dwelling into God's temple; our hearth into a burning fire for the Lord of the Seraphim?

Every family should gather for the blessing; no outside disturbances should prevail; take the phone off the hook; no radio, no TV: no interference but a few, and, oh, so few moments of rededicating holy service of blessing to the God of heaven and earth. It is not an impossibility; it is, however, an effort to change society, and society will not be changed until individuals and families change.

"This home is blessed to the service of the Father, and of the Son and of the Holy Spirit. Amen!"

40

> *"With the changes in Eastern Europe in particular, the other aspect of the secularization of the New World is blatantly obvious. The faith, which sustained East Europeans in the depths of their hearts, can now be more public and evident. The shallowness of our own belief will be more scrutinized. Do we really believe that God is the ruler of history, or do we think that man is "all in all?"*
>
> *(November 1989)*

As the regimes of Eastern Europe began to fall, Archbishop Nathaniel saw clearly the irony for Americans. On Thanksgiving Day, 1989, he asks his flock to examine their own faith, contrasting it with the real sufferings of the millions behind the now shattered Iron Curtain. Twenty years later, we must ask ourselves whether we have responded to His Eminence's call to "transfigure the society in which we live."

Give Thanks to the Lord for He is Good! Alleluia!

Modern man and his children tend more and more to forget to "Give thanks to the Lord", considering that he, himself, the creature, is really the "source" of his well-being, and the Creator is "somewhere" out there, in the sky, or in the nebulous heavens but far removed from the actual life of man and his offspring.

Americans and Canadians pride themselves on their special day of "Thanksgiving", considering it a mark of uniqueness on the calendar of nations to have a day set aside for national giving of thanks.

However, slowly, slowly, even the tie to giving thanks to THE LORD is being eroded, and the day is rapidly becoming secularized for eating, watching sports events, etc.

The New World also favored itself during the last few decades as a "believing" New World, one based on faith in God and on the truth of his existence and his direction of human history.

With the changes in Eastern Europe, in particular, the other aspect of the secularization of the New World is blatantly obvious. The faith, which sustained East Europeans in the depths of their hearts, can now be more public and evident. The shallowness of our own belief will be more scrutinized. Do we really believe that God is the ruler of history, or do we think that man is "all in all"?

Some Orthodox reject the uniqueness of these national holidays, either because they are not "Church" holy days or because we say, "Everyday is a day of thanksgiving!" However, in that the Church has always sanctified time and space, we should not shrink from doing the same for a day that, in historical foundation, was intended to be a "religious" holiday.

But, the crisis comes in that to REALLY celebrate the day, we are ABSOLUTELY CERTAIN that we must have turkey, etc., etc., etc., and act and do what others do on the day. Instead of sanctifying the day, our nation, and ourselves, we have been swept up in the secularization of the day, neither gaining from it nor adding to it.

To give proper thanks, we must first of all give it to the Author, Savior and Sanctifier of Life, the all Holy Trinity; and, we must give it to God alone for God alone is GOOD, as our Lord said. Secondly, we must celebrate the day as Orthodox Christians who, as good citizens of our nations, nevertheless have the divinely appointed task to transfigure the society in which we live, instead of being changed by society.

What appeal can we make to celebrate our holiday and still make it a holy day? Stop! Reflect! Consider who is the real source of life for us and for our children and confess that, really, we cannot add nor subtract to our life unless it is the will of God and by his grace.

Let us give thanks to the Lord, FOR HE IS GOOD! Praise the Lord! Alleluia!

41

> *"Although these scientific findings and biblical research clarify events which happened and especially clarify poor translations and ignorance of the past, they do not alter the essential: Jesus Christ was born at a definite time in history, He was expected by the Jews and written of by the prophets, and God, through nature, drew attention to this intervention of God in human history."*
>
> *(December 1989)*

Science and pseudo-science are indirectly addressed as His Eminence outlines the various theories and questions surrounding the actual date of the birth of Christ. While acknowledging the validity of and the necessity for scientific research, Archbishop Nathaniel reminds us that controversy over incidentals in no way threatens the core truth of the Incarnation. In this article, we see hints of His Eminence's general attitude toward science: that the material truths of science may be disputed or confirmed, but that the Truth of God's love manifested in the Incarnation, Crucifixion and Resurrection of His Son is never in doubt.

The Star of Bethlehem: Fact or Fancy?

After Jesus had been born at Bethlehem in Judaea during the reign of King Herod, some wise men came to Jerusalem from the east. *"Where is the infant king of the Jews?"* they asked. *" We saw his star as it rose and come to do him homage"* (Mt.2:2).

Astrology is fast becoming a popular pastime. Many people turn immediately to the "predictions" for the day in the papers. Some folks follow them, basing their lives upon the "sign" under which they are born. Others merely laugh at the column and its followers. This interest in astrology is superficial.

In the past, astronomy was a respected science. The difference between astrology and astronomy is this: the first is practical astronomy, the art of judging of reputed occult influence of stars upon human affairs, while the second is the science of the heavenly bodies. Ancient astronomers were very scientific in their methods. However, it was the astrological interpretations that the Church rejected. Man has free will and can choose his destiny. He is not ruled by external forces, though he is influenced by them. He is responsible for his own actions.

After the birth of Christ, some men came from Babylon to Bethlehem. Although they observed the stellar conjunction of three stars and predicted it in Babylon, they traveled to Palestine. These men attached special meaning to every star. They gave particular importance to the one at the birth of Jesus. The stars which came together and shone as one were Jupiter, a "lucky" star, and Saturn, a royal star supposed to protect Israel which appeared at the same place as Pisces, the sign of Israel.

Since Nebuchadnezzar's time, thousands of Jews had lived in Babylon. Some studied astronomy at the School of Astronomy in Sippar. These Jewish wise men understood the meaning of this heavenly occurrence. It pointed to the appearance of a mighty king in the west, in the land of their fathers. The intention of these men was to travel to Palestine, to see with their own eyes, to experience this great event.

They had observed the first encounter of the stars from the roof on the School in Sippar, May 29, 7 B.C. But as it was summer and exceedingly hot to travel, especially a long and dangerous journey, they waited, knowing that the stars would make a second conjunction about October 3. They predicted this future conjunction, just as today we predict sun and moon eclipses. It was noted that October 3rd was also the Jewish Day of Atonement that year, and it was meaningful for them to depart then. The trip, taking about 6 weeks, would bring them to Jerusalem about the end of November.

On arriving, the first question, the important one for these Jewish wise men, burst out: "Where is the infant king of the Jews? We saw his star as it rose and have come to do him homage." The Holy City knew nothing of schools of astronomy. The entire city was shocked by the news. The King, Herod, was angry, for he was not himself a Jew but an Idumaean! The people were pleased, for they felt that the nation would finally rise against the foreign dominations that bound Palestine. There are historical accounts testifying that after the conjunction of these stars one year later, a strong messianic movement began, and though Christ came and fulfilled it, the people rejected him until the nation was destroyed by the Romans in 70 A.D.

The King called the chief priests and scribes to ascertain where the Messiah was to be born. They found it in the book of the prophet Micah: *"But you, (Bethlehem) Ephrata, the least of the clans of Judah, out of you will be born for me the one who is to rule over Israel: his origin goes back to the distant past, to the days of old"* (Micah 5:2). Herod then sent the wise men to Bethlehem. On December 4, the conjunction of the stars occurred for the third time.

On the road to Hebron, five miles from Jerusalem, lies the village of Bet Lahm, the Old Bethlehem of Judah. The ancient highway lay almost due north and south. The third appearance of the conjunction of stars appeared to have dissolved into one great brilliant star. In the twilight of evening, they were visible in a southerly direction, so that the wise men of the east on their way from Jerusalem to Bethlehem had the bright star in front of their eyes all the time. As the Gospel says: *"And there in front of them was the star they had seen rising; it went forward and halted over the place where the child was"* (Mt. 2:10).

The Gospel rendering of the star has been authenticated by the identification of the cuneiform texts of the School of Sippar deciphered in 1925 by the German scholar, Schnabel. According to him, the texts give special importance to the conjunction of Jupiter, Saturn, in Pisces, an occurrence over 5 months in the year 7 B.C.

Also, with modern biblical research, textual glosses are made clear. In the old Authorized Version of the text, we read: his star "in the east". Normally in Greek, the plural is used for the direction, east. But in scripture, it is the singular, "en te anatole" not "anatolai" which in astronomical terms implies the early rising of a star, the heliacal rising. Thus, the obvious meaning of the wise men was that "we have seen his star appear in the first rays of dawn", or his rising star. These correspond to the exact astronomical facts. Also, if it were in the east that the wise men saw the star, they would have to travel towards the orient, Persia, India, for Palestine is WEST to Babylon. Thus, the meaning is clearer with biblical criticism.

Although the Church celebrates December 25 as the liturgical date of the birth of Christ, historians and astronomers agree that December 25 of the year 1 A.D. is not the date, neither day nor year. Responsibility lies upon the Scythian monk, Dionysios Exiguous. He lived in Rome and in 533 worked backwards to fix the beginning of the new era. He forgot the year zero which should have been between 1 B.C. and 1 A.D., and overlooked the four years when the Roman Emperor Augustus had reigned under his own name of Octavian.

According to the Bible, we know better. Herod was King, and he died in 4 B.C. Thus, Jesus must have been born before this. The star appeared in 7 B.C., and thus, a more likely date. The month of December is challenged because of St. Luke (2:8): *"In the countryside close by there were shepherds who lived in the fields and took it in turns to watch their flocks during the night."* Meteorologists recorded the temperatures at Hebron and found that frost is heavy and rains fall the most in December, January and February. No cattle or livestock would have been in the fields during this time. In other references, it is noted that livestock is taken into the fields in March and returned at the beginning of November, remaining in the open for nearly 8 months. Today, shepherds and animals are under shelter during the Christmas season. Thus, St. Luke points to the birth before the beginning of winter, and St. Matthew points to the brilliant star of 7 B.C.

Although these scientific findings and biblical research clarify events which happened and especially clarify poor translations and ignorance of the past, they do not alter the essential: Jesus Christ was born at a definite time in history; he was expected by the Jews and written of by the prophets -- and God, through nature, drew attention to this intervention of God in human history.

The church expresses this beautifully in the Troparion of the Nativity of Jesus Christ:

"Your nativity, O Christ our God, has dawned to the world the light of knowledge, for in it, those who worshipped

the stars, were taught by a star to adore you, the Son of righteousness and to know you the celestial dawn, O Lord, glory to you!"

42

"Thus, Beloved, while looking hopefully for change upon this earth, and awaiting the restoration of man and nature, let us reflect these things in our own lives. Let us rekindle in our hearts the "Joyous Light", the "Light which illumines all mankind", Christ himself. Let us celebrate the day with proper hymns of praise and thanksgiving, venerating the holy icon of the Lord's resurrection and partaking of the Paschal Lamb who was sacrificed for us."

(April 1993)

In this Pastoral Letter, His Eminence brings us face to face with the reality of the Resurrection. He urges us to embrace that reality and to make our own lives icons of it. He lifts us beyond mere observance of the Feast, to real celebration.

Resurrection Pastoral Letter 1993

To the Worthy Clergy and Pious Faithful
of the Romanian Orthodox Episcopate of America

Dearly Beloved in Christ:

Christ Is Risen!

Throughout the year, Christians celebrate various feast days which commemorate the earthly but divine activities of our Lord and God and Savior, Jesus Christ. There are other special feast days on which we commemorate the Ever Virgin Mary and the saints, those faithful witnesses who in all generations are pleasing to God.

As wonderful as all of these celebrations are, there is none that compares with that of Holy Pascha, the Resurrection of our Lord. It is the "feast of feasts and festival of festivals, on which we bless Christ forever!" Pascha is the most beautiful, most splendid and illuminating of all the feasts of our Orthodox Faith. Saint Gregory of Nazianzus says that "...as the sun outshines all the stars, so this holy day is above all the others." Let us take heed, therefore, to celebrate it fittingly.

Our Christian faith is based on the very reality of Christ's resurrection from among the dead; the words to the hymns we sing are of joy and praise and thanksgiving for the resurrection; the icons we "write" are portrayals of the resurrected Christ and of the saints who are alive in him; the architecture of our churches and the structure of our worship are based on the fact of the resurrection of Jesus Christ. For we know that, "...Christ has in fact been raised from the dead, the first fruits of all who have fallen asleep" (1 Corinthians 5:20).

"In Christ's holy resurrection, all who are in him arose, and life, resurrection and the dawn of a new day were granted to those sitting in the shadow of death," states Saint Gregory of Nazianzus. Orthodox Christians are in Christ through holy baptism; and thus, in a special way, we were buried with him, arose with him and now live our lives in the knowledge of this new dawn and new era bestowed upon the universe.

The resurrection was not a vision, not the good feeling of the apostles nor of the early Christian community, but a physical reviving of the body of the Lord. Saint Thomas had to put his hand into the wounds in the Lord's side and in his hands. He believed without having to also touch the wounds in the Savior's feet! Says Saint John of Damascus: "The risen Lord by his own body, bestowed the twin gifts of resurrection and subsequent incorruption even on our own bodies."

The reality of the Lord's resurrection is God's finger on the page turning to the next chapter of his divine plan, which is the resurrection of all mankind. Saint Athanasius the Great explains: "The Savior came to accomplish not his own death, but the death of men, and he was concerned about the resurrection of the body."

Indeed, this is a great mystery, meditates Saint Gregory of Nazianzus, "...the purpose for us of God, who for us became man and became poor, to raise our flesh and recover his image and remake man, that we might all be made one in Christ." What great love God showers on us! What steadfast patience and kindness he has toward our stubbornness and our doubts!

In that this day is above all others, we must guard ourselves against merely observing it instead of celebrating it. Even if the world only gives it lip service and purposes to gain from it in a mundane commercial manner, Orthodox Christians must keep the feast pure in its full power and meaning. We are warned by the Nazianzan, "Fear God! This is your only guide for life here below, to be guided through the disorder of the things which are seen and changeable, to the things which stand firm and are unmovable." We believe that the fact of universal resurrection stands firm.

Although the truth of the resurrection is universal, we must participate in transfiguring the world around us by sharing this Good News and being admirable witnesses to the risen Lord. How to do this? Listen to Saint Polycarp, patron of the first hierarch of our Episcopate, Policarp Morusca: "Strengthen yourselves by serving God in fear and in truth, putting away empty vanity and foolish decisions."

We have just sung, "It is the day of resurrection! Let us reflect the feast and let us embrace one another. Let us say 'Brother!' to them that hate us, and let us forgive all things because of the resurrection!" This holy embrace, however, is not all that we must do. We are told by the Nazianzan, "...let us offer to him who suffered and rose for us, let us offer ourselves...let us give all, offer all, to him who gave himself as ransom and reconciliation for us."

Let us embrace the ecstatic words of wonder of St. Gregory Nazianzus who says, "I can hardly wait for the voice of the archangel, the last trumpet, the transformation of the heavens, the transfiguration of the earth, the liberation of the elements, the renovation of the universe!"

Thus, Beloved, while looking hopefully for change upon this earth, and awaiting the restoration of man and nature, let us reflect these things in our own lives. Let us rekindle in our hearts the "Joyous Light", the "Light which illumines all mankind", Christ himself. Let us celebrate the day with proper hymns of praise and thanksgiving, venerating the holy icon of the Lord's resurrection and partaking of the Paschal Lamb who was sacrificed for us.

For Christ is risen, and we arose with him! Christ has burst from the tomb and our own graves stand emptied! Christ is risen, and life is renewed; and we are all made alive in him to whom be all honor and glory, together with the Father and the Holy Spirit. Amen.

Christ is risen! Truly, he is risen!

43

"The Great Paschal Fast prepares us to appreciate and celebrate fully the resurrection of Jesus Christ from among the dead, allowing us to enter with him and the apostles and disciples into that point in time at which death was destroyed by the Anointed One, the Christ, thereby setting all humanity free from the fear of bondage to death and the end to our personal existence."

(March 2003)

Simply, without esoteric theological ornamentation, His Eminence calls us all to embrace and engage in the season of Great Lent. The imagery is mundane, but the message is clear – the Fast is a milestone in our lives, an occasion for real rebirth and the beginning of new life.

The Great Paschal Fast

The Chancery Office receives statistic cards from each parish priest. There are four cards: a pink one for baptism, yellow for conversion, white for marriage and blue for burial. Each month the statistics are published in the **SOLIA** newspaper; and once a year, a total is made and reported. The one statistic that cannot be changed is the one for death, because that is the end of earthly experience; there are no more decisions or choices to be made.

On the other hand, a baptized person may neglect and even abandon the faith; a conversion may be temporary, and a marriage may end in divorce. Life is a matter of choosing, and choosing means to do one thing before another. To live a life in Christ is to live for him and for the Church, that is, those who are part of his body. On the other hand, to live our life in Christ also means to live for those who are not baptized into Christ but who are also children of God. "If we live, we live for the Lord; and if we die, we die for the Lord, so that alive or dead, we belong to the Lord" (Romans 14:8).

We, as Church, help one another along the road of life. The celebration of baptism, conversion, marriage, and death, are each part of the life of individuals and the community. As part of that assistance and mutual support, we have established activities at certain times and seasons which are meant to remind and restore us along our way of living. There are times of celebration and times of intense individual and communal reflection. The Great Paschal Fast (sometimes referred to as "Great Lent") is one of those communal reflections experienced individually, as well as in unity with others.

"Orthodox" wall calendars, those wonderful timetables whose printing is usually sponsored by our local Funeral Director, have color indications as to weekly fast days, particular fast days and the seasonal fasts. A list of these is given in the *SOLIA Calendar 2003* (pages 66 & 69). But even though we are reminded of these days of recollection and renewal as printed on the calendar, and even though our parish bulletins recall them to us, it is up to each one to embrace the fasts as a personal spiritual health program.

Our world stands in a state of awareness, awareness of the fragility of peace, of possible instability, of disharmony among peoples. People also have faith in some supreme being whom they beseech to protect, to uplift, to direct them along the way of their lives. Prayer with fasting is prescribed by our Lord, Jesus Christ. Prayer, because God wants to know what is in our hearts; and, it is in prayer, private and communal, that we express ourselves to him. Fasting from foods, from words and inappropriate actions is also required to help us refocus on who we are and what is our service to God and neighbor. Fasting helps us focus on first things, first.

The Great Paschal Fast prepares us to appreciate and celebrate fully the resurrection of Jesus Christ from among the dead, allowing us to enter with him and the apostles and disciples into that point in time at which death was destroyed by the

Anointed one, the Christ, thereby setting all humanity free from the fear of bondage to death and the end to our personal existence.

It is good for us to gather together at this time of the year to prepare for the great day. It is a tonic for the sadness in our hearts and the anxiety and concern which comes from forgetting that "the Lord is King, robed in majesty: the Lord is robed in power, he wears it like a belt. Holiness will distinguish your house, O Lord, forever and ever" (Psalm 93).

God said to his people: "Be holy, for I, the Lord your God, am holy" (Leviticus 19:2, 1 Peter 1:16). To be holy means to pull out all that is mundane and negative into what is good, positive and of everlasting value.

Having noted our wall calendars and our bulletins, let us decide to step into the Great Paschal Fast and stick to it, preparing ourselves as serious athletes for their competition, out to seek the "gold", the highest award, which can be bestowed on us. The golden reward can be described in words, but it can only be fully experienced by having worked for it and struggled to renew ourselves. This is our invitation, to take up the baton and run the course of the fast until we are crowned at the Paschal Feast of Feasts with the joy of breaking bread with the Master and with the communion of saints. One day, our name, too, will be written on a "blue" card: but until then, let us become fully alive in Christ, enjoying our baptism in Him, so that we can reap the glory of his resurrection through him and from him, having followed his own example to pray and fast.

Historical Notes

44

"Some were content that, at last, the Archbishop stepped down and they could foster 'new relations;' others still work to undermine what the diocese has come to be over the years; still others thought that chaos would reign, that the machinery would come to a dead stop."

"An Archbishop retires, a bishop is consecrated; a priest retires, a man is ordained; a layman falls asleep in the Lord, a soul is baptized; one may retire from a ministry but not from the apostolate to the Gospel."

(June 1985)

In 1984, Archbishop Valerian retired and Bishop Nathaniel was elected by the Episcopate Congress to succeed him as ruling hierarch of the Romanian Orthodox Episcopate of America. In this first anniversary tribute to his predecessor and mentor, His Eminence reflects on the life and commitments of a priest and hierarch.

One-Year Retirement Anniversary

It is one year since His Eminence, Archbishop Valerian D. Trifa chose to retire on the occasion of his 70th birthday. Laying aside the office of administration of the Romanian Orthodox Episcopate of America, he remains an Archbishop of the Church and a member, although retired, of the Holy Synod of the Orthodox Church in America.

Every American anticipates retiring, and the clergy, in growing numbers, do too. Perhaps, in the past and in the "old world", clergy did not retire; in the "new world," the life of the parish priest, as well as of the hierarchy, is different, and retirement is a normal part of Church life.

Orthodox priests serve parishes whose membership is not conveniently gathered around a church; daily visits to hospitals and homes demand much of the day; meeting with the faithful are, because of the working schedules, relegated to evenings; counseling and planning demand further time, and the burden of parish administration rests mostly on the shoulders of the priest. Services are not held on weekdays, because working people cannot attend, and the retired and others are often miles from the church and without transportation or depend on others for it. The church of America is a "new world" Church.

Other priests, in addition to serving a parish, may be involved in outside work to supplement the income that the parish provides. Clergy with families are also in need of clothing, food, insurances, education, transportation, etc., etc., etc.

The family life of the priest is shaped by the demands of the parish. The Preoteasa must equal the patience of Job, the attention of Martha, love of Mary and faith of Paul. Children need education and the saving for this great burden weighs heavily on the clergy. The "unexpected" must always be anticipated. The family life of the priest is molded by his availability to others.

It is no wonder that more and more clergy do retire and lay aside the burden of administration while continuing to be interested in and giving time to other church programs. The physical limitations, desire to have more time to dedicate to personal prayer and work, prompts them to make way for younger clergy to shoulder the burden, the "light" yoke in the vineyard of the Lord.

What is said for the parish priest may also be said for the hierarchy. More traveling, wider concerns, constant demands for availability and visibility take time. Physically, one can do so much and then, in good grace, one retires to give attention to personal details, prayer and writing.

Usually, one prepares for one's retirement to be among friends and family, in surroundings both pleasant and familiar. No one anticipates being alone or in a strange place; no one wants to retire to the unknown.

Archbishop Valerian has been in exile for one year; his retirement is, however, not a retirement but a search for one; his time is not his own, because he is at the beck and call of strangers. Although time may be available for some writing, some reflecting, it is not the promised time rewarded for many decades of service and dedication.

Some were content that, at last, the Archbishop stepped down and they could foster "new relations"; others still work to undermine what the diocese has come to be over the years; still others thought that chaos would reign, that the machinery would come to a dead stop.

The Church is not one individual but all of the members. Each has a function, a duty, blessed by talents. When one passes from the scene, another is called. Parish council, organizations, parish priests and hierarchs pass from active administrative involvement to various other roles within the Church.

Our Diocese/Episcopate is based on faith in Jesus Christ who is the same yesterday, today and forever. The mission of the Gospel continues, because the members of the Church continue to live their life in Christ. Our roots are firmly planted in the soil of the new world, and her ways have been tried and found trustworthy. The people of God, ordained and non-ordained, have clearly shown and uphold that the diocese will continue her witness to Orthodoxy serving the Romanian-born, the American-Romanian and the American, as part of the Orthodox Church in America.

An Archbishop retires, a bishop is consecrated; a priest retires, a man is ordained; a layman falls asleep in the Lord, a soul is baptized: one may retire from a ministry but not from the apostolate to the Gospel.

"All baptized in Christ have put on Christ, Alleluia. The Lord reigns forever, your God, O Zion, from age to age."

Your Eminence: La Mulți Ani!

45

"Orthodox jurisdictional unity must not remain on the drawing table nor put on the back burner. Time does not permit it nor does the Gospel condone disunity to actions. The Church, already existing on these shores for two centuries, is falling farther and farther behind the opportunities God-given by the civil liberties of this land."

"May God grant that we celebrate, and soon, a united witness, a single light, a strong voice in the name of Him who said, "Go out and make disciples of all nations."

(November 1985)

With just a year of his archpastorate under his belt, then Bishop Nathaniel already was calling for unity among the Orthodox of North America. In this article, His Eminence refers to the two occasions then uppermost in the minds of his faithful: the coming Thanksgiving holiday and the monumental project of restoring the Statue of Liberty. After reminding us of our good fortune as Americans, His Eminence then lifts us beyond nationalism and ethnicity, calling us – as he will so often over the next twenty-five years – to true unity and discipleship in Jesus Christ.

Restoring the Lady

Decades ago, American children gathered their pennies and small coins to help set up the Statue of Liberty in the New York Harbor. That united effort extracted from hundreds of thousands of individuals is an example of what unity of purpose and strength in solidarity can do.

Now, after years of weathering the storms and wages of the elements, "The Lady" was found to be in need of restoration in order for preservation of the sculpture and safety of those who visit her. Again, appeals have been made and corporations and businesses vie with one another with matching funds to "Save the Lady".

In her uplifted arm, "The Lady" holds a lamp to light the way for those coming from afar, from bondage, from suppression, from the many negative aspects of far away lands from which the millions of immigrants came, willingly and unwillingly. They came for a "new life;" for a more bounteous life, for educational benefits, for spiritual liberty and intellectual freedom.

For many, "The Lady" seems to have become more of a symbol of all the United States than is "Uncle Sam", the shrewd New England "Yankee." After all, Uncle Sam is more of a northern figure than one for the entire nation.

Be these things as they may, it appears that a part of the infatuation with "The Lady" may, in fact, be a longing on the part of Americans for the real lady, "Our Lady", the Mother of God. While being careful not to be "nationalistic" nor fall into the obvious trap of making nationality a "religion", one can observe the deep desire of Americans to find spiritual meaning in our present day society. It offers, indeed, all the wonderful material gifts of this bountifully blessed land, but society has not come up with "the" answer, who is Christ. As "The Lady" appears to be a symbol to all of America, so the Mother of God is a symbol to all mankind before the Creator.

Somehow, in a "secular mystical way," the Lady in the Harbor conjures up hope, strength, and trust. She calls forth courage, effort, dedication and rewards. In fact, it is not difficult to transfer these virtues to the Mother of God who told the stewards at the wedding of Cana, "Do whatever he tells you to do."

For decades, the "tired, hungry, homeless" have passed by "The Lady" as through portals to a new life. So one of the titles of "Our Lady" is "the Gate," the one who points out Christ as the gate of new life, the door into the pasture of our heavenly Father's kingdom, the way through the vineyard.

In her arm, the Birthgiver of God carries Christ, the true Light who enlightens all mankind; and he, being the source of life, holds the book of life in his own hands. She presents the "Lamp" himself who leads from the bondage of sin and suppression to eternal freedom. "Many will come from the east and from the west, from the north and from the south" to the banquet of the

Kingdom of God, we are told; and certainly, those who come to America's shores do not come only for the cornucopia of our "amber waves of grain" but for a "new life," which for the Christian can only be a life of rebirth through the saving water of the mystery of baptism.

Intellectual and cultural freedom means to see all things, all areas of human experience in the light of the Gospel. If we, as Orthodox Christians, see our faith as just one of many; if we consider the Lord Jesus Christ as just one religious leader among others, we have lost the taste of salt, we have hidden the light under the bushel, we have become inert yeast, dead to itself, dead to its purpose of witnessing.

November is the American month of "thanksgiving". The traditional turkey dinner satisfies the body, but only the Eucharist can satisfy the soul and body, the entire person. We thank God for the many freedoms that the founding fathers of our nation were enlightened by human sentiments to express and frame in the documents of the day. Free enterprise, equal opportunities, all the advantages which man can legislate for man are available, although these are not the total solution.

We cannot be forgetful of others who have not the material blessings of this world, and moreso, who are not able to freely pursue an open path of salvation in public and without fear of recriminations. God has put a price on the lamp in the Lady's hand: the price of dedication, of witness, of vigilance. The gift of salvation, however, is free and comes from the Sun of Righteousness, the Only-begotten Son.

America has a duty to all nations to share the wealth of her material riches with others. In turn, we have received the gift of Holy Orthodoxy from others, and in looking to "The Lady" in the harbor, we must see THE LADY who by giving birth to the Lord Jesus Christ, guides us to the harbor of the salvation of our souls.

One thing that this month of thanksgiving and "The Lady" should remind all Orthodox Christians of, is that only with the same unity of purpose and intense solidarity in scope of all Orthodox can we present the True Faith to our brothers together in one single effort to bear a witness to civil liberties; so we must take the same road and become "like children for the promotion of the Kingdom of God" in unity.

Orthodox jurisdictional unity must not remain on the drawing table nor put on the back burner. Time does not permit it nor does the Gospel condone disunity to actions. The Church, already existing on these shores for two centuries, is falling farther and farther behind the opportunities God-given by the civil liberties of this land. One begins to look with question on those of us who do not see "lost opportunities," "right occasions" slipping by because of the weakness inherent to fragmentation of jurisdiction.

We have long ago learned that in passing under the lamp of "The Lady," one does not necessarily lose one's personal identity nor cultural preferences; but we have learned that in separation, there is weakness, and in weakness is judgment both from God and from man. In passing under the "light of Christ which illumines all men," we have no fear of losing particular identities but instead are really one in Christ. Let us learn that the Church, too, is weathering the storm of secularism, of fragmentation through human preferences, that she has a need to be for everyone, "a place of refuge and safety in times of trouble." It is not money that the Church needs, but unity in witness.

May God grant that we celebrate, and soon, a united witness, a single light, a strong voice in the name of him who said: "Go out and make disciples of all nations."

> *"We thank you, Christ our God, that you have satisfied us with the blessings of this earth. Grant that we may not be unworthy of the kingdom of heaven, and as you were present among your disciples, O Savior, giving them peace, come also among us, unify us and save us."*

46

> *"SOLIA did not receive the rich financial support available to the public newspapers; no advertisements, no added income helped to pay the staff. Included in the generous offerings of time and talent is the wonderful group of photographers who took photos, developed and gave them to SOLIA.*
>
> *"In the struggle to keep the church free from communist infiltration and takeover, SOLIA was the media necessary and the only one having credence.*
>
> *"One of the great marks of Archbishop Valerian as editor of the paper was that it did not sink to the level of polemics nor of verbal battles."*
>
> (February 1986)

As the diocesan newspaper, SOLIA, celebrated its fiftieth anniversary, Archbishop Nathaniel paused to reflect on its long history – from its founding by Bishop Policarp, through the editorship of Archbishop Valerian, to the early years of His Eminence's own tenure. The terrible struggles of the 1950s are only incidentally alluded to – the words of retrospection are transfigured into a statement of gratitude for the past and hope for the future.

SOLIA's 50 Years: a Sketch

This year, this month, the SOLIA newspaper, the official organ of communication of the Romanian Orthodox Episcopate of America is celebrating its 50th anniversary.

Communication between individuals and nations is of the utmost importance. What is in one's mind must be communicated in external forms to others in order to have some reaction, to promote an interaction for the benefit of more than one party.

Such, in fact, is the example given to us by the Almighty himself in the Holy Trinity. By taking on our human nature, God became man and communicated to us. What was in the mind of the Father was made known to us through the incarnation of his Word, Jesus Christ, the second person of the Holy Trinity. The impression made on us and in our hearts by the Lord Jesus is made to bear fruit through the indwelling of the Holy Spirit, which illumines our minds to God's message and brings us to respond.

The Lord Jesus preached to man; and, in turn, his followers repeated his words and told of his activities in behalf of mankind. In time, the oral preaching was enhanced by being written down, and thus the good news of salvation was transmitted farther and farther around the inhabited world.

Through the history of the Church and of nations, it was often the clergy who wrote new alphabets in which to write the Gospel. Sts. Cyril and Methodius made up an alphabet for the Slavs. St. Innocent of Alaska did the same centuries later with the Eskimos and Aleuts. There was even a newspaper printed in Cyrillic in the Eskimo language as an early means of communicating the Gospel to a new people.

At the turn of this century, when a large immigration of Romanian people came to America, numerous newspapers were initiated; but almost as rapidly as the ink dried, they disappeared. The effort to communicate, to "keep in touch," was very strong and necessary. The Romanian Orthodox parishes, which were established in the first three decades of the century, were, in fact, individual units, having a loose tie of fraternity and common interest between them, but no formal administrative or canonical basis. It was not until the 1929 Church Congress in Detroit, held on April 28-29, that the Episcopate or diocese was established. Each parish was invited to enter within the Episcopate in order to create a diocesan center, or a central authority to coordinate and supervise the life and direction of the Church in anticipation of seeking canonical approval for a diocese and its own hierarch.

In order to convince the people, with the parishes, that a diocese was necessary, some form of communication was needed. The idea came about that since there were no funds, as of this time, it was not feasible for the parishes to have their own organ of information. Mr. Joseph Drugociu of Detroit, publisher of the

Romanian language newspaper, TRIBUNA ROMANA, offered one full page of his newspaper for the use of the parishes in behalf of offering information about the needed establishment of the Episcopate. In December of 1930, the first page for the parishes appeared in the *Tribuna Romana.*

Some of the more frequent authors were Fr. John Stanila of Youngstown, editor and Fr. John Trutza of Cleveland. At that time, there were 17 parishes making up the body of the Church Congress. In 1932, the "Episcopate" page was discontinued for reasons yet unknown.

In December of that same year, an official newspaper, carrying the title, *Glasul Vremii*, was published through the efforts of Fr. Stefan Opreanu in Detroit. Mr. N. Moga of Cleveland, in charge of the paper's administration, had only 52 subscriptions after the 5th edition, and for lack of support from the people for financial assistance, the paper ceased publication.

With the coming of His Grace, Bishop Policarp Morusca, came the hope of buying a print shop. Thus in 1935, there was a plan to purchase the old *Viata Noua* press. This had been founded by a group of individuals who had hoped to make a commercial business of printing Romanian language publications. However, for lack of interest in Romanian language news and because of other reasons, the company failed. The Episcopate, itself not having sufficient funds to purchase the equipment, once again was thwarted in having its own official organ of communication.

The *Viata Noua*, which changed it name to *Solia Noua,* did, however, print a newspaper for the Episcopate. In 1936, it folded and was sold.

Bishop Policarp wrote in general asking for support of the idea of an Episcopate newspaper, and among the suggestions he received were that it be founded first on donations received and then on advance subscriptions.

Interesting to note are the words of Fr. Victor Barbulescu of Chicago who commented that there was a general lack of interest in reading newspapers, no matter how serious they may be. His second observation was that some attention should be given to writing in English for the benefit of those of the younger generation (1936) who did not read Romanian. At least a part of the paper must be given over to educating the young through the English language.

In general, the idea was accepted and support aroused. The Bishop, however, stated that he would write some articles but did not have the time to dedicate to the administration and actual publishing of the paper. Once again, Fr. John Stanila offered to be in charge, and the *Solia* newspaper first saw light on February 23, 1936 in Youngstown at the Youngstown Printing Company where a Romanian printer, Mr. John G. Gaspar was employed. *(February 23 is the feast day of St. Policarp, a tribute to the first Bishop of the Episcopate.)*

The main concern of the *Solia* was to provide spiritual information for its readers.

The newspaper continued to be published in spite of many changes of address, of editors, or rising financial costs. It continued to be the means by which all the parishes were informed of the activities of the other parishes and of the Bishop. When he left America in 1939 for Romania, the *Solia* was given over to the clergy for administration.

Following the departure and permanent absence of Bishop Policarp, the paper again was moved from place to place, under the direction of various editors, until 1950.

With the arrival of Viorel Trifa, later elected Bishop of the Episcopate, the paper was to have a permanent and experienced administrator. Having worked with his uncle, the priest Joseph Trifa in his print shop in Romania, the new editor gave heart and soul to putting the *Solia* on a firm financial basis and lifting it to a level of appreciation, which never decreased. The new editor-administrator, however, was elected bishop and had to share the burden of the *Solia* with others.

Mr. John Sibisan of Cleveland and Fr. John Surducan were charged with the administration after the election of Bishop Valerian. By 1953, however, the *Solia* faced serious problems. Frs. John Trutza and John Surducan gave their time, and Messrs. N. Smarandescu and Petru Lucaci, all of Cleveland tried their best, but costs of publication rose and subscriptions fell. A big change was initiated at the Church Congress of 1954.

The *Solia* was brought to Detroit to the press of Mr. Gaspar; the large newspaper format became smaller with double the number of pages; instead of being a weekly, it became a bi-monthly, and all parishioners received the paper and an appeal to voluntarily support it.

At this time, Fr. Vasile Hategan was given the editorship of a larger English language section. Subscriptions from outside the diocese came in. Authors included: Princess Ileana (Mother Alexandra), Rev. Frs. George Preda, John Dinu, George Zmed, John Surducan, Victor Barbulescu and Mr. D.C. Amzar.

In Detroit, the *Solia* also came under the fine administrative hand of Mr. Traian Lascu, whose involvement with the *Solia* continues to this day. Mr. Lascu, versatile in both English and Romanian, added a thorough and clear style to the pages of the *Solia*. Through the years, he came to know the operation of the paper from all angles. His association with the Archbishop made a formidable team for the Romanian free press. Help came from good hearted people in the area in assisting in the tedious wrapping and mailing of the paper: Mary Gaspar, Elena Perianu, Vioara Vintan, Marta Gavrila, Elena Capeti, Mary Busila and others.

Following Traian Lascu as Business Manager was Mr. Leonte Copacia, a young Romanian-American with fresh administrative ideas. In turn, Mr. Andrew Peru took his place as Business Manager and under his concern in 1968, the *Solia* found a new and permanent home on Woodward Avenue in Detroit. At that time, the *Solia* also printed newspapers for other Romanian language groups, and an added source of income provided a wider basis for operation.

Although busy with consolidating the Episcopate, shaping the auxiliaries, building churches, the Archbishop's schedule really revolved around the publishing of the paper. His briefcase was usually full of photos and articles written about the previous day's activities as hierarch. He did enjoy the support of many fine people who gave assistance to him.

The *Solia* has enjoyed the dedication of Mr. and Mrs. John Mercea who were ever present and totally given to the service to the Church through Mrs. Mercea's office as Secretary of the Publishing Department. Keeping track of the subscriptions, of the expenses, of the needs of the subscribers, Mrs. Mercea had the burden of the daily operation of the publishing department. There are always difficulties when business is carried out with friends, the issues are more sensitive: complaints, concerns, questions; all fell on the ears of the patient lady behind the front desk.

Solia did not receive the rich financial support available to the public newspapers: no advertisements, no added income helped to pay the staff. Included in the generous offering of time and talent is the wonderful group of photographers who took photos, developed and gave them to the *Solia*. The work of many of these photographers is truly art: Mr. Lou Martin of Cleveland, Mr. John Farcas of Youngstown, Mrs. Sylvia Baia Lupsor of Detroit and others.

One of those who, like Mrs. Mercea, knew everyone and worked on the editorial staff was Rev. John Toconita. His was the difficult job of presenting the statistics for publication. No easy thing to know how the immigrant, his children and, in turn, their children, spelled the same name. His was also the job to re-type and edit many of the hand-written articles which passed over his desk in anticipation of the press.

Over the years of publications, the *Solia* has accumulated a vast wealth of articles of spiritual value written by an impressive number of contributors. Within its pages, one can follow the history of the Episcopate and its parishes. The auxiliaries have their own history and personalities printed on its folios; struggles and the good order of the Episcopate are chronicled in *Solia*.

The plan to communicate suggested growth, and with growth a deepening of roots into the American soil. During the years, the pages of *Solia* reflected the life of the faithful Romanian Orthodox in taking part in the American life. In the struggle to keep the Church free from communist infiltration and takeover, *Solia* was the medium necessary and the only one having credence.

News of the Church throughout the world was provided so that the faithful would not remain ignorant of the sufferings and joys of the universal Orthodox Church.

In the last few years, the *Solia* had to be the official mouthpiece of the Episcopate in support of its Archbishop whose only authentic forum for defense was in the pages of the *Solia*. Certainly, it was the privilege of the *Solia* to defend the man who made her the free, authentic voice of the Romanian Church.

One of the great marks of Archbishop Valerian as editor of the paper was that it did not sink to the level of polemics or of verbal battles. In fact, one column entitled, "Cu Duhul Blândeții" (In a Humble Spirit), the fallacy of enemies of the Episcopate were wisely and logically put down. The *Solia*'s pages were never abused nor became a means of personal vendetta or attack. The 3 decades of the *Solia* under the careful guidance of Archbishop Valerian are years of spiritual growth in the diocese, prestige in the Orthodox community and respect in the world of Romanian language newspapers.

In 1972, the *Solia* appeared as a 24 page monthly paper, half in English and half in Romanian. The paper was sent to each member of the Diocese without charge. There were, as before, wonderful volunteers in the Detroit area who, by their assistance, helped to keep the cost of operation lower: Mr. Petru Muresan, "Mr. Solia;" Draga Nicoara, Zenovia Guia, Virginia Precop, Mary Stoia, Vioara Sepetan. New writers and contributors giving assistance to the continued efforts of Fr. Hategan were Frs. Vladimir Berzonsky, Nathaniel Popp, Mark Forsberg, Roman Braga, and Deacon Victor Angelescu.

These few paragraphs about the past 50 years of the *Solia* are not sufficient to sketch a total picture. One must turn to the pages of the work of His Eminence, Archbishop Valerian D. Trifa: *SOLIA, Istoria vietii unei gazette romanesti in America (Solia, The Story of the Life of a Romanian Newspaper in America)*, from which most of the data for these lines was taken. As a complimentary in English, Dr. Gerald Bobango's work: *The Romanian Orthodox Episcopate of America, The First Half Century, 1929 – 1979*, provides many pages concerning the role of the *Solia*.

The *Solia* is entering a new phase: a relocation in Jackson, Michigan; plans to be self-composing; a renewed outreach to the new immigrant. Mr. Traian Lascu, recently moving from the area, also retired from the office of Romanian editor, which was given to Mr. Marin Mihalache, a recent arrival from Romania and having literary talents. As a bonus, the *Solia* has a monthly column by the Rev. Fr. Gheorghe Calciu, who adds an authentic voice to the Romanian spiritual articles.

Solia continues its function as the direct means of communication between the hierarch and the faithful, between the diocese and the parishes. It stands out among all the foreign language papers for its long and fruitful history of service and intention to be of even better service to the Romanian Orthodox community and the Orthodox Church in America.

There are many individuals whose names should be printed in this article. Thanks are rendered to all of them as part of the wonderful body of collaborators in communicating the Good News of the Lord Jesus Christ.

Hard at work in the Solia office, 1980s

47

"The glory of Orthodox Christianity is, indeed, that it does become indigenous. In America that means diversity but not disunity in jurisdictions. If the Gospel is to be preached in power, it will not endure the stress of the American scene in its present disunity."

(March 1986)

Archbishop Nathaniel uses the concept of "annunciation" to bring home a recurring point: that the Church must finally unite in a real, visible and functioning way if the Gospel is to be preached in America. His Eminence makes the connection from the Feast of the Annunciation to that of an American saint, Saint Innocent of Alaska.

In a time when it became fashionable to wonder whether the American Church is 'mature' enough to assume her own identity, His Eminence acquired a reputation for his unrelenting insistence that she is, indeed. A generation later, his words and those of like-minded hierarchs appear to be on the verge of bearing fruit.

The Annunciation in American History

On March 25, Orthodox Christians celebrate the wonderful event of the Annunciation. On this day, we relive the encounter between the Archangel Gabriel and the Virgin Mary of Nazareth. God, through his messenger Gabriel, invited the pious young virgin to become the mother of his only-begotten Son, Jesus. By the power of the Holy Spirit, the Son of God was conceived in the womb of the maiden who is "more honorable than the cherubim and more glorious beyond compare than the seraphim," and she gave birth in the flesh to our Savior, Jesus Christ.

The message of the forgiveness of sins and reconciliation with God the Father was preached by the Redeemer, "beginning with the House of Israel" and then, as to the Canaanite woman, the Roman centurion and others, to the whole of mankind.

We know from the prophets that salvation is for all men and to all nations and ages. It is, therefore, pertinent to us to reflect on the second celebration this month: the feast of St. Innocent, Bishop of Sitka, Alaska, U.S.A.

This first bishop of our Orthodox Church in America was also an "angel of good news," for he brought Orthodox Christianity to the Americas. It was the burning desire to bring to yet another nation, a different people, the news of forgiveness of sins and reconciliation, to teach the words of praise and worship in another tongue that gave Bishop Innocent the title of "Illuminator of the Americas." It was his dedicated life which was recognized by the Church which confirms him as "holy" or a saint, one through whose life God is glorified.

Some would like to say that St. Innocent is not "theirs;" that is to say, his is of another ethnic origin. Obviously, there can only be one "illuminator" to a new land, one "first" bishop, and with that single person the annunciation is made, the Good News shared, the seed planted, and the Body of Christ increases and glorifies God.

Orthodox Christians in America, both the United States and Canada would do well to thank God for HIS wisdom and plan, and stop arguing over who is first and second, whose place is at the right and at the left. For whatever reason known to the Almighty, monks DID come from Russia; the first bishop was a Russian. Perhaps God was giving a gift from a land that would later be so bathed in blood of new Christian martyrs and torn by atheistic persecution, that the new cutting, the slip of the vineyard was brought here. What is important is not in what language the message was preached but that it began to BE preached!

The glory of Orthodox Christianity is, indeed, that it does become indigenous. In America that means diversity but not disunity in jurisdictions. If the Gospel is to be preached in power, it will not endure the stress of the American scene in its present disunity.

No one should not celebrate the feast of St. Innocent of Sitka anymore than the Greeks should not celebrate Peter or Paul; the Slavs, Nicetas of Remisiana; the Romanians, Cyril and Methodius, and so on.

No more can we rephrase the Gospels than can we revise our history to celebrate one of "our own" as the "first" in America. The message is clear: God asks the cooperation of all peoples and all nations, and his glory is precisely in this, that all folks are invited to respond: some do, some procrastinate.

48

> "*Valerian D. Trifa was not a mere potential prime minister, a possible great politician. He never apologized for his great role as a shepherd of a flock for which he felt both compassion and, at the same time, oneness. He was most fulfilled in the life that he willingly accepted: the outstanding position of the apostles, a hierarch, a disciple of Christ."*
>
> *"Let his crown be valued for what it is, not for the lesser value of what it might or could have been had the hand of God not directed him to the United States. It is too resplendent a crown to need 're-plating'."*
>
> (March 1987)

Archbishop Valerian fell asleep in the Lord in January 1987, after two and half years of voluntary exile in Portugal. At his request, no eulogies were offered; only this brief tribute exists to record the love and humility with which Archbishop Nathaniel remembers the man in whose footsteps he would lead his flock for the next generation.

Archbishop Valerian: Bishop, Man of Prayer

How amazing it is that an obituary in a local newspaper, the obituary of a loved one, condenses an entire life into a few inches of printed characters. Just the barest of information is revealed: name, place of birth, of death, age, list of relatives, clubs and associations, last place of occupation, church affiliation, and thud, funeral arrangements. Brief, and to the point!

Only those close to the deceased truly know the entire life, the good days and the downers, the talents and falls, the effort and struggle, and they would not be unlikely to state that "books" could be written about the deceased.

We habitually scan the daily newspaper to "see" who has died, little thinking of how many years and what stories are encased in those meager letters which flee before our eyes until we have to prepare just such an obituary or "funeral" notice for someone we love and find it impossible to force that life into a few lines. It seems like a dishonoring, a sacrilege to their memory.

With the news of the death of Archbishop Valerian also came his final directions: "No eulogies, but just the testamentary letter." No eulogies were pronounced; the letter was read, translated and read.

For someone not born in Romania, it is impossible to liken the Archbishop to any particular Romanian hero or great personage. I would fall short of the task. I did not know him as a leader of the young students, nor as a theologian, or as editor of the SOLIA.

In the annals of history of this nation, there are very few church leaders who are outstanding or to whom I could liken him. Thus, Valerian D. Trifa is unique to me as both a Romanian national outside of Romania and a church leader in America where this small community of Orthodox has very little recognizable impact on its history.

But there is an enigma: although bishop for this limited community of Romanian Orthodox, he was one of the outstanding promoters of Orthodox unity in America and was a champion for upholding its visibility and good name; and, he was known to the upper ranks of American church leaders. He was one of the torchbearers for making known this sub-culture in America called "Eastern Orthodox Christians."

His role is testified to by his contemporary hierarchs who worked with him and learned from him, by the many and sincere clergy who also looked up to his integrity and zeal for Orthodoxy in America. The knowledgeable laity also know him and appreciate him for his forward-looking actions as a bishop for the youth, for Orthodox literature and publications, for involving the Church in 20th century America.

One of the reasons for establishing the 40th day memorial on March 8th is precisely because it is the "Sunday of Orthodoxy," the day on which American Orthodox celebrate the unity of faith and the fellowship in the Holy spirit. It is a day which Archbishop

Valerian valued as year by year more clergy and faithful came together, growing in strength to provide a more visible image of the Orthodox Church to their fellow citizens. He never held back his clergy from cooperating and fostering brotherhood. His theme was always to join together, not separate and fragment. This attitude prevailed on most occasions when Orthodox gathered for celebration in common.

Some would extol the Archbishop for his dedication to his land of origin, its traditions, language and particular customs and history; nevertheless, his crown of victory comes from accepting to be a pioneer bishop in the new world. Let's not fantasize about what "might" have been or "could" have been. This is to demean what actually took place: the transfiguration of a follower of Jesus Christ in a particular time, at a given place with all the possibilities and limitation implied.

Valerian D. Trifa was not a mere potential prime minister, a possible great politician. He never apologized for his great role as a shepherd of a flock for which he felt both compassion and, at the same time, oneness. He was most fulfilled in the life that he willingly accepted: the outstanding position of the apostles, a hierarch and disciple of Christ.

Let his crown be valued for what it is, not for the lesser value of what it might or could have been had the hand of God not directed him to the United States. It is too resplendent a crown to need "replating."

Perhaps this is why Archbishop Valerian wanted no eulogy. Eulogy means literally, a "good word." A eulogy is often a repeated set of phrases, hollow words, echoed for the benefit more of the speaker than for the person remembered. If we say too little, it is paltry. Each man values himself, and that is the eulogy which counts.

The testamentary letter, read both in Romanian and in English, is both an obituary and a book, résumé and panoramic exposé, in a word, the wise choice of a wise man.

After the newspaper clipping fades and shreds, and the book thumbed through, the real value of the life of another continues to live in the lives of others who hold that "memory eternal". Memories are alive and motivating, invigorating and encouraging. Stories will be told and recounted and become part of a legend, a true force of eulogy lived and not fabricated.

Of all the experiences shared with Archbishop Valerian, one remains always in my heart and gives light to the darkness of the world of politics, economics, intrigues. It was in May of 1970, Metropolitan Theodosius, then a bishop, returned with the Tomos of Autocephaly, and special services of thanksgiving were called across the land.

We went to the church in East Lansing and after the service of gratitude, the Archbishop went to the center of the church and turned to address the congregation assembled. Looking over those faithful, turning back to the clergy, he asked: "What are we doing here today? We are doing something great and wonderful. You are asking yourselves, just what has taken place? What does this mean? What have those in power and authority done and how does it affect me? What is expected of me, of my family, my parish? I don't know what I'm supposed to do or what can I do? What is my own role in this moment of history?"

He stopped for a few moments (they seemed very long to us) and let the words sink in. His answer to his own questions was slow and deliberate, brief and to the point: "Pray."

Now therefore, that one word, that one dynamic statement has more power than all political maneuvers or governmental formation. Not a politician, not a prime minister but the shepherd boy from Campeni, at home and at ease among his flock with the Word, which gives peace, understanding and value to man's existence.

What can be said? How can we eulogize? What limitations to put on our words or what stops to pull to give full voice to our grief? Our lives will be a living eulogy; our unity will be his eulogy; our Episcopate will be his eulogy; and the Orthodox Church in America, which he served without reserve, will be his eulogy.

Thanks be to God for those who tread steadily over the dust of this world and push forward against its adverse winds, for they follow in the path of the Master, the Creator and the Savior of our souls. Thank You, Lord, for your simple shepherd who taught the most profound wisdom: "Pray."

49

"For the Orthodox Christian, there is no "Memorial Day Weekend," but every day is an occasion to remember both the living and the dead. In enjoying the civil holiday, we ought to bring up our children to indeed, make it a "memorial day" and visit the cemeteries, resting places for our loved ones, and remind ourselves that though separated from sight, we are still one with those who have gone before us."

"Our children, we ourselves, need the reality of belonging to the previous generations and being obliged to those coming after us. We are one with Christ and so we, together, await the glorious and awesome second coming."

(May 1987)

In this Memorial Day article, Archbishop Nathaniel returns the civic holiday to its spiritual roots. While acknowledging the notion of remembrance – even out of his own sense of patriotism – His Eminence takes the opportunity to instruct his flock as to the proper understanding of death, that is, the fact of the continued existence and intercessions of those fallen asleep. He notes the spiritual and psychic ills that follow from the lack of connectedness to previous generations, urges parents, especially, to bring up their children in the spirit of belonging to those gone before and those who will come after us.

Memorial Day "Weekend"

It's one of "those" holidays…a weekend of three days off the usual work-schedule toward which we look forward to spending some time at home, on a short vacation or being with others for some recreation.

At one time, it was called "Decoration Day," for it was the time when most Americans went to the cemeteries where their loved ones lay asleep, cleaned the graves and "decorated" them with flowers and spring blooms. The name changed to a more general "Memorial Day," a national observance for the deceased in our military who had offered their lives for their nation, in addition to remembering all the dead.

But does America, in fact, "remember" all the dead? Hardly! Our national makeup now has swung from a "Christian" populace (even if it was mostly in theory) to a general "whatever-you-wish-if-you-wish" population. Among our friends and neighbors, indeed, among new relatives, are both those who do not believe in an after-life or hold to a theory of "reincarnation." This stands for the idea that when an individual dies (we can't even say "a person," because our Christian concept of person is totally unique from others), the spiritual aspect (again, we can't use the word "soul," for that, too, has a unique Christian meaning) goes into a different being which could be on a higher or lower level of the scale of existence.

Christians who "remember" the dead do so in a unique way. Some sects and denominations which like to define themselves as Christian (Christian Scientists, Jehovah's Witnesses, Mormons, Armstrongites) are not Christians, precisely because they do not hold the Christian belief in an afterlife which is consistent with the Bible and the teachings of the Christian Church.

Orthodox Christians, those who worship and believe in the "right" *(orthos)* way, remember the dead as still being members of the Church. Once "baptized into Christ," we remain forever united to the Savior, and even death cannot destroy that link with the Lord Jesus. This is the pivot of our Christian belief, that Christ suffered death, was buried and stood up, alive, after three days. He is the "first" among us to do so, and he is the "pioneer," the "forerunner" of all humanity to die, rise up; and uniquely as God, he is also our Judge as well as our Savior.

While we who are still alive continue to "fight the good fight" in the ranks of believers who follow the Lord Jesus, those who have "fallen asleep" in the Lord intercede for us. Intercession is a sign of continued existence. The dead do not "cease to exist" for a while and then come into existence again! Their status is different from ours, but they nevertheless, remain members of the same body, the organization, the Church, the bride of the bridegroom Jesus.

This is what is know as the "communion of the saints," the saints being all believers in Christ, both those alive on earth and those "fallen-asleep" in the Lord. Our unity is not broken. Our oneness does not cease. In confessing that we believe that God created both the "visible and non-visible," we confess our belief in the reality of the soul and its continued existence after the death of the body. This is why we say that when someone "dies," they really "fall-asleep-in-the-Lord," implying a continued existence and not a total annihilation or a "transmigration" of the soul.

It is in the celebration of the Divine Liturgy that we "remember all the saints"; and "remembering the all-holy Birthgiver of God and all the saints," we too offer ourselves and one another to Christ our God. The liturgy, established by the command of the Lord to "remember his cross, grave, third day resurrection, second and glorious coming," unites heaven and earth, the bodiless powers (angels) and ourselves, the living and those fallen asleep in the Lord. The prayer offered after the consecration of the gifts (see pages 88-91 of 1975 Liturgy Book) is *"So that for those who partake of them* [the body and blood of Christ] *they may be for (1) awakening of the soul, (2) for forgiveness of sins, (3) for communion / fellowship with your Holy Spirit, (4) for fulfillment of the kingdom of heaven, (5) for confidence towards you but neither to judgment nor to condemnation. Again we offer you this spiritual sacrifice for those fallen asleep in the faith...*[the saints are remembered]*...for the hierarchy...for the city in which we dwell...send down your mercies on all of us."*

Thus, in the mind and experience of the Church, the faithful are ever united although separated briefly by death. The transition from the ones "fallen-asleep in the faith" and for "all of us" is without distinction. Time has no power or force in the Church, and the memory of the faithful is for those from Adam and Eve to those "who are still alive" at the coming of the Lord.

There are other occasions on which the memories of the departed are specifically remembered with fitting hymns and prayers; and, in America, in Canada, we have national days of observance which we Orthodox Christians would do well to sanctify with our prayers and services.

Such is the reason for the annual Memorial Day services at the Vatra: to celebrate the Divine Liturgy and partake of the Body and Blood of the Lord, the cup of salvation; to remember those in the service of our nations who have given their lives, so that we can worship and enjoy the liberty we have; to remember the departed with our specific rites and prayers in St. Mary Cemetery.

For the Orthodox Christian, there is no "Memorial Day Weekend," but everyday is an occasion to remember both the living and the dead. In enjoying the civil holiday, we ought to bring up our children to indeed, make it a "memorial day" and visit the cemeteries, resting places for our loved ones and remind ourselves that, though separated from sight, we are still one with those who have gone before us. If we fail to remember the efforts and sacrifices of those gone before us, we fail our children and ourselves.

In today's society, the importance of community is not stressed. The desires and whims of the individual are placed above the common good. However, it is on just the "one-to-one" basis that extreme loneliness is felt and a sense of being afloat, of having no ties with the past, the present or future, which pushes to the brink of despair and great stress. Our children, we ourselves, need the reality of belonging to the previous generations and being obliged to those coming after us. We are one with Christ, and so we, together, await the glorious and awesome second coming.

Memory Eternal!

50

"The birthing pains were hurtful and even today, scars remain. The history of the Church in America is humble and unusual. Certainly, no other Church in any other nation has such a history as has Christ's Body in the New World."

"Looking into the history of local churches in the Middle East, the Mediterranean and Europe, one finds real pressures of politics. America, North America, is the home to various peoples and on whose lands all religions are equal. There is no sign of local governmental politics affecting the Church of America."

(May 1988)

On May 18, 1970, the Orthodox Church in America, and with it the Romanian Orthodox Episcopate of America, received full independence from European control, through the Tomos of Autocephaly granted by the Church of Russia. In this anniversary article, His Eminence has no illusions about the difficulties of autocephaly – he calls for "a new Pentecost in the Churches," leading to "a unified hierarchy and a unified Body visible and acting as THE CHURCH." In the wake of the Episcopal Assembly in May 2010, His Eminence's words seem almost prophetic.

1970-1988: Eighteen Years of Autocephaly

On July 30, 1741, the first Divine Liturgy was celebrated in America in Alaska by Priestmonk Illarion Trusov and Priest Ignaty Kozierveski. From that time on, the Holy Sacraments of Christ's Church have been celebrated in the New World.

As immigrants from various nations came to Alaska, Canada and the United States, clergy of those same peoples came to minister to them in their particular rites and languages.

In the beginning, however, we are aware that it was a definite missionary effort by the Church of Russia to bring the native Alaskans to Orthodoxy. Although the first clergy did serve the needs of the Russian traders, by 1793, a planned missionary movement was begun, not merely to serve the particular needs of the Orthodox Christians, but to bring the light of truth of God to the North American continent and its indigenous people.

By 1796, the first Orthodox Christian church in America, Holy Resurrection, was constructed and completed in Kodiak, even having bells sent over from Russia.

Over the centuries, the Church in the New World grew and matured. At one time, there was a unified hierarchy; after the Bolshevik Revolution in 1917, however, the various Churches in the Old World sent out "national" bishops and established "new" jurisdictions on the already existing missionary jurisdiction of the Church of Russia.

Perhaps, had the Revolution not occurred, the Church in America would be in different circumstances; no, it would definitely be. We know that liturgical books had already been translated into English at the turn of the century; that they were pushed aside after the Revolution and a conservative, dig-your-heels-in attitude took over, a fragmentation of the Unity of the Church resulted.

In 1970, more than two hundred years after that first Liturgy, Patriarch Alexis of the Church of Russia, on April 10, signed the TOMOS OF AUTOCEPHALY. In the name of the Church in America, the Bishop of Alaska, His Grace, THEODOSIUS, went to Moscow to receive the TOMOS. This was on May 18, 1970, eighteen years ago.

The birthing pains were hurtful and even today, scars remain. The history of the Church in America is humble and unusual. Certainly, no other Church in any other nation has such a history as has Christ's Body in the New World.

Looking into the history of local Churches in the Middle East, the Mediterranean and Europe, one finds real pressures of politics. America, North America is the home to various peoples and on whose lands all religions are equal. There is no sign of local governmental politics affecting the Church of America.

Why is there a hesitation on the part of other Orthodox Christian Churches to see the Church in America in a light or mirror, reflective of their own beginnings? Here no government will assist or resist the birth of the Church...it is the Church herself who is giving birth to herself.

The early Christian Community in Jerusalem and then in cities throughout the Roman Empire spoke out as a single unit to society, whether to a favorable government or to an inimical one: there was a unified voice, a unified hierarchy and a unified Body visible and acting as THE CHURCH.

Thanks to God's mercy, all Orthodox Christians in the New World do recognize one another; children of the same Mother are related through the waters of rebirth.

Now, after eighteen years, in reflecting on the Autocephaly, we see that there is still the need for a single voice, a single heart speaking out to America and an "official" move to recognize the Church by the Church!

Fast approaching the 21st century, the world lunges forward in all human sciences and fields of endeavor. Governments are trying to promote some better understanding among nations. New and various religions are coming to the New World. Where is Orthodoxy as THE VOICE? THE BRIDE OF CHRIST? THE COMMUNION OF SAINTS? How can the Church effectively respond when she is divided?

One looks forward to a new Pentecost in the Churches, to an opening of the heart of Orthodox hierarchies to the grace of the Holy Spirit to act with concern and trust now.

51

"Had there been a different person on the episcopal throne, the attacks would have come the same, a different angle, another plan; nevertheless, no one believes that the attack against Valerian Trifa was merely a personal one but one created against the leader and intended for the faithful. How often the Biblical expression comes to mind: "Smite the shepherd and scatter the flock!" But the shepherd was not smitten; and, thus, the flock remained because he resisted, not for himself, but for his people."

(January 1990)

In the first weeks after the fall of the Ceausescu regime, the customary annual memorial for Archbishop Valerian was celebrated. Archbishop Nathaniel reflects on the past struggles and enduring legacy of the Episcopate's now legendary shepherd.

Archbishop Valerian Remembered

Parishes of the Romanian Orthodox Episcopate of America will remember the late Archbishop Valerian Trifa of thrice-blessed memory with appropriate services on Sunday, January 27, 1991.

It is four years since the death of Valerian Trifa, and one year since the Freedom Revolution in Romania; and, the causes for which he fought are still causes for which struggle continues. No one would think that the necessary changes, which must occur in Romania, can happen overnight, over the next year or few years. Decades of stifling communist rule, the planned degradation of man and values cannot be equally altered over one year, as much as the heart would hope that might be possible.

During the years when Valerian Trifa was the shepherd of the Romanian Orthodox Episcopate of America, he shouldered the blows and attacks launched against his flock. The flock remained united, because it found in its shepherd a mighty pastor who resisted the personal attacks of slander, falsehood, press sensationalism, and speculations. The flock knew that the blows falling on Trifa were meant for the flock, and that he, in rejecting the communist intention to control the American community, was calling down on himself the powers of hell and its allies.

Had there been a different person on the episcopal throne, the attacks would have come the same, a different angle, another plan; nevertheless, no one believes that the attack against Valerian Trifa was merely a personal one but one created against the leader and intended for the faithful. How often the Biblical expression comes to mind: "Smite the shepherd and scatter the flock!" But the shepherd was not smitten; and, thus, the flock remained because he resisted, not for himself, but for his people.

The book of the life of Viorel-Valerian Trifa is not finished; chapters remain to be written and the real conclusion revealed. Part of the authorship is time, which slowly unfolds the past, the present and the future. Nor is the book of the history of these past decades written, but it is still in the process of solidification. The events of last December and the following months have not been "put to bed." There is no "dead-line" for a "conclusive edition" of the real revolution; the truth will come out.

Part of the process of change, for freedom of the Romanian people, for non-interference in the life of Romanians outside its borders, continues like the staunch stand of Valerian Trifa. He was not for himself but for the people whom he loved and for which he gave himself, his life, his talents. The flock continues to scrutinize those recent events and still is not ready to look down in peaceful gaze but watches, left and right, to note, to take into account, to continue that which Valerian Trifa hoped would come true. His own image will be exonerated by truth.

In his Paschal Letter of 1953, he wrote: "No tears exist which Christ will not wipe away . . . nor is there any injustice which will be overlooked." We look forward to the "will" becoming "is" and the "is" becoming "has." Until then, we remain grateful to God for the efforts of the young man from Campeni, a studious person, a serious soul, a man searching for justice and peace for his people. Memory eternal.

*With Archbishop Valerian,
1980*

52

"A great part of this tension, this great burden, the best effort, was expended in that process of conserving while also sharing; of defining while adapting, of being comfortable in the familiar while venturing courageously into the unknown North American scene. This knowledge of how to balance between the needs of the Romanian immigrant and those of the American born citizen does not come easily, and the personal sacrifices are rarely considered by others."
(January 1993)

Keenly aware of his place in the historical context of his diocese, Archbishop Nathaniel never fails to honor those who came before, both out of respect and love. Here he reminds the faithful of the sacrifices of their great leader and archpastor, Archbishop Valerian Trifa.

Fifth Anniversary: Archbishop Valerian

"I am leaving this world with gratitude in my heart towards our Heavenly Father for granting me the privilege for 33 years of serving His Holy Orthodox Church, my Romanian heritage and my beloved adopted country, the United State of America."
--- *Testamentary Letter,*
Archbishop Valerian Trifa

This opening statement of a single-page, seven paragraph testamentary letter was left by Viorel/Valerian Trifa, son of Dionisie, retired Archbishop of the Romanian Orthodox Episcopate of America, to describe the value he placed on his lifetime's activities. A witness to the faith of his fathers, staunch believer in his people and their land (Țara Moților in

Transylvania), and tenacious citizen of the land to which he had immigrated; such, indeed was Viorel Valerian Dionisie Trifa.

January 28, 1993, will mark the fifth anniversary of the death which came suddenly on him while he was yet in exile far from those who had benefited from his talents and dedication, away from those who would have wanted to be with him in his last moments but were unable.

This testamentary letter tells of his joy on being "called and elected" by the Romanian Orthodox faithful; the "great burden" which nevertheless, gave him true happiness; having put forth "my best efforts in all"; with thanks to "those who understood my intentions and efforts." It continues, "Find it in your heart, I beg, to forgive me, as I have already forgiven anyone who has erred before me or wronged me;" and in closing, "be very conscientious in this great responsibility (the destiny of the Episcopate)."

The letter, I believe, was written in Romanian, and post mortem, was quickly rendered by someone into English. If one re-thinks it into the Romanian language, one can arrive at something a little warmer and more like Valerian. The English seems to be more of a strained and necessary translation than the personal testamentary and fatherly farewell it most certainly was intended to be. In particular, there are a few final thoughts, which after re-reading, stand out in these ultimate words and on which it is an appropriate time to reflect.

In the last paragraph, which in scope is an exhortation to unity, just before the closing benediction, we hear him say, " . . . maintain the full freedom which was obtained with so many sacrifices . . . for the pride of our Romanian origin and of the beloved adopted country in which you now reside."

These last of Valerian's final lines, even if not intended by him, subconsciously identify him and his ministry primarily or at least closely with those who themselves are from Romania, with those who, like him, were born in Romania and found themselves residing in North America, in an "adopted" country. Of course, the letter was addressed to the clergy and laity of the Episcopate which jurisdiction includes Canada and the United States and which would necessarily include those who were, in fact, living in their own country of origin and not merely "residing" in an "adopted' country.

The meaning of these last, culminating lines of a few words, I believe, reflects the tensions, the struggles, the "many sacrifices" demanded of numerous European/American church leaders like Archbishop Valerian. They only hint at the intense personal demands made on such leaders in the ethnic North American communities, demands which are all-consuming, because they entail one's entire force of being, one's own identity.

Valerian Trifa, elected to be the hierarch for the Romanians "outside Romania" (if he held to his claim to succeed Policarp Morusca and the original mission entrusted to the first hierarch by the Romanian Church, which he did), remained personally concerned with Romania, its people and history. Nevertheless, he put his talents to work in the New World Episcopate, which had called him to serve. None would dare say that he did not give himself to his ministry. He wed his love for his homeland to that for the flock he pastored in North America.

He was an "ethnarch" in the traditional sense of the word, and most of his troubles came because of this. Those inimical to him and Romanian people "outside Romania" cleverly so identified him as the leader who was to bear the burden of his people, his "millet' in the understanding prevalent in the old Ottoman Empire.

He remained a "Romanian" Bishop in the New World while witnessing to the "catholicity" of the Orthodox faith, overseeing the particular Romanian tradition of that timeless faith and carrying into the New World the universality of the truth. Valerian, like many others, had to live with his feet straddling two continents while reaching with his heart for heaven from the earth.

A great part of this tension, this "great burden", the "best effort", was expended in that process of conserving while also sharing; of defining while adapting; of being comfortable in the familiar while venturing courageously into the unknown North American scene. This knowledge of how to balance between the needs of the Romanian immigrant and those of the American born citizen does not come easily, and the personal sacrifices are rarely considered by others.

Valerian Trifa, son of Dionisie the schoolmaster, however, was able to find peace even amidst unrest; to make decisions although confronted with apathy; to look for happiness even in tribulation. He loved his complex flock, and he earnestly tried to identify what was good about North America so as to gain as much as would be useful while giving effectively.

He did much to foster a united Orthodox witness in North America. He was not narrow in his ethnicity or critical of others, but he did demand that his own native land and its history were due the equal respect that was given to other people.

We owe to his memory and to our sense of honor to recall him on the fifth anniversary of his death.

Thank you for answering our call! We also made sincere efforts to help you carry your burden! If you tried to call out the best in us, we certainly also responded! Your flock supported you since your election, each person in particular ways. While to err is human, to forgive is Divine, and God does forgive! The destiny of the Diocese, the Episcopate, the Church of the first pioneers was, has always been and remains foremost in our lives. We shall not forget God's mercy on the Romanian people in Europe, nor shall we or our children belittle his blessings on the New World.

Finally, let us invoke on him his own final benediction on the Episcopate: "May the Lord and Savior Jesus Christ have you in his loving care now and always."

53

The Constitution and Bylaws of the Episcopate were revised in legislative sessions of the Episcopate Congress, lasting two years, 1993-1994. His Eminence takes time to educate the Congress delegates as to the reasons behind some of the more important changes to be debated.

(June 1993)

1993 Church Congress: Legislative Session

The Romanian Orthodox Episcopate has been organized since 1929, when a general Church Congress of clergy and lay delegates held in Detroit, Michigan, April 25, decided to unite together all the parishes which existed in North America. The majority of the parishes did send delegates; and thus, the formation of the Romanian Church on the North American continent began.

The first Constitution and By-Laws of the Episcopate were adopted at the Church Congress held on October 30, 1932 in Cleveland, Ohio.

Under the advice of Bishop POLICARP, the second Constitution and By-Laws were passed in Youngstown, Ohio, September 5-7, 1936.

Due to the communist take-over in Romania under which the Church was held captive, a special Church Congress, March 28, 1947, abrogated the 1936 Constitution and By-Laws and re-enacted those of 1932. This was due to the 1936 change that had allowed the Romanian Patriarchate to elect, consecrate and install the bishop for the Episcopate, and fears were that a bishop sent from Romania might be more of an agent than a shepherd. Also, the clergy and faithful wanted to have a voice in choosing their archpastor.

Thus, the Church Congress of that same year, 1947, meeting in July, adopted the revised Constitution and By-Laws, particularly reasserting the autonomous character of the Diocese.

This right to change the Constitution and By-Laws was tested in the U.S. Federal Courts and the Court of Appeals, with the conclusion that the parish representatives convened in the Church Congress "were entitled to revoke their previous by-laws and to re-establish the by-laws of 1932."

The 1947 By-Laws were subsequently revised, amended and updated by Church Congresses held in Canton, Ohio, 1953; Vatra Romaneasca, 1967, 1978, with amendments in 1980.

Over the past decade and an half, the Episcopate Council has received parish and deanery suggestions for amendments or revision of the By-Laws. Since that 1978 revision until his retirement, Archbishop VALERIAN gathered these various suggestions. He was of the opinion not to change the By-Laws frequently and yet, on the other hand, to not deny the need as it became apparent.

A committee of members of the Episcopate Council has worked on the Constitution and By-Laws, meeting at St. George Cathedral for various sessions: His Grace, Bishop NATHANIEL; V. R. Laurence Lazar, Episcopate Council Secretary; Deans: V.R. Simion Pavel, P. Stanciu; Dn. John Schmidt; Dr. Eleanor Bujea; John Serban; Pauline Trutza; Emily Lipovan.

Considering that the Episcopate is not the only Orthodox Church in North America, and knowing that other jurisdictions also have Constitutions and By-Laws expressing their experiences in North America, the Episcopate Office began in 1985 to procure copies from various other Orthodox dioceses to compare the administrative structure of these others.

The following were read in our process of review:
1. The Statute of the Orthodox Church in America
2. Parish By-Laws/Diocese of the Midwest (OCA)
3. By-Laws of the Diocese of the South (OCA)
4. By-Laws of the Diocese of the West (OCA)
5. Proposed Bylaws/Archdiocese of Canada (OCA)
6. Special Regulations & Uniform Parish Regulations/Greek Archdiocese
7. By-Laws/Orthodox Diocese of Johnstown

In addition, we reviewed the Pastoral Letter sent by Bishop **POLICARP**, Cleveland 1935, in which his thoughts about the Church in general and the Diocese in particular were offered to the faithful.

In the Constitution, Article II, Purpose, will be a proposed addition: (d) "To work toward the realization of a unified Orthodox jurisdiction in North America."

The Articles in the By-Laws about which clergy and faithful have expressed most opinion have been: **the Bishop I; The Episcopate Congress III; The Episcopate Council IV; The Parish IX.**

Article I: The clergy, at the annual conferences, in deanery session and in private are of the opinion that the Procedure to Fill the Vacancy in the Office of Parish Priest Art. IX, Sec. 22, (2) should eliminate the system of "electing" the parish priest.

Reasons: It is the traditional prerogative of the Bishop to appoint his clergy to the parishes. The bishop knows his clergy better than the faithful and is concerned to find the right priest for the particular parish. This system pits the priests one against another; it is an unfortunate situation for the "losing" priest to return to his home parish, "defeated", which can result in a changed attitude of the parish toward him. The laity have expressed similar opinions; that the parish easily divides into "parties, pro and con" for a particular candidate; that intrigues arise among members who begin their own "campaign" to bring their own relative or friend. There are many costs involved with an "election".

Article I would mean that only the Bishop shall appoint, transfer and remove priests and deacons. **Article IX, Sec. 22, (2)** would be removed and **Sec. 24**, eliminated. In **Article IX, Sec. 30, (a)** the word *"elect"* would be removed.

Article II: The Vicar was amended in 1980 and will be introduced under the title of The Auxiliary Bishop.

Article III: Competence of the Episcopate Congress, **Article III, Sec. 20**, would be added: **(p)** *"Establish, enforce and amend, as necessary, obligatory parish standards for clergy remunerations."*

A few years ago, this issue came to the Congress, and the entire body voted in favor of this. However, there was some disagreement as to how it related to the existing **Article IX** authority and duties of the Parish General Assembly, **Sec. 30, (a).**

Article IV: A proposed change is offered concerning the auditors on the Episcopate Council, **Art. IV, Sec. 5, (f):** *"Two auditors, parish members who need not be members of the Episcopate Council or Congress are elected. The auditors should have training or experience in financial accounting or auditing, or bookkeeping. In the alternative, the Council may resolve that during the term of office in question, all or any portion of the auditing function may be discharged by a public accountant under a regular retainer agreement."*

Article V: Which has to do with Deaneries, **Section 2**, is proposed to add **(k)**, *"To coordinate the leadership and active participation of all parishes in the Deanery in common programs with other Orthodox Christians.*

Article IX: The **definitions** of *Parish, Membership, the Parish Priest,* were reviewed and much attention given to them, inasmuch as these are the areas that affect the basic structure of the Episcopate.

There has existed a certain tension in the parishes when it is perceived that the priest is either an "employee" or is merely a "glorified altar boy" whose sole function is within the walls of the church and, in particular, in the altar. Some artificial dichotomy has grown to consider the parish as both a spiritual base and a social one, as though Christianity is limited to the altar and has no purpose or role in sanctifying all realms of human experience and endeavors. There are those who even say, "Father, you belong in the altar; leave the rest to us," with various different refrains.

Also, there is a mistaken idea that there is the parish priest **and** the president of the parish. There is an elected person who presides at the meetings of the parish council, but no one can claim to be the lay "head" of the parish. There is the priest and then, there is the "President of the Parish." Such a role and title does not exist in our present nor past By-Laws. It is an idea which has been growing and maturing because of the wrong idea that the parish, meaning in its widest form the Church or Diocese, is both a spiritual and non-spiritual entity with areas of concern for the spiritual leader, the priest/bishop and that of the general, worldly, administrative arena which belongs only to the non-spiritual leadership, someone elected from among the laity.

In this regard, the Parish was re-defined in the following terms: *"The parish is the local community of the Church under the jurisdiction of the Romanian Orthodox Episcopate of America, having an appointed priest who as spiritual leader cooperatively administers the parish with the parish council, duly elected by its general assembly."*

Thus, in **Section 4,** the following is added to consideration given to parish properties: *"In administering them, the parishioners and the officers elected by them must remember the religious nature, purposes and goals of the parish and act as trustees of God's property, not man's. The parish serves God and cares for God's work in the world, as does the whole Church, and all decisions concerning parish administration should be inspired by that care and by the spiritual needs of the Church."*

Much attention was given to reviewing "Membership", which is the area that touches most people. It was felt that the emphasis on membership as payment of dues was detrimental to the fundamental purpose of the Church which is not an institution, not a society nor club, but which is the Body of Christ and the community through which comes salvation.

The introduction to Membership reads: *"By virtue of his or her baptism and chrismation, an individual is a member of the Holy Orthodox Church which is the Body of Christ, and as such is called to live in accordance with her teachings, traditions and rituals, and to regularly support the Church through the local parish.*

(a) **To become a voting member of a parish, a baptized Orthodox Christian man or woman must:**

(i) be at least eighteen years of age;

(ii) partake of the sacraments of confession and communion in one's home parish at least once a year;

(iii) have belonged to/attended the parish for six months;

(iv) have accepted and adhere to the Constitution and By-Laws of the Romanian Orthodox Episcopate of America;

(v) fulfill such financial obligations as the Episcopate and the parish establish;

(b) Such an individual applies to the parish priest to become a voting member of the parish. With the approval of the priest and the knowledge of the parish council, the person is enrolled on the list of voting members of the parish.

(c) Newly enrolled members may exercise the right to vote in the parish assembly and to be elected to an office in the parish:

(i) upon payment of all established financial obligations,

(ii) after having been so enrolled for more than six months prior to said assembly.

Regarding the Parish Priest: *"The parish priest, by virtue of his canonical ordination and episcopal appointment, heads the local parish of the Church. He has the right and the duty to perform all religious services in the parish. He must follow and respect dogmas, Holy Canons, teachings and traditions of the Orthodox Church, as well as the directives of the bishop. According to the teaching of the Church, the priest is the spiritual father and teacher of his flock and the celebrant of the liturgical worship established by the Church. He teaches and edifies the People of God entrusted to his spiritual care with no partiality and sees that all activities within the parish serve the religious purposes of the Church. No activities within the parish can be initiated without his knowledge, cooperation, approval and blessing; neither should he do anything pertaining to the parish without the knowledge of his parishioners and parish officials elected by them, so that always there may be unity, mutual trust, cooperation and love."*

These are some of the proposals sent to the delegates of the Church Congress and which will be debated in Special Session, July 2-3, at the Vatra.

54

> *"Now, 65 years after the installation of the first bishop of the Romanian Orthodox Church in America and Canada in the person of His Grace, Bishop Policarp, and already having the apostolic seal of three bishops as well as many significant realizations, together with a great material and spiritual potential, the Romanian Orthodox Episcopate of America and Canada has its own traditions shaped by the extended conditions of exile and of a new generation of faithful born and raised in the Americas, and the great tradition of Orthodoxy from today and from all the ages."*
>
> *(March 2000)*

Deeply conscious of his place in the history of the Episcopate, and in the succession of its hierarchs, Archbishop Nathaniel never loses an opportunity to credit his predecessors and to keep their memory alive in the minds of the faithful. Here, His Eminence offers some thoughts on the 65th Anniversary of the installation of the first ROEA hierarch, Bishop Policarp Morusca.

65th Anniversary of the Installation of Bishop Policarp Morusca

The first Romanian Orthodox parishes in the United States and Canada were founded at the beginning of the twentieth century.

In the years following World War I, a series of discussions were held regarding the establishment of a Romanian Orthodox Episcopate in America. Knowing this, the Holy Synod of the Romanian Church sent Father Trandafir Scorobet to America to work out a solution for the problem.

Having come and assessed the situation, Father Scorobet suggested that a church congress be convened. In Detroit, Michigan, on April 25-26, 1929, 20 priests and 24 lay delegates unanimously decided upon the founding of an autonomous Missionary Episcopate, under the jurisdiction of the Romanian Patriarchate of Bucharest.

On October 30, 1932, a Church Congress held in Cleveland, Ohio adopted rules and statutes of organization and function for the new Episcopate and the parishes under its jurisdiction. These were later ratified by the Holy Synod of the Romanian Church at its meeting of August 22, 1934. Among the most important of these statutes was the right of the Episcopate Congress to elect its own bishop.

Only Archimandrite Policarp Morusca, Abbot of Hodos-Bodrog Monastery, showed a desire and willingness to be a candidate for the position of Bishop of the Romanian Orthodox Church in America and Canada.

Thus, on January 26, 1935, the Holy Synod of Bucharest elected him bishop and shortly thereafter he was consecrated. The new hierarch arrived in America in June and was officially received and installed at the time of the Church Congress held in Detroit, Michigan on July 4, 1935.

Bishop Policarp (whose name before monastic profession was Pompei) Morusca was born on March 10, 1883 in Cristesti, Alba County. His father was a priest. He graduated from the Theological Institute of Sibiu in 1905 and published a number of articles, theological and apologetical works, and treatises on Christian morals. Following a pilgrimage to the Holy Land in 1925, the young priest felt called to the monastic life and later became Abbot of Hodos-Bodrog Monastery. It was from this position that he was elected Bishop of America and Canada.

It may be said that Archimandrite Policarp had the qualifications to be called to the high office of the Episcopacy. He also sincerely desired it and was determined to handle the responsibilities of the office. The newly elected bishop was relatively young and physically strong and healthy. He brought with him his appreciable experiences as a parish priest and administrator in positions in the Metropolia of Sibiu and as Abbot of the monastery. He was marked with the gift of apostolic love and determination, and he was a Transylvanian, as were the majority of Romanians in America.

Bishop Policarp was peaceful by nature, with a pleasant personality. He was a spiritual man but also very practical. He was a convincing speaker and a good writer who did not lose himself in minute theory, but expressed himself in a simple style, formed by the burning of missionary zeal and desire for progress.

Following his consecration as bishop on March 24, 1935, Policarp, with canonical documents of consecration in hand, accompanied by a priest and a deacon to assist him in his pastorate, set sail for America, full of the desire to be a true spiritual leader of the flock scattered across the vast continent of the new world.

His official installation in July 1935, drew a large number of participants, but after the celebration and festivities were over, the Bishop, not having been provided with a suitable residence or offices, withdrew to the cramped quarters of his hotel room to there formulate his plans and ideas, some of which came to be and others as time would show, remained unattained dreams.

He first resided in Cleveland, Ohio, but then returned to Detroit, Michigan, in anticipation of residing at the property newly purchased by the Episcopate in Grass Lake Michigan, which would be known as "Vatra Romaneasca."

It seems that the rural setting of the "Vatra" met with Bishop Polycarp's concept of establishing an Episcopal residence outside of the bustle of a large city. Having tasted the peacefulness of a secluded spiritual life at the Hodos-Bodrog Monastery, Bishop Policarp favored the idea of forming a similar religious center where the basic elements of Orthodox religious life and Romanian traditions would be integrated. Such a center, in a rural setting, could later comprise, among other things, an official Episcopate residence, a monastery and church, a farm worked by monks, a home for the elderly, a village of retired Romanians. It would be a place equipped with everything necessary for receiving guests and for ethnic meetings, religious courses and recreation, plus housing a research center, etc. Many of these projects of which Policarp dreamed would be realized by others in later years.

It should be said that in the short pioneer activity (less than 5 years) of his pastorate in America and Canada, Bishop Policarp brought forth much spiritual and administrative fruit, visiting the parishes and, in 1936, founding the official Episcopate publication—the "Solia" newspaper, which even today reaches all the faithful. The annual publication of the Almanac/Calendar "Solia" was begun by him.

In 1938, with his blessing, the women's auxiliaries in the parishes joined together into a unified organization called "Asociatia Reuniunilor de Femei Ortodoxe Romane din America" (A.R.F.O.R.A.).

During the time he lived in America, the Bishop ordained four priests: Eugene Lazar, Paul Craciun Jr., Peter Moga, and Traian Vintila.

During his prolonged absences, Bishop Policarp kept contact with his faithful through the "Solia" newspaper and encyclical letter which he sent to the parishes.

Although Bishop Policarp understood the necessity and even encouraged the foundation of organizations for the youth as well as religious education classes, a national organization A.R.O.Y. (American Romanian Orthodox Youth) was not founded until 1950.

Having acquired the property in Grass Lake, Michigan in 1937, Bishop Policarp called the Church Congress to meet at the Vatra that year. On July 4, 1938, during the Congress, surrounded by an enthusiastic 3,000 people who had gathered for the inauguration, he laid the cornerstone for a chapel. From that moment, maintaining and transforming the Vatra into a center for Episcopate activities became his principle preoccupation, and he left many of the Episcopate's problems to the Episcopate Council to resolve.

Financial support was usually insufficient to effect many of the bishop's plans, for there was little inclination to sacrificial giving in behalf of the Episcopate. Under these circumstances, and disregarding the advice of his closest supporters, Bishop Morusca returned to Romania in August 1939 with the intentions of participating in the meeting of the Holy Synod to report on the situation of his Church in America and Canada, and probably to ask for greater funding for his plans for consolidating the parishes into a viable Episcopate.

World War II caught him in Romania, and though he most probably could have returned to America, something held him back, and later he was unable to alter the situation. During this time, Bishop Policarp sent letters and communications to the Church Congress to maintain contact with the Episcopate at the Vatra.

During the War, he fulfilled the function of a vicar bishop to the bishop of the Romanian Armed Forces, and later served as locum tenens for a vacant Episcopal see. He was unable to return to his throne as Bishop in America, and was unable to obtain a similar position in Romania—a position which he perhaps desired. The communist authorities, who came into power in Romania, in the meantime, ordered him to his home village to live under forced domicile in retirement.

Although he did not renounce his position as Bishop of the Romanian Orthodox Church in America and Canada, through his letters he could not effectively fulfill his duties as bishop. Due to the gravity of the situation, in 1951 the Church Congress elected His Grace, Bishop Valerian as Vicar Bishop.

On October 8, 1959, old and all but forgotten, Policarp Pompei Morusca died, broken-hearted and disillusioned, a virtual prisoner in his own country. It was then that Bishop Valerian was installed as ruling Bishop of the Episcopate.

Bishop Valerian built upon the firm pioneer basis laid by his predecessor, Policarp, and upon the foundations laid by other forerunners of Romanian religious life in America and Canada. He led the flock until June 28, 1984, when he retired. Bishop Nathaniel Popp was elected as Vicar Bishop in 1980 and elected ruling bishop at the Episcopate Congress held in Cleveland, Ohio on October 20, 1984 and installed on November 17, 1984 at St. George Cathedral in Detroit, Michigan.

Now, 65 years after the installation of the first bishop of the Romanian Orthodox Church in America and Canada in the person of His Grace, Bishop Policarp, and already having the apostolic seal of three bishops as well as many significant realizations, together with a great material and spiritual potential, the Romanian Orthodox Episcopate of America and Canada has its own traditions shaped by the extended conditions of exile and of a new generation of faithful born and raised in the Americas and the great tradition of Orthodoxy from today and from all the ages.

Romania

55

> *"Mr. President . . . We also bear witness to you for our brothers and sisters who are also struggling mightily to break loose from a repressive and devastating regime of almost five decades in the Socialist Republic of Romania."*
>
> *"If what is happening in Romania were to occur in England, Ireland, France, Germany, Italy or the Scandinavian nations, the uproar would be deafening."*
>
> *(July 1989)*

Under Archbishop Nathaniel, as under Archbishop Valerian before him, the Romanian Orthodox Episcopate of America earned a worldwide reputation as the only Orthodox Church body to consistently and openly defend the freedom of the Romanian people against the repressive communist regime. In this letter, written before the still-unforeseen events to come just five months later, His Eminence directly addresses the President of the United States. He protests the destruction of sacred places such as churches and cemeteries, but even the homes of defenseless Romanian citizens by their own government. In this action, Archbishop Nathaniel and his diocese stood alone until the fall of the regime in December of the same year.

A Letter to the President of the United States

The Honorable George H. W. Bush
President of the United States
Dear Mr. President:

The Romanian Orthodox Diocese of America, meeting over the 4th of July weekend in its 57th Church Congress at the Romanian Hearth, Grass Lake, Michigan, under the Presidency of His Grace, NATHANIEL, Bishop of Detroit, Orthodox Church in

America, with delegates from across the nation and from the Dominion of Canada, greet you with sincere good wishes for strength and wisdom as you lead our nation through demanding and exciting years ahead.

Around the globe, peoples who for long decades have been enslaved under repressive communist regimes are struggling against great odds to free themselves from these tyrannical rulerships forced on them and shored up by military force.

The heroic students of China, the working class of Poland, the proud folk of the Baltic nations are reclaiming the right to the freedom which we enjoy, cherish and defend in this blessed land.

Mr. President, our hearts are joined to those of millions and millions of world-wide citizens who are watching, praying, and working for the blossoming of freedom in the world's people. We read and are witness to their sacrificial actions to regain freedom. We also bear witness to you for our brothers and sisters who are also struggling mightily to break loose from a repressive and devastating regime of almost five decades in the Socialist Republic of Romania.

Surrounded on all sides by communist states, without a window to the West, this ancient people is being systematically destroyed, materially, intellectually, and spiritually, by a government which intends to remake man in it own image and likeness of total sub-human existence.

Mr. President, two months before this 4th of July Independence Day celebration, you received a letter signed by at least 119 Members of Congress! The letter urged you to construct a new policy toward the government of Romania, addressing its continuous egregious human rights abuses. Our voice has been strengthened by theirs!

One hundred and nineteen freely elected representatives of our Nation acknowledge publicly the horror of life in Communist Romania, and high-ranking Romanian Communist party officials themselves spoke out against its own people. Our voice now has more witnesses to the truth!

The churches in which our grandparents and parents were baptized and married, the cemeteries in which many of them were laid to rest, the very homes of generations of families, all are being systematically razed to the ground; and, the suffering of all generations of the people is unspeakable.

If what is happening in Romania were to occur in England, Ireland, France, Germany, Italy or the Scandinavian nations, the uproar would be deafening. Finally, the European nations have broken their silence and are taking strong measures of protest.

President Bush, the American-Romanian community is not a large one, nor is it wealthy; it is not politically powerful and has created no lobbies or special interests. It minds its own families and children and is the quiet type of citizen that makes politicians glad to serve the public.

Our presence in the New World goes back to colonial times, in a limited number. Our talents and efforts have been strong for the past 100 years. Do not overlook the humble character of our people nor let us continue to suffer because of seeming insignificancies. We are pleading for 23,000,000 souls behind the still existing, and yet un-penetrated, Iron Curtain. They are not seeking to immigrate; they love their native land, but they have no one to speak out for them against the harshest of regimes, except for our persistent voice from the free world.

Like those 119 Members of Congress, we also urge further action! Past policies of our government must be reshaped to fit the reality of today and to let America again be a leader in democracy for all peoples; but, in particular, Mr. President, please for Romania.

With respect, trust and great hope, we address you on behalf of the Romanian Orthodox Diocese of America.

Rt. Rev. NATHANIEL
Bishop of Detroit
President of the Church Congress

56

"When, Romania? When?...In the delight of the Christmas season, as we in the free world gather with family and friends, as we travel from here to there, as we go about our preparations for the new year, we can also repeat, daily, the prayer of Sarah, in behalf of the Romanian people who already have it etched on their hearts, in their tears, over their bowed and bent heads."

(December 1989)

Always outspoken and fearless in its defense of the Romanian people and Church in the face of tyranny and oppression, the Romanian Orthodox Episcopate of America once again found her voice in this passionate cry from her hierarch, then Bishop Nathaniel.

On December 23, 1989, just a few days after His Eminence published this article, the regime of Nicolae Ceausescu was toppled, and forty years of communist domination came to an end in Romania.

When, Romania?

"Blessed be your name, O God of our fathers; who when you are angry still show mercy, and in the time of tribulation forgive the sins of those that call on you.

To you, O Lord, I turn my face, to you I direct my eyes.

Your council is not in any man's power. But of this everyone is sure that worships you, that his life, if it is under trial, shall be crowned; and if it is under tribulation, it shall be delivered: and if it is under correction, it shall be allowed to come to your mercy.

For you are not delighted in our being lost; because after a storm you make a calm, and after tears and weeping, you pour in joyfulness.

O God of Israel, may your name be blessed forever!"
-- Prayer of Samuel's mother, Sarah (Tobias 3:13)

One by one, the governments of Eastern European nations are falling, like dominoes, cascading one on top of the other; except for one, Romania.

One by one, each people has raised its voice powerfully but peacefully, to cast aside the stubborn yoke of oppression and elitism of the communistic rulers; except one, the Romanian.

During these recent weeks, various individuals have asked: "Why haven't the Romanian people raised their voice and demonstrated for their rights and freedom?

Some, in the recent past, have claimed that the noose of atheistic communism was wrapped around the throat of the nation, because the people themselves are so very bad as to "deserve" from God this castigation!

Others, usually those coming from or intending to "return" to Romania, say, "things aren't all that bad; it has been worse before!"

Each nation has a unique geographical situation among the nations of mankind; each people has its own history of development and progress; each its own heart, its own breath and genre.

While we cannot luxuriate in speculation on the motives or reasons why a nation acts one way or another, we can, nevertheless, refresh ourselves in the reality that no man lives forever nor do tyrants last beyond a given length of days. Those in power will surrender all with their last gasp, and others will wrest away all that was bloodily gained or, rather better said, raped from the people and the land.

What about Mr. Gorbachev? Why doesn't he visit Romania and put pressure on the Ceausescu government to "reform"? Perhaps it is because at least 87% of the food produced in Romania is sent to Russia, and with the Russian economy the way it is, Gorbachev cannot afford to cut off this essential source of food. If Romania is "liberated", that food will no longer go out of the nation but will be kept to feed the starving Romanian people, the very producers of the food being taken from them for use by the Russians.

When, Romania? When? Always plundered by strong neighbors, both subservient to its geography but also divinely blessed precisely because of it. Romania will always have to struggle to maintain its identity and integrity. History shows that there have been "golden" ages and, please God, may there yet be more.

In the delight of the Christmas season, as we in the free world gather with family and friends, as we travel from here to there, as we go about our preparations for the new year, we can also repeat, daily, the prayer of Sarah, in behalf of the Romanian people who already have it etched on their hearts, in their tears, over their bowed and bent heads.

Ours can be the hope for that calm and joyfulness, for that mercy and forgiveness, for that crowning and mercy. Let us who can raise our voice, do so, alone, together, in private and in our churches, that "the God of our fathers may be fittingly praised and glorified in time of tribulation and trial, under correction, that our joy may be all the greater" when the rainbow of promise dawns, and the Joyful Light expels the deep darkness of atheism and slavery.

And let those, who for whatever reason choose not to publically and boldly say the prayer, at least in the quiet, in the inner recesses of their private hearts, mouth the word of hope and praise.

On the last day of the decade which is the Lord's Day, December 31, 1989, we ask all the faithful gathered for the Divine Liturgy in their parish churches, to recite together with the parish priest, the Prayer of St. Sarah, mother of the Prophet Samuel after the final blessing, and before venerating the cross and receiving the holy bread, that the bells of the church be tolled for a minute and a half and then pealed for the same number of minutes.

May God listen to our prayers, and may our hearts be stirred with renewed hope as we hear our bells ring out for freedom, just as 200 years ago the Liberty Bell sounded across this free and blessed land. God is with us!

57

"Our community, almost 100 years old in Canada and the United States, has not been living in splendid isolation from the burden of Romania's woes . . . While we anticipate better relations, we also remind others that we have a long life and an established one. Our government has been steadily the same; unlike the history of yours. Our way of life is stable, and we look forward to positive growth and understanding. Your progress will be watched with pride, your achievements, ours, too. Nevertheless, as we have fought to keep an identity in the New World, we shall continue to maintain it as we see fit for us, for our children and our institutions."

(January 1990)

The fall of communism brought expectations for some that the Episcopate would automatically revert to the jurisdiction of the Romanian Orthodox Church. His Eminence is quick to empathize with the suffering of the brethren in Romania, and equally quick to assert the separate identity of the Romanian Orthodox community in North America.

The Plight Of Job

"Glory to God in the highest heavens and peace on earth to men who enjoy his favor!"

The psalmist states: "O Lord, a thousand days are like one to you" but for man, one day can seem like an eternity, especially when he is suffering minute by minute and hour by hour. When such a state extends through years and even decades, the light of a man's eyes can even begin to fade, and hope may seem to be a silent sound which stirs only an echo in the heart, a spark in the darkest inner resources of his being.

Recently, while on a "Red-Eye" special from New York to Detroit, I overheard an animated conversation between two gentlemen passengers seated behind me. "It took Poland ten years; Hungary 10 months, Germany 10 weeks, but Romania will be in 10 hours . . . and bloody!" I shuddered at the prophecy, but on that December 18 flight, I had no idea as to what the next few days would bring.

On the next day, December 19, the pent-up suffering of almost 50 years burst like a volcano; the violence and might of which no one would have imagined, and only the most evil power would have tried to contain.

There is still much to be made known and that which was hidden brought to light and shouted "from the housetops." The news that came to be transmitted, the photos sent racing across the satellites to beam down on nation after nation brought shudders of anguish and deep anger for what was being witnessed, what was being portrayed.

While the U.S. press had been fair in covering the event of the downfall of a tyrant, European coverage has been constant and intense. Romania is, after all, a part of Continental Europe and one of the sister countries, and the interest there would be greater. But, in fact, it has been so intense, so supportive, that in America we have little idea of the profound effect the plight of the Romanian people has made on their European fellows.

Financial support, foods, clothing, needs have flowed into the country like a newly formed branch of the Danube which meanders across and ties so much of Europe together.

The joy of East Germans, of Czechoslovaks, Lithuanians, Poles and Hungarians in the changes in their respective nations silenced into prayers that rose to a mighty roar to heaven: "Lord, Lord, look down on this vine, visit and protect what your own right hand has planted!" Turning from their national moments of gladness, they turned to the east, to the last stronghold of bestial tyranny and shouted for the Iron Wall to be torn down by tears and hearts and human sacrifice, if that was the only way to do it.

There are some who will say it was this event or that person, this combination or that which incited the revolution; it was the hand of God Almighty who alone could have chosen the moment and the need for the change. After the times have been calculated as to when the army entered the picture and what the Soviets pre-determined and the mistakes Ceaușescu fell into, it will still be the same truth; God is the author of history and the only one who gives meaning to man's suffering. No one has more of a right to be a collective "JOB" than the Romanian People, but like the biblical Job, we bow to the reality that God in his wisdom acts as he does and no one can sit at the conference table opposite him and ask "WHY, WHEN, HOW?"

Pious platitudes? Retrogression into the "dark ages"? Opium of the people? Even after the display of human mistreatment and the darkness of personal greed of the tyrant, there will still be those who will find "meaning" in what he did and descry our thanks to the Creator of the created. What power for good man has been given; what forces of darkness he can miscreate! There is no hope for mankind if salvation and perfection rests within his own breast, and there alone.

There are signs of hope: the churches are overflowing beyond capacity, and people are actually seen to smile; under the cold of winter, a new warmth of rebirth and fraternity is stirring. Perhaps the peace, which is beginning to come over the land, will be a lasting one brought on by cooperation and trust, a difficult art at this time and place.

Articles will continue to be written, photos shown and documents revealed; and as the healing process goes on, we can wish well to those who now have their first taste of freedom with a price tag.

What cost liberty? What price freedom? Responsibility. Love for neighbor and for God. It may be easier to love God at this time than to embrace one's neighbor who yesterday might have been on "that" side. It may be too simple to rest on "ignorance" than to embrace the novelty of individual and collective responsibility.

One danger that the Romanians will face is from the "carpetbaggers from outside," each one now eager to set out his corporate shingle, each one ready to "assist." Like the South after the end of the War Between the States, Romania must weigh each visitor, know the goal and purpose. As the Gospel story says: "A clean house swept must fill with something good, otherwise the evil which was flushed out will come back and be worse than the first."

A second danger will come from within; the temptation to settle scores, to instigate old hatreds and animosities, to "take the laws into one's own hands." A decent settling of equal rights of all citizens and all faiths can be legislated by government, but only men can put it into action, de facto.

The Church must wake up from lethargy and renew herself in her people and hierarchy. The Gospel must be the touchstone for the majority of the nation, and those who are not Christian ought not to fear. The greatest lesson that the Church faces, however, will be that it is not a favored and integral part of the government. Separation of Church and State so long resisted by Byzantine style is no longer supportable. The democratic process in vogue throughout the world favors no one, belongs to all and leaves the responsibility to the individual. A hard lesson to learn; one with which the American Church is still floundering.

Finally, the third danger is from Romanians from abroad who may want to return from "exile" and expect to be "welcomed" back. While talents and experience will be welcome, it is difficult to think that a nation of 23 million does not have enough people to create a sound future for itself. Our support will be financial, with humanitarian interests and vigilance, concerned that the process does continue and that abuses be brought to light. But those who have bathed the land with blood and those who have resisted have the right to shape and mold; the rest, accordingly, even if exiled, must await the sign of welcome and not presume to plunge into what belongs to the tenacious to hold.

Through the decades, since childhood in the 40's, I have been aware of the sufferings of my forefather's people; I have known of churches, Uniate and Orthodox, destroyed and abused, of clergy maltreated and killed, of faithful massacred and decimated. We, outside the nation, have also felt suffering, and our lives have also been shaped by the events there.

We have no physical scars on our backs, but we have them in our hearts and minds. Our childhood was not so carefree and happy that, at the back of our minds, we didn't know that "over there" things were bad.

Our community, almost 100 years old in Canada and the United States, has not been living in splendid isolation from the burden of Romania's woes; and, we, too, all too much, felt the long hand of communism in our communities, among our societies and organizations, tantalizing, taunting some to eat "Salami din Sibiu şi Ţuică din Ţară," instead of the bread of integrity.

Our days in courts have been long and costly; our name dishonored and despised; our efforts were sabotaged and undermined, and the names of our leaders and community abused.

Yes, the freedom to speak and gather, to write and read, to publish and produce, we had all the time; but, it too had a price, because we also felt the burden of poison, the venom dripped on us, on our churches and communities.

Brothers and sisters, we have also suffered and longed for this day and not merely as by-standers but as participants; and, thus, our joy is all the more real and powerful, because it is the same as yours, from within, and not from without, not as strangers but as fellows.

While we anticipate better relations, we also remind others that we have a long life and an established one. Our government has been steadily the same; unlike the history of yours. Our way of life is stable, and we look forward to positive growth and understanding. Your progress will be watched with pride, your achievements, ours, too. Nevertheless, as we have fought to keep an identity in the New World, we shall continue to maintain it as we see fit for us, for our children and our institutions.

58

> *"It is unrealistic to imagine that everything from the past 45 years could be overcome at once or that the black can become white as before; years of corrosion cannot be polished bright with one swipe of the cloth....It is, however, a time for reflection and thought, to think before speaking, to consider before acting."*
>
> *(February 1990)*

No one waited more eagerly for news of the events in Bucharest and the rest of Romania than Bishop Nathaniel in early 1990. In the aftermath of bloodshed and upheaval, His Eminence ponders the words of Mother Alexandra and the challenges ahead for the nation of his ancestry.

"An Entire Nation Stood Up, As One Man"

As the last remaining days of 1989 rushed by, the opening weeks of 1990 seemed to drag along, each day being long, and demanding more than the previous one. The scarcity of news from Romania about relatives and friends almost overshadowed the general news of the freedom revolution.

There was no doubt that the Ceaușescu regime had fallen, but the terror that reigned before was still evident. There was still no peace in Timișoara, in Bucharest, in Los Angeles, New York, Cleveland, Toronto.

Slowly, new images formed and the picture became somewhat clearer, but there were still many things not yet in focus.

It is unrealistic to imagine that everything from the past 45 years could be overcome at once or that the black can become white as before; years of corrosion cannot be polished bright with one swipe of the cloth.

It is, however, a time for reflection and thought, to think before speaking, to consider before acting. The pent-up rage has initially spent itself, but peace is yet only on the surface.

The most difficult thing for men to do is to work together; the democratic process is not an easy one. To accept the majority vote as one's own, to accept the right of disagreement, to respect the difference of others; it is not an easy road.

But, as we read in V.R. Mother Alexandra's article, "Suddenly it was there! An entire nation stood up as one man, from the youngest to the oldest." It is possible to make one from many, to unite that which was scattered, to join that which was separated.

The Episcopate's delegation to Washington saw that government officials were hesitant, cautious to consider that the people could, in fact, unite into one voice and one mind. Doubt was obvious that the many could become one. "There is no experience for democracy, no past examples or models. There is too much division to foretell what can actually take place, or what the people will actually want."

The article, "Excerpts from a Letter," indicates, too, "there are deeper problems which will be harder to change." But in many societies, deep-seated difficulties are long in being overcome. We in America are still working against racism; in Canada, the "Native problem" runs deep.

One advantage, however, that the Romanian people have is a unified history and culture, language and traditions. The coming of white settlers into the New World is still a scar; the introduction of black slaves made the equality of men a mere phrase. The Romanian nation has certain positive elements of its national identity which should cause it to heal rapidly and more justly than in other historical situations.

One of the more memorable tragedies of American history is the famous "Johnstown flood" when the quiet city nestled between the hills of middle Pennsylvania was literally swept away by the relentless power of the deluge of floodwaters. After some hours of terror, of great loss of life and property, quietness came over the valley. The mountains were as before; the land retained its shape.

It is similar in Romania's history. The terrorizing ugliness of communism has borne down on the population for the last forty-five years, sweeping away life and culture, destroying, devastating, scarring the people and the land. But, now, by God's hand, the flood is gone and the time for cleaning up and restoration has begun. The City of Johnstown is today greater than it was, but only through work, cooperation and trust in one's fellow and neighbor.

The floodwaters were indifferent to the "good" or to the "bad," to the young or old, rich or poor. So, it appears the same in Romania. Of course, favoritism ruled and the floods drowned some, washed over others and simply swirled past others. But it is gone and all elements of society have to join together to reconstruct.

In Johnstown, it was civic pride and spirit that rebuilt. In Romania, it must be national pride and the Holy Spirit that heals. There cannot be a restoration of a nation to what it was or rather to what it would like to be, unless it is through the operation and overshadowing of the unifying Spirit of God. As the Spirit hovered over the tumultuous waters and saw that light was brought from darkness, so too, it must be that Heavenly King, that Comforter, the Spirit of Truth which recreates a new Romania, which cracks the facade of the dark kingdom and lets in new light, the Light of Christ which "illuminates all."

Meanwhile, in the New World, we can gather our assistance and compassion packages and send them to bodies, but we must also collect our prayers and petitions for the souls and, from our homes, from our parishes and communities, watch that reconstruction. For we know that restoration comes from within, not from without, and that renewal comes from a desire to live and bear fruit, new fruit, new witness; but only after the pruning has been completed and new sap rises. Then there will be blossoms of promise and harvest in due season.

59

"The children in the orphanages will receive better care and slowly assume their place in the sun. But is there anyone to join Rachel in crying for her children because they are no more? Who will join Liberty to weep because HER children are no more?"

(March 1990)

As the stories of Romania's orphans began to reach Westerners, His Eminence reflected on their plight in the light of the treatment of children and the unborn everywhere in the world. A short time later, he co-founded the charitable organizations, Help for Romania and Help the Children of Romania.

Romania's Orphans

At one time, the SOLIA appeared on a weekly basis. Frankly, right now, I am glad that it doesn't. Our staff is not able to keep up with all the events taking place in Romania, and, although we may be sure that some of our faithful are concerned that we are already taking up many pages and much space with reporting on those events, we feel that forty five years of suffering of that people merits a few editions of this publication.

The events which have rolled across our TV screens, entered into the sanctuary of our homes via the newspaper and penetrated our reading habits with splashy magazine coverage have left us exhausted and emotionally angry.

At first we were told about the bloody revolution, the victims of which we are not even yet certain and whose numbers will always be contested; after the exhumation on TV of corpses in cemeteries, in woods, in desolate places, the likes of which reveal the faceless brutality of a system that does not place any value on man; after the continued and continuous harassment of civilians by snipers and vengeance strikes by retaliating neighbors. After all this we find more atrocities, and the world swoons with disbelief.

Now the story is about orphans and the elderly, the "non-productive" and, yes, there is still more, there are the children with AIDS. Behind that simple statement, however, is the reality that if children were infected through transfer of infected blood by unsanitary needles, how many adults may yet be discovered as new victims?

The West crooned over the plight in which the orphans found themselves; few attendants, insufficient nourishment, lack of hygienic care. It was from these neglected kids that recruits for the "Securitate" were extracted, going from innocence and poverty to security and death dealing. The telephone at the Episcopate rings continuously with requests for information as to how to adopt a "ROMANIAN ORPHAN". In the meantime, large amounts of food, clothing, toys, even tons of chocolate, were disgorged into a system that wasn't able nor ready to handle this outpouring of concern. Who can resist the sad eyes of a hungry, frightened, neglected infant? Who doesn't want to wipe the face of a tear-stained, smudged little face?

As aid was being blanketed on those hundreds of little tykes, old news, old information came to light that AIDS was already suffocating an entire generation for itself!

TIME magazine's photo of February 19 portrays, no, that is too gentle a word, broadcasts a victim of AIDS being bathed. It is a still life study of "Life Struggling to Die". The little body is arched not upward to light, to the sun and life, but downward, to darkness, to the earth and death. The eyes see but do not care; the mouth is open but waits to be shut; the body wastes and its members are intolerable to strength and resistance. AIDS, however, claims victims of all ages.

It is like the Medieval portrayal of Death with the great scythe, cutting its huge swath across every social strata, through all generations, with its grim reminder that all men bear the seed of death while trying to eclipse the real truth that even in death there is a life-bearing pod of eternal existence.

Coming back to the "ROMANIAN ORPHANS", we note that the line to adopt forms from the bowels of Western nations, from across oceans, transcending borders and boundaries. Those same nations whose rate of abortion is the entire population of Romania itself, now trek to that little known country which was bound and hobbled, like the feet of the old Chinese nobility to not grow, to remain stagnant, to be considered quaint but ineffective. These are the nations who claim that the "pre-orphan", that is the fetus, is merely "property" of the carrier, "chattel" as described by civilized law.

A child is a child and though each nation may think, and permissibly so, that its children are the sweetest, there is nothing exceptional about "ROMANIAN ORPHANS"; except, they are alive and, presumably available for adoption. When Ceauşescu created his "kids for currency" system, the world was shocked. Now, people are angry that the Romanian government, temporary as it is, will not allow mass adoption. Even though the couples be parentally perfect and wonderful folks, the doors of the orphanages have not been flung open. I think this is a courageous stand.

Is the government concerned for its "ROMANIAN ORPHANS," or is it just that no special plan has been formulated? Is it because a nation without children is doomed, and these children are seen as numbers for the future work force? No one knows, here in the West; what we do know is that we have laid waste to our own "pre-orphans," to the unborn, and this for 17 years.

A month ago, Americans for life marched in the nation's capital to protest the Roe vs. Wade decision of this nation's highest court. Yet, there was not much ado in the media, except to intentionally ignore the march. What great coverage though, for the "Innocent Little Victims of AIDS", for the "ROMANIAN ORPHANS", for those living although almost dead.

Can the issue be so simple that in the womb it is an "IT," and only after birth "IT" becomes a person? Is there really that much difference between "Kids for Cash" and "Kids who are Trashed?" Our society is in need of deep soul searching and re-evaluating of life from conception to death.

The authors of informative articles want us to believe that the AIDS problem is due to Ceauşescu's denial of birth-control and sex-education when, in fact, AIDS in this instance is caused by poor hygienic practices rather than by sexual transmittal.

The Orthodox Church has always exhorted abstinence as the first mode for conception control, especially between unmarried couples. Secondly, the sanctity of marriage calls for a single partner and the honoring, one of the other. Finally, the Church does recognize conception control under the guidance of the spiritual father and with concern for new life and ability to sustain it. But never, never, can we consider that what exists in the womb is not human and not to be protected. Furthermore, never, never is that which carries the fetus merely a "carrier," but rather, a mother, demonstrating a unique, beautiful relationship, which only some can experience and others admire.

Those little folks, the AIDS-infected, have a short life; God grant a cure! The children in the orphanages will receive better care and slowly assume their place in the sun. But is there anyone to join Rachel in crying for her children because they are no more? Who will join Liberty to weep because HER children are no more?

We are still angry, because there is no undoing 17 years of wrongdoing. But we have hope that those who may be allowed to adopt may convince others that there is a place for all life, that life in the womb is sacred, that "ROMANIAN ORPHANS" are "GOD'S ORPHANS," and that the FETUS in the Womb is God's Lifegiven Child. We hope that lesson comes soon, Lord, because it hurts so very much; because we are exhausted by the struggle for life over death and light over darkness.

60

> *"We sat in the comfort of our homes and saw the innocent children in Timisoara cut down; we watched the youth go out to embrace the bullets of the Securitate. We should be moved to join them now, spiritually, in song, to sing the powerful hymn of the resurrection of Christ."*
>
> *(April 1990)*

The first Pascha following the fall of communism provides the Archbishop with pause for reflection and joy. He exhorts us all to join the newly liberated in giving thanks to God and in proclaiming the Good News of the Resurrection.

In the Light of the Resurrection

We cannot but wonder at how the Romanian people, and for that matter, all Christian people who have just recently been freed from the communist yoke, will celebrate the "Feast of feasts and Festival of festivals." For this year, for the first time in decades, the faithful may be able to celebrate the feast as never before. Perhaps more will go to their parish church to confess their sins. to ask and give forgiveness, to "approach with the fear of God, with faith and love," to receive the Lamb of God who takes away their sins and the sins of the world.

There are certainly those who, having experienced the bitter sting of betrayal, will not go to the holy mysteries, who will resist because of the clergy. While we do not judge them nor chide them, we recall the Liturgy of St. Basil in which the priest says: "Do not withhold your grace from these holy gifts because of my sins." This is true of all the sacraments or mysteries of the Church: true of the mystery of confession, true of the mystery of the priesthood, true of the mystery of baptism and so on.

Part of the change for the future comes with change now, through the holy mysteries, for it is time for a new start, and Pascha is the time for personal response. As the processions form in the streets, winding between the churches and the surrounding buildings, how could anyone not want to take part; how could anyone absent themselves from what is taking place? When the winding sheet of the crucified Lord is placed in the tomb in the sanctuaries of faith, after the quiet of the darkest moments of the night, the celebrant will come out of the altar bearing the lighted candle and exclaim: "Come! Take the light, which does not fade! Let us glorify Christ who is risen from the dead!" Who will refuse it? This is the chosen day, the acceptable time, the moment of cleansing and catharsis. This is the hour of preparation for what is shortly to come. Armed with the power of renewed faith, sanctified with the holy Body and Blood of Christ, the clergy and faithful will be illuminated with the light which does not fade and will be led to lead new lives, a new and holy life, in a new and holy Pascha.

We can imagine the tears flowing from eyes which previously dared not be seen to weep; to hear the choked voices of response that "Truly He is risen!" from lips which chose not to form the words before. We can conceive of the emotions of those who enter the church and smell incense for the first time in years, who light a candle for parents, grandparents and ancestors for the first time in decades.

The ecstasy of this year's Pascha may be unique, for it is a year of jubilee, a year of celebrations, a year of liberation, which will be felt in a different way than before. However, each year is a year of personal liberation, of renewal, of the Church's steady pilgrimage to her Lord and Savior.

There are those of us who, year after year, have been able to fully celebrate Pascha, but out of neglect failed to or chose to partially celebrate in a perfunctory manner. We had the occasion to confess our sins in the holy mystery of confession but ignored the invitation from the Church; we had the call to renewal in our parish churches but elected to do other things of little importance instead. We have no excuse; we had no excuse.

We sat in the comfort of our homes and saw the innocent children in Timisoara cut down; we watched the youth go out to embrace the bullets of the Securitate. We should be moved to join them now, spiritually, in song, to sing the powerful hymn of the resurrection of Christ.

Now is the acceptable time for us, too. This is a jubilee year for us, as well, for Christ's victory knows no limits in time, in space, is all-pervading and holy. It is the time to take the light that does not fade, the light which illuminates all men and which penetrates the darkest recesses and pierces the heaviest curtain, of iron or of the human heart, in Romania, in America and everywhere.

61

"Save us from pride, O Lord, for we do not seek the riches of this world but only this day's bread and freedom to worship you without fear of oppression and to love you, to bear witness to you with one mouth, one heart and one mind, in unity with all peoples who love your name, now and ever and unto ages of ages."

(December 1990)

In this simple prayer, His Eminence gives glory to God for all things, and focuses our thoughts on the truth that salvation comes only by our repentance and God's grace.

Prayer on the Occasion of the First Anniversary of Romania's Revolution

O Holy God who created the nations and set every people in its given place; who, because of our transgressions allowed many years of suffering and slavery to come on the Romanian people, as you allow for all those who bear your name; you sent Godless people, barbarians, who profaned your way, that is, your Holy Church, demolishing the places of worship and praise of your faithful people.

You, Lord our God, have taken mercy on us and forgiven us and lead us forth again into freedom. As your holy apostle, Peter, you have released us from bondage and prison. Now grant us your Holy Spirit to put us on the right path of life, lest we sin in your sight again. Bestow on the Romanian people the unity of faith, so that the body of your Holy Orthodox Church be not dismembered. Grant that the liberty you have given us be not unto perdition but unto the salvation of souls. We have abandoned you, O Lord, but do not abandon us. Bestow your peace upon us, not as the world gives peace, but the true peace, which is to have Christ Jesus dwelling in our hearts. Give us this, O Lord, so that we may fulfill our role in history, which you have given to us to do. Grant, too, O Lord, that the death of those thousands of youth and children given in sacrifice for the freedom of the Romanian people be not offered in vain. Receive their souls in paradise and direct our lives here on earth, that we may be prepared to receive you at your second coming. Prepare a place for the people at the resurrection in the life to come. Accept the prayers of the monks and nuns, the martyrs and Carpathian hermits, of those who died in prison, in labor camps, deprived of confession and the Eucharist and a peaceful end to their lives, but who gave of their lives for the salvation of the people.

O Lord, do not allow those who are atheist to rule your nation. Save us from pride, O Lord, for we do not seek the riches of this world but only this day's bread and freedom to worship you without fear of oppression and to love you, to bear witness to you with one mouth, one heart and one mind, in unity with all peoples who love your name, now and ever and unto ages of ages.

Amen.

62

"In visiting parishes and in speaking with the faithful, I was heartened by the keen interest shown in continuing the assistance program initiated in January of 1990, and the explicit promise to respond again when the need was stated. Now is that time; we do have funds, much more limited than in the beginning, but if programs are to be planned, we have to have the 'money in the bank'."

(November 1991)

In two years, the Episcopate's "Help for Romania" fund became the premier assistance agency for Romania, sending nearly $85 million in goods and funds to those in need. Founded by Archbishop Nathaniel, the fund worked directly with the Romanian Patriarchate to determine areas of need, and entrusted the Romanian Church with the responsibility of overseeing distribution. In this appeal, His Eminence reminds the faithful that their help is still needed, even though the news media have turned their attention elsewhere.

An Appeal for "Help for Romania" on the Second Anniversary

Through the past 24 months, the faithful of our diocese have been aware of the extensive program of assistance that we have offered to the Romanian people. Our primary purpose was to show our human concern for them in the recent days of political change; and secondly, to share with them goods which might help them physically, intellectually and morally.

Shipments of food, clothing, medicines and medical equipment have been sent; grain and vegetable seed and implements have reached the farms; books of medical studies, engineering, and other topics have reached the shelves of the libraries; office equipment, printing equipment was shipped.

Through the efforts of the Department of Christian Assistance, with our two coordinators, V. R. R. Grabowski in the United States and Fr. D. Tatulescu in Bucharest, and working with Brother's Brother Foundation of Pittsburgh, we have sent an estimated $20 million in goods to the Romanian people.

The Episcopate Office made one single appeal to the parishes and auxiliaries in 1990, and approximately $275,000 has been contributed for this assistance work as reported in the 1990-1991 REPORT TO THE CONGRESS.

Considering that almost $20 million in goods was sent and that future projects need to be funded, we are asking that the SUNDAY FOLLOWING THANKSGIVING DAY, DECEMBER 1, 1991, be a Day for Romanian Assistance Collection in all parishes throughout the Episcopate, and that this collection be taken at the conclusion of the usual Divine Liturgy on that day.

I am making this appeal to you as your Bishop, recognizing the limitations imposed on everyone by the present economic status in Canada and the United States. We all have observed and experienced that when we work together, we can accomplish much in the name of all. In visiting parishes and in speaking with the faithful, I was heartened by the keen interest shown in continuing the assistance program initiated in January of 1990, and the explicit promise to respond again when the need was stated. Now is that time; we do have funds, much more limited than in the beginning, but if programs are to be planned, we have to have the "money in the bank."

The Appeal is in the name of HELP FOR ROMANIA, the official assistance program of the Episcopate and by which we are recognized in Romania by the officials as a "Charitable Organization."

We thank the good God for his grace, which moved you to respond two years ago to our only appeal, and we pray that you will again open your hearts and share with the people of Romania some of the blessings which God has bestowed on us in North America. Both Canada and the United States have an official "Thanksgiving Day"; it would be an extension of these celebrations to our Romanian brethren, if they could continue to receive from the bounties of hearts and from the HELP FOR ROMANIA program which depends on YOU for its continuation and expansion.

It would be a beautiful act of "thanksgiving" if each local auxiliary, every individual in all parishes combined their love and made it concrete with a financial gift to say: "Yes! We want to see this movement of love and concern from our parishes and diocese to continue; we want to show to the world that our love is not a veneer, and that our aspirations for the Romanian people continue for their further development and growth."

A major project now underway is to provide the New Testament and Psalms for spiritual nourishment, and the continued flow of assistance as well.

Being filled with the good things of this earth after Thanksgiving Day and anticipating the blessings of the Birth of Our Lord Jesus Christ, let's lay at the feet of the newborn Christ child whatever offering we can and know that together, we will offer back to him the Romanian nation.

With blessings, thanks and deep admiration for your previous offerings in behalf of our Romanian brothers and sisters.

With Corina Phillips, daughter of "Help for Romania" director, +Archpriest Richard Grabowski, Akron, 2009

63

"With the assistance sent to Romania by the Episcopate, we showed that we still feel for the Romanian people and have responded from the depths of our hearts and material goods. By choosing, intentionally, to work through and with the Church in Romania and the Patriarchate, we demonstrated our love for the faith of our fathers and our acknowledgement that the Church is the Body of Christ; and, we want, as Church in America, to work with the Church in Romania. We do not challenge the Mother Church or judge, nor do we expect to be challenged or judged. However, we have a history that cannot be ignored, denied or rejected; to do so would be an injustice to those who 'fought the good fight and kept the faith'."
(November 1991)

In this 1991 article, Archbishop Nathaniel reminds the world that the good intentions and Christian charity of the Episcopate and her faithful should not be misunderstood. The Romanian community in North America has its own, unique identity and history.

Episcopate? Patriarchate?

Last year, 1990, a special Pastoral Letter was sent by the Holy Synod of the Orthodox Church in Romania to Romanian faithful everywhere. The general thrust of the letter was that the "bonds of the faith of our forefathers and fraternal love overcome all boundaries, all distances and any human frailties."

The heart of the message was: "Seeing the goodness and forgiveness of God toward us, let our hearts be open and our souls be illumined and the desire for communion (fellowship) and unity flow in us . . . we send a holy and paternal call to unity in faith and fraternal communion in the name of the resurrected Christ."

Finally, there was an extension of willingness " . . . to work together for the spiritual rebirth and renewal . . . to come to an understanding, to forgive and to come to a reconciliation between us brothers of the same nationality and faith."

In response to this Letter of Reconciliation, the delegates of the 1991 Church Congress passed a resolution, which was also printed in the August SOLIA of this year. The thrust of the resolution was to hope to " . . . set aside differences of the past and normalize relations . . . as brothers in the Lord, and as those who also share a common ancestry, to have respect for one another."

The resolution was sent to the Holy Synod as information, but the hierarchy responded with the Patriarchal Letter 6391-1991, which responds to some of the resolution, but not all.

It has come to our attention that some of the faithful wonder, "What does the Letter mean? Are we now under the jurisdiction of the Romanian Patriarchate? Are we no longer part of the American Orthodox Church? Is there now only one diocese/archdiocese/episcopate? Do we concelebrate with the clergy of the Romanian Missionary Archdiocese? What is the result of the recent correspondence between the Patriarchate and the Episcopate?"

Our resolution did not seek to "return" to the Church in Romania nor to "withdraw" from the Autocephalous Orthodox Church in America. We are still an integral part of the American Church and are not "under" the Church in Romania.

The Episcopate and the Missionary Archdiocese are still two separate church entities, each with its own history and existence. The Romanian Orthodox Episcopate of America is within the Orthodox Church of America, and the Romanian Missionary Archdiocese is within the bosom of the Romanian Patriarchate in Bucharest.

Although the Patriarchal Letter states that the Holy Synod recognizes the canonicity of the diocese (Episcopate) and the validity of the hierarchal succession, it does not state in what manner these are perceived.

Is the Episcopate recognized within the Orthodox Church in America? This is not stated, as such. Is it understood to be under the jurisdiction of the Patriarchate, which claims concern for all Romanians? This can be deduced.

The Letter recognizes the "Episcopate of the Vatra" as distinct from the "Missionary Archdiocese of Detroit." In fact, there is no "Episcopate of the Vatra" per se, but the Romanian Orthodox Episcopate of America with its See in Detroit, which has its administrative center in Grass Lake, Michigan, on the grounds named, "Vatra Romaneasca." For the ROEA, it considers itself to be the continuation of the original diocese of Bishop Policarp Morusca with his successor being Archbishop Valerian D. Trifa.

The Missionary Archdiocese, on the other hand, was founded on June 5, 1950, and incorporated with an address on E. State Fair, and now has its administrative center on Riopelle Street and its Cathedral in Windsor, Ontario.

Thus, to the question: Are there two dioceses? The answer is that this is how both the ROEA and the RMA perceive themselves, and the Romanian Patriarchate likewise.

At this time, there is still no concelebration between the clergy of both bodies; such a change in policy will have to result in consultation and understanding as time grants and God's grace moves us.

What, then, are the results of this correspondence between the Episcopate and Romanian Patriarchate? Exactly as can be realized, "to seek fraternal love, to overcome boundaries and distances and frailties to come to a reconciliation between brothers," and "to set aside past differences and normalize relations."

This is a futureable and needs the input of the Missionary Archdiocese, which has been in America for 40 years while still remaining under the jurisdiction of the Church in Romania. It can act as a bridge or a wall. It has a role, but it must discover it. If no role is seen, then nothing can be done, for there is not merely an Episcopate-Patriarchate relationship, but an Episcopate-Patriarchate-Archdiocese relationship.

With the assistance sent to Romania by the Episcopate, we showed that we still feel for the Romanian people and have responded from the depths of our hearts and material goods. By choosing, intentionally, to work through and with the Church in Romania and the Patriarchate, we demonstrated our love for the faith of our fathers and our acknowledgement that the Church is the Body of Christ; and, we want, as Church in America, to work with the Church in Romania. We do not challenge the Mother Church or judge, nor do we expect to be challenged or judged. However, we have a history that cannot be ignored, denied or rejected; to do so would be an injustice to those who "fought the good fight and kept the faith."

We pray the good God to enlighten the hearts of our clergy and faithful to pray for and work towards the fulfillment of our Congress Resolution and "for peace and stability of the Holy Churches of God."

64

"Indeed, how does one dare 'publish' the suffering of souls? Can the depths of human endurance be measured, weighed, appreciated, or judged? Only God, who created the heart of man and knows the depths of his soul, knows what his servants have "suffered for the sake of righteousness!" We can only weep and recoil, mediate and admire.

(October 1992)

As the literature of the communist-era underground began to emerge in the 1990s, His Eminence published several samples and excerpts in the pages of Solia. Here he introduces us to a collection of poetry springing from the experience of political imprisonment.

Poems From Communist Prisons

This is not a 'book review' but an introduction, an offering to our readers of selected works from ***Poems from Communist Prisons***, translated from the Romanian book of the same name.

There are a limited number of twenty-nine poems presented in this slim volume, which were translated by the Very Rev. Mother Alexandra of thrice-blessed memory, first Abbess of the Holy Transfiguration Monastery, Ellwood City, Pennsylvania.

These twenty-nine are but a fraction of the thousands of literary works that are coming to light from the dark bowels of the Communist political prisons in Romania. Without doubt, there exist unpublished millions of works of testimony from other peoples and nations which were enslaved, and who likewise suffered/suffer unspeakably under diabolic atheistic Communism.

A fuller and richer volume of poems published in Romanian as ***POEZII DIN INCHISORI,*** collected by Mr. Zahu Pana and published by the Canadian newspaper, "Cuvantul Romanesc/The Romanian Voice" in 1982, is the source of the English book. Can we hope that the rest will also be translated for the wide English-speaking public?

Indeed, how does one dare "publish" the suffering of souls? Can the depths of human endurance be "measured," "weighed," "appreciated," or "judged?" Only God, who created the heart of man and knows the depths of his soul, knows what his servants have "suffered for the sake of righteousness!" We can only weep and recoil, mediate and admire.

The purpose of the book and the reason for which we are publishing these poems is to share the bounties of the spiritual fruit which these elect of the Lord carefully planted, nurtured, protected, and pruned in the inner garden of their heart, while yet constrained within the sterile "killing fields" of Communist prisons.

Furthermore, it is not possible for us to ignore nor attempt to whitewash the decades of vicious and inhumane treatment perpetrated against the victims of Communism just because it seems that changes are in the wind. We must not only gain from their words but must also make their words be respected. Not only do the relics of these individuals cry out to heaven for recognition, but the prison stones themselves would shout out in rage should the blood poured forth and splattered on them, staining them forever, not be acknowledged, however humbly so in these few printed works.

One must read Mother Alexandra's Foreword which in itself is like a personal echo, her own poem and confession of sympathy, of understanding, and which is a type of spiritual participation, "common union," if you will, with the suffering of the authors of ***Poems from Communist Prisons.***

"This is true poetry of the soul," she states, "that expresses various emotions of those unjustly imprisoned by the Communist Party, for the crime of independent thought. These poems should not be read too quickly, for their meaning may be difficult at first sight to comprehend. There is much symbolism in them, and however bitter in parts, they are full of Christian fortitude and forgiveness."

It is our intention to publish these poems as a kind of "remembrance" or "pomelnic" to the authors, individuals who have scratched into the hard walls of this life the graffiti of their innermost feelings, and which cannot be ignored nor made light of. Without pen and paper, they committed to memory and later shared their soul's monologues with their prison mates. By God's will, they have been delivered to us like some special "St. Valentine's" greeting of old.

Each issue of **SOLIA** will carry at least one poem, one testament, and we pray that "the suffering which is so real will also explain the final strength to forgive." It is this Christian virtue, which is the basis for the unique and light-filled out-pouring of these illumined souls, a virtue without which the world cannot change and which itself is the touchstone of the true message and person of Jesus Christ. It is a virtue sorely absent from our own Western Capitalist/Consumer/Agnostic Society.

It is not our intention to stir animosity against those particular individuals who were in authority at the time; there are others who will be charged with meting out justice and other ways that will be employed.

We have been asked: "Did the corporate body of the Romanian people know of these languishing souls, and could they not, by some action, have changed the course of that imprisonment and that of their own national history? Without a doubt the suffering of the prisoners was known at least in part, so to what extent is a moot point.

We are reminded of the time, just months ago, when people asked why something had not been done about the orphans. Did not the people know? Could they not have done something? We ourselves pass our prisons and our own public and private institutions, and can we say that we know what is really going on inside? If there is a universal responsibility of the entire nation, is this not a question that must be asked by those there and not by us here? On the other hand, if such a question can be posed there, it can also be formulated for us.

We in the free world have been blessed to now come to meet these individuals through their poetry. Once locked behind impenetrable walls, unjustly imprisoned, they have become part of the action of purification and renewal resulting from their sufferings and through their intercessions in behalf of their fellow citizens. They became, in fact, some kind of collective conscience of the nation.

Certainly, it is not necessary for us to know that others are praying for us in order for us to benefit from their love. God's plans work unhindered by thick walls, violent beatings and extreme deprivations; and, he selects his servants as he wills. So, too, the Romanian people need not have known the intensity of the poets' suffering for them as a nation to have reaped the benefits of their witness to God.

Nations, groups, individuals are all part of the fabric of our earthly life, and hidden between the visible warp and the weft are invisible threads of the grace, the light and love of God. We may notice only one side of the cloth, but the other side is there and bears the perfect pattern and is the "right side up," revealing God's hand in human history, making it sacred history.

We have selected for the first poem, "Jesus In The Night," by Radu Gyr. It is in the night that one's mind, body and heart come to rest in the hours after heavy labor; and yet, it is in those moments that our soul so often "as a deer thirsting for water seeks the living God." Sit with Radu on his bed and behold the tall, sad Savior who has come to give balm to his heavy heart.

Our thanks to the Very Rev. Mother Christophora, Abbess of the Holy Transfiguration Monastery, for permission to publish this series of poems.

May these ***Poems from Communist Prisons*** move those of us who did not live through such times and bring us to contrition, to thanksgiving and to personal and collective renewal as Children of God and as our brother's keeper.

65

"During the Communist Iron Curtain decades, the Voice of America and Radio Free Europe broadcast truth and gave these same people hope. American politicians promised to liberate them. East Europeans thought that they had an honest ally in America, 'Sweet Land of Liberty of whom we sing!' Now, when it is possible to show signs of authentic welcome, our government is pulling the Welcome Mat from under their feet."

(January 1994)

One of the ironies of the fall of communism was the simultaneous tightening of travel restrictions by the United States. His Eminence takes on the issue, speaking out for the many who were denied permission to travel to America, just when their new freedom seemed to make that dream possible.

New Iron Curtain: "Made in America"

According to Marc Ballon, a writer for the *Prague Post* and former reporter for the *Los Angeles Daily News*, a new Iron Curtain has descended on countries of Eastern Europe; and, across it could be stamped the words, "Made in the USA."

The "Land of the Free and the Home of the Brave" has slammed the door closed on thousands of Romanians, Poles and Bulgarians who simply wish to visit the land of the "Lady with the Lamp." After four and more decades of Communist darkness, America is actively excluding these people, "This is ugly betrayal," says Ballon.

The Czech Foreign Ministry recently complained to the U.S. Embassy in Prague (where Mr. Clinton himself as a visitor was recently warmly welcomed) that its citizens seeking tourist visas were routinely humiliated during interviews by American officials who accuse them of lying and planning to emigrate.

7% of the Czechs were denied visas last year but the Poles had 60%, the Romanians 44% and Bulgarians 28%. "In effect, their chances of visiting the U.S. are little better now than when the Soviet soldiers lived down the street," observes Marc Ballon.

According to procedure, the words "Application Received" are stamped by U.S. officials in the passports of rejected applicants. This brands them as suspect and makes it far more difficult to obtain visas to other Western countries. *"Under U.S. law, consular officers must view every applicant as a probable immigrant until the applicant proves otherwise. A person is considered "GUILTY" until proven innocent."*

During the Communist Iron Curtain decades, the Voice of America and Radio Free Europe broadcast truth and gave these same people hope. American politicians promised to liberate them. East Europeans thought that they had an honest ally in America, "Sweet Land of Liberty" of whom we sing! Now, when it is possible to show signs of authentic "Welcome", our government is pulling the Welcome Mat from under their feet.

The U.S. should add East European countries to the 22 mostly West European nations currently exempt from tourist-visa requirements. It would also be fair. Americans no longer need visas to travel in Eastern Europe, except to Romania.

In conclusion, Ballon states: "If Congress opposed granting waivers, it could at least amend the Immigration and Nationality Act so that visa applicants are viewed as POSSIBLE rather than PROBABLE immigrants. After all that East Europeans have gone through, this is the least the United States can do."

We agree with the author. The thinly disguised, prejudiced formal attitude of our government toward Eastern Europe and the obvious kowtowing toward Russia is the beginning of another sick foreign policy which is written in blood and tears for some, and aggression and privilege for others. Down came the Berlin Wall and up goes a new one, a heavier one appears to be erected: "Made in the U.S. of A.?" Let's hope not!

66

> *"Mountains, hills, plains, forests, lakes, rivers, streams! It is understood that political pressures must have been very harsh at the turn of the century to pry anyone loose from the natural beauty of this area to go to a foreign country."*
>
> *"Across the river to the North was Slovakia and Ukraine; on the West, Hungary. To keep an identity through the decades, the people clung to the Orthodox Church as the truly Romanian institution of national unity."*
>
> *(October 1994)*

A few years after the fall of communism, His Eminence, accompanied by a retinue of clergy and staff, made a personal pilgrimage to the land of his ancestry. Here is a brief report and reflection on that trip.

Return of a Pilgrim

During Holy Week, Orthodox Christians walk a spiritual pilgrimage in time and space, following in the footsteps of the Lord on his road of suffering. On the Great day of Holy Pascha, they stand with the angels at the empty tomb, rejoicing in Christ's resurrection.

Our visit to Romania during Bright Week was a continuation of that Paschal joy as we visited cathedrals, monasteries, parish churches and monuments which stand for the thousands of years of Christianity in the Romania of yesteryear and reflect the image of a national resurrection, the reward for being faithful stewards of the Faith through decades of oppression.

Our group traveled in two vehicles: Toyota Van I and Jeep Cherokee Car II. Autovan I: Very Rev. R. Grabowski,

Archimandrite ROMAN (Braga), Mr. Dinu and Mrs. Manuela Cruga and the Bishop. Red Jeep II: Very Rev. Frs. C. Alecse, L. Lazar, S. Pavel, and C. Tofan.

Traveling together as a group of Orthodox Christians from America to the land of our forefathers, our journey was from May 7-22, when the nine of us were together. After that date, Car II left Romania, and the remaining five continued the trip until May 26. Our excursions began early in the morning and concluded late in the day, filled with wonderful sights, smells and sounds.

Among the cities we visited and in which we stopped were: Alba Iulia, Arad, Baia Mare, Blaj, Bucharest, Constanta, Craiova, Galati, Jassy, Oradea, Ramnicu Valcea, Satu Mare, Sibiu, Slobozia, Suceava, Targoviste, Tecuci, Timisoara.

Romanian cities have their own particular characteristics created by history. The citizens of the metropolitan areas are very proud of them; and, in the years since 1989, much renovation has taken place and is still being done. Nevertheless, each city continues to reflect its particular image fashioned by time and events.

Our hosts were many. Among the hierarchy whom we met and who showed extraordinary kindnesses are the following: His Beatitude TEOCTIST, Their Eminences Metropolitans ANTONIE of Transylvania, DANIEL of Moldova and Bucovina, NESTOR of Oltenia, NICOLAE of Banat; Their Eminences Archbishops BARTOLOMEU of Vad, Feleac & Cluj, CASIAN of Tomis, LUCIAN of Constanta, PIMEN of Suceava and Radauti, VASILE of Targoviste; Their Graces ANDREI of Alba Iulia, EMILIAN of Caransebes, GHERASIM of Ramnicu Valcea, IOAN of Oradea, IUSTINIAN of Maramures and Satmar, NIFON of Slobozia, TIMOTEI of Arad, Ienople & Halmagiu; Their Graces Auxiliary Bishops DAMASCHIN (Severineanul), IRINEU (Slatineanul), IUSTIN (Sigheteanul), TEODOSIE (Snagoveanul), TEOFAN (Sinaitul), VINCENTIU (Ploesteanul).

The large and beautiful Metropolitan cathedrals are newer in most cases, being constructed during the time of the monarchy and a unified Romania. They remind us of the time of great building and status achievement accomplished before the dulling ignorance of the communist philosophy spawned its static "socialist" structures.

We concelebrated the Divine Liturgy in the Patriarchal Cathedral with His Beatitude, TEOCTIST and His Grace, TEOFAN; in the Metropolitan Cathedral of Sibiu with His Eminence, ANTONIE; and in the Cathedral of Timisoara with His Eminence, NICOLAE. It was a joy to concelebrate the consecration of a parish church in Zabrani with Their Graces, TIMOTEI and EMILIAN.

Who can adequately describe the ancient churches with their tall vaults and domes, some recently renovated, others still blackened by fires built in them by Austrian and Turkish occupiers who did not allow them to be restored or used? It is difficult to understand that many churches and monasteries were left with their roofs collapsed, open to the elements as a sign of the power of the present occupiers of the country, in particular in Transylvania! To suppress the Church was identified with suppressing the people, the nation itself.

Some of the monasteries we saw include the following: Agapia, Antim, Cernica, Cornetu, Dragomirna, Gaiu, Hodos Bodrog, Hurezu, Lainici, Moisei, Moldovita, Neamtu, Polovraci, Putna, Recea, Rohia, Sambata de Sus, Secu, Sihastria, Sucevita, Techighiol, Tismana, Timiseni, Toplita, Varatic, Voronet.

The monasteries stand as living sentinels to the role they played in the development of the Romanian nation. It is obvious that these historical places were and are the sites from which the Romanian language, history, and culture was shaped. Not unlike the great Benedictine monasteries of Western Europe which were centers of learning; so, too, these Orthodox beacons of faith and culture nourished the Romanian spirit through dark days of invasions and suppression.

We watched nuns and monks working to renovate monasteries or build new ones. The destruction of hundreds of monasteries under the forced "Unia" and the Austrian General Bukow could be undone only after almost four hundred years!

We visited the Theological Faculties of Bucharest, Jassy, Timisoara; the Theological Institute of Sibiu; and the Theological Seminary in Neamtu, and were sung to by seminarians from Targoviste and Slobozia in their respective cathedrals. Church print-shops and candle factories were high on the list of places to be seen, as was Plumbuita where liturgical vessels and the like are fabricated.

Following in the footsteps of the work of **Help For Romania**, in Bucharest, we went to Colentina Hospital to visit children with AIDS. We dined at Chirila Orphanage for children between 7-18, about 100 residents. It was a distinct pleasure to meet in person, Dr. Pavel Chirila, founder of CHRISTIANA hospital. We met the nuns who are learning to be medical nurses and visited some sick people in the wards. Later in our trip we went to the senior citizens' home at Recea Monastery. Oh! To have tons of money to give in support of such wonderful works of charity and love!

In most instances, where possible for our number of nine, we were house guests of the hierarchy; otherwise, we were guests of the monasteries. We were made very comfortable.

Our original plans did not include visits with government officials; although, at the invitation of a few hierarchs, some civil authorities were present at some events - the Prefect of Alba and the Mayor of Alba Iulia; and the Prefect of Arges and the Mayor of Ramnicu Valcea.

Our group was treated with great kindness and fraternal love; there was no time at which we felt or were made to feel uncomfortable, nor were we put into unpleasant situations nor drawn into negative discussions. On the contrary, the hierarchy, clergy and laity who introduced us explained the fact of the existence of Orthodoxy in America, the presence of Romanian communities, and the fact of two dioceses, one under the Patriarchate and one in the Orthodox Church in America.

There were informal discussions with Church leaders, but without any agenda or any scope other than to come to better know one another and to be informed. We were interviewed by radio and television stations, newspaper reporters and by individuals.

Our theme for the visit was the dual one of the 200th anniversary of Orthodoxy in North America and the 65th anniversary of the Episcopate's founding. Each of the members of the group was invited to speak at one time or another.

A variety of Episcopate publications had been pre-shipped to three places in Romania to make it easier for us to distribute them on the various stages of our journey. It was a great blessing and joy to have 100,000 icon prints of "Our Lady, Joy of Romania" to distribute throughout the country. This was made possible through generous financing by Ms. Margie Caciavely in memory of her mother Marica and brother Tom.

Through the kind preparations of His Grace, ANDREI of Alba Iulia, we were able to concelebrate a parastas with him at the grave of His Grace, POLICARP Morusca. Bishop POLICARP's niece was present, and she brought with her a photo album with pictures of long ago, mostly of the Vatra and of many of you "Old Timers." At a pomana, we enjoyed identifying individuals and sites for her.

It was impossible in the time allotted to visit Campeni, the home of Archbishop VALERIAN; but, in a newly-constructed wood church in Alba Iulia, we did have a parastas for him and his family. The Archbishop's brother, Ionel and a niece came by bus from Campeni to be present for the occasion.

We visited monumental churches where we revered the relics of many saints: Stefan the Great and Holy, St. Demetrius of Bessarabia, The Righteous Parascheva, St. John the New of Suceava, The Righteous Philothea of Curtea de Arges, St. Nicodimus the Sanctified, St. Joseph the New of Partos, St. Calinic.

At the tombs of Kings Carol I and Ferdinand and their consorts at Curtea de Arges, we served a parastas, also remembering "Domnita Ileana," Mother Alexandra, at the site of her forefathers' resting place.

In Bucharest, we visited the Tomb of the Unknown Soldier and also the Cemetery, "Eroilor Revoluției," where the young people who were killed in the December 1989 Revolution are buried. A monument church is being constructed there by parents and friends of those who lie asleep in the shadow of the still unfinished structure. How terribly sad to see the row on row of porcelain photos of very young people who were massacred for freedom.

Likewise, in Timisoara, after the Divine Liturgy on Sts. Constantine and Helen Day, our entourage crossed from the Cathedral to the cross monument erected for those slain in the square, laid a wreath in their memory and placed our lighted candles among the many hundreds burning there day and night.

In Bucharest, we presented ourselves at the American Embassy where we met Mr. Jonathan Rickert, Consul, who was glad to hear of the work of **Help for Romania**.

We stopped at village and city churches under construction where the people together with the priest are doing the actual work. Towns in Maramures, which had been denied the right to build churches by the Austro-Hungarian and later Communist regimes, were erecting them now for the first time since the destruction of their old churches in the 1700's. Romanians in their own land could now have large churches as need be and were not controlled by other ethnic groups or foreign religions.

In Blaj, a group of Orthodox Christians forced out of their church by the Greek Catholics, were building their own altar from the basement up. In some areas, there were neo-Protestant churches, old and new. Large old Gothic Roman Catholic Hungarian and German churches dotted the countryside; Hungarian Reformed and Unitarian churches were also present in Transylvania. In larger cities, we noted synagogues standing silent; most of the Jewish population had chosen to immigrate to Israel some years ago, and these buildings were left standing silent and vacant.

In Zabrani, in the Diocese of Arad, while driving to the church to be consecrated, we were asked to visit the Swabian Catholic Church as a sign of concern for the people who had no priest. After we had entered the large Gothic structure and had greeted the people, Fr. Grabowski addressed them in the German language. It was a very touching scene.

On our way out of Romania, through Transylvania, on one day alone, we witnessed three Hungarian wedding parties complete with Gypsy violins, palinka, bride and groom and guests walking down the village street on their way to church.

The final leg of the trip had been intended to have been the first, but Maramures was patient and the whirlwind visit left many haunting impressions. Frs. Braga and Grabowski accompanied the Bishop through his tours in the area from which his own family originates, Satu Mare County.

Mountains, hills, plains, forests, lakes, rivers, streams! It is understood that political pressures must have been very harsh at the turn of the century to pry anyone loose from the natural beauty of this area to go to a foreign country.

Across the river to the North was Slovakia and Ukraine; on the West, Hungary. To keep an identity through the decades, the people clung to the Orthodox Church as the truly Romanian "institution" of national unity.

These few lines cannot paint a full picture of this visit, and in the 1995 edition of CALENDARUL SOLIA, it is our intention to present a photo image of "A Pilgrimage to Romania."

67

"We consider the result of the meetings with the Patriarchal Commission in Bucharest as positive and encouraging for the mission and life of our Episcopate in the United States and Canada, the healing of the estrangement of the two Romanian Orthodox eparchies in North America, and the movement toward the unity of all Orthodox in North America – which the Church of Romania agrees is needed and inevitable."

(March 2008)

In February 2008, Archbishop Nathaniel led a delegation to Bucharest, to discuss with the Patriarchate certain issues concerning the Romanian American Orthodox community. One result of that meeting was the unprecedented "Agreed Statement" reproduced in this article, and an informal decision to continue the recently interrupted dialogue with the Romanian Orthodox Archdiocese of the Americas. Unfortunately, a subsequent series of misstatements in Patriarchal publications caused the dialogue to cool almost as quickly as it had resumed. In 2010, the problem of unity remains unresolved.

The Dialogue with the Romanian Patriarchate

To the Beloved Clergy and Faithful of our holy Episcopate:

As announced at the 2007 Congress, in our letter of February 12, 2008 to the clergy and parishes, and via the Press Release posted at www.roea.org, the Episcopate engaged in dialogue with the Church of Romania.

These discussions were initiated at the recommendation of our Joint Dialogue Commission, and approved by the Episcopate Council and Congress, in order to clarify and seek mutual understanding of certain historical issues in the relationship between our Episcopate and the Church of Romania, the sufferings of Bishop Policarp and Archbishop Valerian, etc. Such direct talks with the Church of Romania had long been considered necessary; and, if met with a positive result, it was felt that they would favorably impact future talks between the Joint Dialogue Commissions of the two North American eparchies that have continued since 1993. Also to be discussed was the recent action of a few disgruntled and misguided clergy to create a third Romanian jurisdiction in America. We do not bless this unwarranted activity, nor has Archbishop Nicolae of the Romanian Orthodox Archdiocese in the Two Americas.

Our delegation was led by His Eminence Archbishop Nathaniel and included Very Reverend Fathers Laurence Lazar (Chair), Remus Grama, Catalin Mitescu, Ian Pac-Urar, Romey Rosco.

Before meetings began, the group took part in the Divine Liturgy celebrated on the feast of St. Policarp at the city's Antim Monastery, and visited nearby Pasarea and Cernica Monasteries. On Sunday, February 24, the Archbishop celebrated the Divine Liturgy in a packed Patriarchal Cathedral, assisted by the Cathedral clergy and the Episcopate delegation. At the end of the service, which was broadcast live by the Church's "Trinitas" national TV station, His Eminence spoke of how our Episcopate has maintained its Romanian identity despite the passage of time and distance, and that its heart had been with the people of Romania through all their historical trials. The next day, His Beatitude Patriarch Daniel cordially greeted the delegation at his residence, and subsequently hosted several private meals. He was kept abreast of the ensuing formal discussions and personally offered daily input.

The dialogue took place at the Patriarchal Palace Monday-Wednesday, February 25-27, with the commission named by the Church of Romania. It was headed by His Eminence Archbishop (now Metropolitan) Nifon of Targoviste, with His Eminence Archbishop Nicolae (Wednesday), His Grace Bishop Ciprian Campineanul, Patriarchal Vicar, Councilors Frs. Mircea Uta and

Ioan Armasi. The frank discussions were held in a spirit of Christian respect. Thankfully, following several readings, a mutually agreed upon statement was produced regarding the matters of concern to both sides, and we were notified after returning home that it was received with appreciation by the Holy Synod of the Church of Romania. *(The Agreed Statement is printed below.)*

To avoid speculation, we also share with you that the representatives of the Patriarchate raised the issue and offered their view of a possible union of the two North American eparchies. We reiterated the specific reasons for our visit, and explained that we had assured Archbishop Nicolae and his Dialogue Commission that we would not discuss such a matter without their knowledge. In the end, the two North American commissions agreed to study further a possible course of action, since any potential union is a matter that can only be decided by our people locally, in Congress.

Referring to the content of the Agreed Statement of February 27, the Romanian Holy Synod, in its meeting the following week, specifically noted that: (a) the hierarchs and faithful in both Romania and North America endured much during the unprecedented years of communist persecution, and that the communist government caused much suffering for the Romanian Orthodox Episcopate of America, Bishop Policarp and Archbishop Valerian, Confessors of the Faith who were persecuted and marginalized; (b) mutual forgiveness had been asked for any politically-motivated actions that had caused division in the United States and Canada; and (c) a union of the two Romanian Orthodox eparchies in North America was desirable.

We consider the result of the meetings with the Patriarchal Commission in Bucharest as positive and encouraging for the mission and life of our Episcopate in the United States and Canada, the healing of the estrangement of the two Romanian Orthodox eparchies in North America, and the movement toward the unity of all Orthodox in North America – which the Church of Romania agrees is needed and inevitable. Therefore, in keeping with its mandate, our Joint Dialogue Commission is pursuing renewed discussions with the Archdiocese. We trust in the goodwill of the commission members, we pray for the guidance of the Holy Spirit in their work, and we repeat that any viable proposal for union will be presented for consideration by Congress.

Beloved, during our Lenten pilgrimage, let us pray for one another, for peace in Christ's holy Church, and that we will do only what pleases him.

With archpastoral blessings,
+ *NATHANIEL, Archbishop*

AGREED STATEMENT

After 60 years of separation from the Patriarchate of Romania, representatives of the Romanian Orthodox Episcopate of America – His Eminence Archbishop Nathaniel, Very Rev. Frs. Laurence Lazar, Remus Grama, Catalin Mitescu, Ian Pac-Urar, and Romey Rosco – met at the Patriarchal Palace in Bucharest, on February 25-27, 2008, with representatives of the Patriarchate of Romania – His Eminence Archbishop Nifon, His Eminence Archbishop Nicolae, His Grace Bishop Ciprian Campineanul, Very Rev. Frs. Mircea Uta and Ioan Armasi – with the intent of seeking a historical reconciliation, and have jointly agreed to acknowledge the following realities:

1) The break between the Romanian Orthodox Episcopate of America – the historical diocese of Bishop Policarp (Morusca) – and the Patriarchate of Romania was the result of the instauration of the communist regime in Romania, and expressed the will of its faithful and of the 1947 Episcopate Congress, whom that Congress officially represented. Given its unrestricted freedom in the free world, the Romanian Orthodox Episcopate of America acted in accordance with its duty to denounce, to reject with the utmost clarity, and to disassociate itself from the evils of atheistic communism, which had separated the diocese both from its Mother Church and from Bishop Policarp, of thrice-blessed memory, whom the Romanian Orthodox Episcopate of America continued to acknowledge as its ruling hierarch up to the time of his falling asleep in the Lord (1958).

2) The Romanian Orthodox Episcopate of America, rejecting communism, found itself compelled to sever its canonical ties to the Patriarchate of Romania, conscious of the fact that, by

doing so, it was defending the faith and identity of the Romanian Orthodox community on the North American continent, particularly in those days when the interference of the communist government of Romania in the life of the Church was blatantly evident.

3) Under the critical and dramatic circumstances of those times, when Bishop Policarp was held against his will in Romania, Vicar Bishop Valerian (Trifa) dutifully sought a solution that preserved the canonicity of the Episcopate, taking the best possible course of action available in those particularly difficult times.

4) The Romanian Orthodox Episcopate of America never rejected or denied the Patriarchate of Romania as its Mother Church but, given the reality of the "Iron Curtain", the only remaining means for her canonical survival was to affiliate canonically with the "Russian Orthodox Greek Catholic Church of North and South America" (known as the "Metropolia", which eventually became the Orthodox Church in America). Within the OCA, the Romanian Orthodox Episcopate of America always maintained the status of an administratively autonomous diocese.

5) The Romanian Orthodox Episcopate of America recognizes that the hierarchs and faithful of the Church of Romania suffered and struggled greatly through the terrible, unprecedented circumstances of the communist oppression. But the actions of the communist government of those times also imposed great suffering on the Romanian Orthodox Episcopate of America, as well as upon her hierarchs of thrice-blessed memory: Bishop Policarp and Archbishop Valerian, Confessors of the Faith, who were persecuted, slandered and marginalized.

6) We happily note that, after the fall of the communist regime, the Holy Synod of the Patriarchate of Romania recognized, in 1991, the canonicity of the Romanian Orthodox Episcopate of America, and the apostolic succession of her hierarchs. Since that time, our relationship has been marked by fraternal dialogue and liturgical concelebration with the Patriarchate of Romania as well as with the hierarchs and clergy of the Romanian Orthodox Archdiocese of the two Americas, by exchanges of hierarchal visits, and by very significant aid provided to Romania through the efforts of the Romanian Orthodox Episcopate of America.

7) On the basis of the above acknowledgements, we ask each other for mutual forgiveness, in the name of our predecessors, for any ways in which we may have offended one another, and we ask Almighty God to bless us, and to guide us on the path toward a common vision of the Romanian Orthodox presence in America, and toward the strengthening of the unity of all Orthodox people on the North American continent.

8) Having recognized the errors of the past, and having asked each other for mutual forgiveness, the representatives of the Patriarchate of Romania and those of the ROEA express their sincere desire for the realization of the unity of all Romanian Orthodox on the American continent, in a canonical relationship with the Church of Romania.

Animated Conversation with His Beatitude Patriarch Daniel, Bucharest, 2008

The Unity of the Church

68

"There is no reason for not having an Autocephalous Church in America of all Orthodox Christians, with a Patriarch heading a Holy Synod, with schools, institutions, monasteries and parishes as is the norm elsewhere in 'Orthodox' countries. Is their faith more 'orthodox' than ours? Are we not 'orthodox?' ... The present state of Orthodox disunity is a form of colonialism which is not based on Scripture, no matter how one interprets the lines of Matthew ('Go and baptize all nations') to mean that one finds salvation only in an ethnic people."

(May 1999)

The bombing of Serbia and the impotence of the Orthodox community in the face of political power are the occasion for Archbishop Nathaniel's return to the theme of Orthodox unity. His Eminence notes that the time for SCOBA has passed, and that only a real, united, autocephalous American Church can speak effectively on behalf of all Orthodox Christians in America.

In Limbo, But Not Willingly

The bombing of Yugoslavia by NATO at the demand of the United States has deeply affected the Orthodox Community in the United States. Among the faithful in America are Albanian and Serbian people, members of the greater American Orthodox Community. Albanian Catholics and Muslims also make up a part of the overall US multi-cultural citizenry. We live in a multi-ethnic society. There is close cooperation between the faithful of the Orthodox Christian communities in North America and a modicum of the same among the hierarchs allowed in The

Standing Conference of Canonical Orthodox Bishops in the Americas (SCOBA).

All Orthodox have felt the sting of the US press; perhaps have even felt "embarrassed". The media has created an image of the "Orthodox Serbs" as being some type of "war-mongering people", and by association, all Orthodox Christians (who are still considered as 'foreign' to these shores no matter how long they have lived here or been born in this continent) are a cut of the same cloth.

We are not aware of any Orthodox lay response to this crisis. Thus, those inter-city, fellowship groups and those who are proclaiming more "lay involvement" are also "paper tigers" when it comes to responding to an issue which reflects on all Orthodox.

Let it be known that the "SCOBA" initiated an effort to mediate a cease-fire for "Western" Easter and Orthodox Pascha, but the Clinton government ignored the hierarchs and even insulted them by choosing neither to honor an established teleconference nor to meet them as a body, as a spokes-group for Orthodox Americans. History will relate that there was at least one serious attempt by the Hierarchs to mediate, but the "White" House steam-rolled over these representatives of 7 million US citizens without the blink of an eye. Is it not probable that American politicians would rather work with one person of authority than a hodge-podge collection of ethnarchs who are tied to foreign bodies? It goes without repeating that "votes & bank notes" count, and that the business of America is business!

Could the "SCOBA", which includes the Serbian hierarchy, have been recognized by the powers that be and have been accepted as a more powerful voice in the public realm in this issue? Probably not. Should it have been? Probably not. There was no press mention of the efforts of the "SCOBA" to mediate. The President and his supporters may welcome some or all of the hierarchs individually to our "White" House, but he correctly perceives them as individuals, representing a particular ethnic enclave having limited voting and campaign value. It is one thing to welcome an Archbishop or Metropolitan but another to stand face-to-face with a Patriarch!

This august body, "SCOBA", was perceived by our politicians to be exactly what it is, a pseudo-composite of various "semi-autonomous," no, not even "semi-autonomous", ethnic communities whose representatives have standing in their own community and respect among the wider Orthodox Communion, but who have no stature in real, not simply polite, but real American politics and power.

Holy Hierarchs, the importance of our individual visits to the "White" House is a mirage! It is a mirage because, while the governing powers may have some interest in particular ethnic groups because of some political and collective or individual financial clout, our individual presence is made vile because it is fractured and unimportant inasmuch as it does not represent the entire Body of Christ, His Holy Church of which we are archpastors. We must have a Patriarch as all civilized Orthodox nations have, someone to stand face-to-face with the civil authority of this land!

Those who are honest will admit that the "SCOBA" has no ecclesiastical precedent or present status. Participating membership by each ethnarch is tolerated or ignored or even unknown by the Mother Churches. It is not THE Holy Synod of an Autocephalous American Church but an arbitrary gathering, which issues "communal" letters at Pascha and the Nativity, toothless and spineless to do the normal and necessary work to balance the civil government of its faithful. Americans are happy to proclaim a "government of the people, by the people and for the people" which should also mean that Orthodox must participate in government not merely on a personal basis but as a body, the Body of Christ, strong, recognized and confident to issue statements to Congress or the "White" House.

"SCOBA" has a self-inflating importance when (or rather if) it meets and then deflates, as in our present crisis, when its powers are limited, precisely because it is not the Holy Synod of an Autocephalous Church. The feebleness of its power is shown useless when confronting such an issue as that which is before us in Kosovo. Had there been a Holy Synod with a Patriarch at its head, the present state of war would not exist. Perhaps the "White" House would still be white and the Orthodox would have been of great service to our nation. We have used SCOBA for too long as a crutch – it is time to stop hiding behind this ineffective body, and walk on "our own two feet".

Each time such a crisis goes by, unresolved or unaffected by the Church, we are put into judgment. We cannot err as we did in Pennsylvania. There cannot be another "Ligonier-non-Ligonier". Then was the time for a new "Tea Party", a "Ligonier Tea Party", but we allowed the time to pass, and we stand in judgment. Did any Mother Church demand a retraction of the signatures of the signators? On what basis? If not, why not?

There is no reason for not having an Autocephalous Church in America of all Orthodox Christians, with a Patriarch heading a Holy Synod, with schools, institutions, monasteries and parishes as is the norm elsewhere in "Orthodox" countries. Is their faith more "orthodox" than ours? Are we not "orthodox"? Where are we "heterodox"? If we are not "orthodox", how is it that we are in communion with one another and with the Mother Churches?

The present state of Orthodox disunity is a form of colonialism which is not based on the Scripture, no matter how one interprets the lines of Matthew to read, "Go and baptize all nations" to mean that one finds salvation only in an ethnic people. We sing the tropar that we are called a new race, the race of Christ. Perhaps we need to call ourselves by the name of our States: "Illini", "Ohioans", "Pennsylvanians", etc. and then, being born into a particular tribe, we, too, can be saved in them. However, if we move from State to State, we might need to import clergy and traditions from our home State so as to be assured of salvation!

The Orthodox Faith does not admit to the existence of a "limbo". Orthodox Americans, however, are existing, unwillingly, in an "orthodox limbo". How to climb out? Let each Orthodox Christian Community (so we do not speak of jurisdictions) with its hierarchs ask the blessing of their Mother Church to be recognized as "Autocephalous", as the Russian Metropolia did in 1970. If no, according to the canons, it takes three bishops to create a Synod.

In bearing witness to Christ, St. John the Baptizer told his disciples: "He must increase, but I must decrease" (Jn. 3:30). It is now time for SCOBA to decrease so that an Autocephalous Orthodox Church of all Orthodox Christians in America may increase.

Living in the U.S. is to not live in Limbo. It is time before the Millennium to rise to the heaven of an Autocephalous Church.

69

"There is no more acceptable time to the Lord than the present 'Now.' There is no reason why the entire Church ought not to be praying with an open heart for the movement of the Holy Spirit to resolve the issue of new local autocephalous Churches as he has in the Church's apostolic age, through the ages and in our own day, and until the Second and Awesome Coming of Christ the Judge. 'It seems good to us and the Holy Spirit' that, indeed, we take action while the day is still with us."

(October 2003)

Unyielding in his vision of a united, autocephalous Orthodox Church on the American continent, His Eminence insists on the unique experiences and history of the local church. He calls out for immediate action – perhaps his words will bear fruit in our own time.

An Orthodox Never-Never Land

According to the Acts of the Apostles, *"They preached every day both in the Temple and in private houses, and their proclamation of the good News of Christ Jesus was never interrupted. About this time, when the number of disciples was increasing, the Hellenists made a complaint against the Hebrews: in the daily distribution their own widows were being overlooked"* (Acts 5:42; 6:1). Controversies have arisen within the Church since her inception, as the quotation from Acts testifies. Nevertheless, whether the controversy was between individuals, such as that between Peter and Paul, or between groups, such as in the above example, through prayer, good will, and an open heart, issues were resolved after gathering together in unity of purpose and calling upon the Holy Spirit. Through the action of the Holy Spirit, the Spirit of Truth, all controversies can be resolved.

The activity of the Holy Spirit in the church is the activity of the Trinity and thus, differences within the Church are resolved by the powerful love of God, guiding the Church to fulfill his will. Through the centuries, and in particular, in the Holy councils of the Church, the formula has always been, "it seems good to us and the Holy Spirit." Each liturgical service begins with the invocation to the Holy Spirit: "O Heavenly King…who are present everywhere!"

It is the same Holy Spirit active throughout the earth today who binds together the faithful into the One, Holy, Catholic, and Apostolic Church. Therefore, it is the same Holy Spirit who also administers the life of the Church, guiding, restoring, renewing, uplifting, correcting and sanctifying. It is the one Spirit who knits all together into the one body, and it is the Holy Spirit who resolves all controversy brought before him in prayer and trust. The Spirit resolves issues in each Church, wheresoever that Church exists in time and space.

In our post-communist era, in this time of raging materialism and divisive individualism, we must be wary that as members of the one body, that individually, we do not come to depend upon our own interpretation of the will of God which can be different from that of the mind of the whole Church. With the diminishing of the control by governments in the life of the Church (even with the understanding that the Church does live in a particular society and respects civil authority as long as it is not contrary to God's laws), there is a particular concept of ethnic narrowness, which harkens back to the verses from Acts. Each church appears to be interested primarily (not to say solely) in her "own" faithful, wheresoever on this earth they may have immigrated. Instead of resolving the issue, as was done in Acts (with the election of the Seven), through prayer in meeting of the "full assembly", the Churches today pretend that equally important issues do not exist in the Church today.

Those who live in "traditional" Orthodox lands cannot experience (and thus not understand) the life of the Church in North America. Regardless of how many visits, short or long, official or informal that patriarchs, archbishops, bishops and metropolitans may make to these shores, they are strangers to our life, to our time and our space, even for all their good will. Just as the Spirit provides the grace for these archpastors in their own Churches in their own lands, so too, the same Spirit provides for grace for the archpastors of the Churches in North America.

There exists an Orthodox "grapevine" (other than the symbolic one referring to our being branches of the true vine, Christ himself). Some say that there will NEVER be a council of the Church to resolve the problem of self-rule in those lands where Orthodoxy has taken root and grown over the last century. Others say that there is a race among some of the patriarchates to establish as many new dioceses, metropolia outside their national borders as they can so that they can "serve" the spiritual and cultural needs of their "own" people, thus in some way making them be citizens living in one nation but with spiritual oversight by leaders of another. The matter of sanctification of the place is thus contrived to be an extension in time and space foreign to the reality of the actual place in which the faithful are living and striving for perfection and salvation, contrary to Orthodox practice.

Others say that, even if a Council is called and even if the issue of self-rule in those lands wherein Orthodoxy has taken root and grown in the last century is brought up, there will NEVER, NEVER be other Autocephalous Churches other than those presently on the roster! How does such an attitude reflect openness to the Holy Spirit's movement within the universal Church? How can any one individual, cleric or lay, dare to define and limit the power and grace of the creating Spirit of God? How can anyone say, "It seems good to ME and the Holy Spirit?"

While no one is praying to create an "American" Church, we are praying for "The Church" in America wherein all Orthodox are guided by a single Holy Synod with a representative, "First Among Equals", patriarch. Until such time, Orthodox Christians are perceived as being somehow under "foreign" authority, having their bodies in North America but their souls elsewhere, as preservers of folklore and foreign traditions inept at reaching out to the lands in which they are living. Saints Boris and Gleb reached out to make converts to Christ and then left those lands. They did not make them "Hellenes", nor "Byzantines", nor "Romans", but Christians. This was the purpose of their mission into those new lands. In England, at the time of the Reformation, the English hierarchy stated, "The Italian missionaries (the Roman Church) can go back to Italy; we can manage our own spiritual lives in England."

It is way past time for foreign missionaries to return to their own lands and to leave the Holy Spirit to complete his work in North America. How contradictory we are to our fellow citizens while confessing the oneness of the Church in faith yet divided in administration: "The Church can be united sacramentally but not administratively".

While preaching to the Jews in Antioch, Paul stated: "We had to proclaim the word of God to you first, but since you have rejected it, since you do not think yourselves worthy of eternal life, we must turn to the pagans. For this is what the Lord commanded us to do when he said: 'I have made you a light for the nations, so that my salvation may reach the ends of the earth'." (Acts 13:46-47) Certainly, his salvation has reached this nation, and the light which shines will be intensified as it focuses into a single beam through unity of all "jurisdictions" in Canada and the United States.

There is no more acceptable time to the Lord than the present "Now". There is no reason why the entire Church ought not to be praying with an open heart for the movement of the Holy Spirit to resolve the issue of new local autocephalous Churches as he has in the Church's apostolic age, through the ages and in our own day and until the Second and Awesome Coming of Christ the Judge. "It seems good to us and to the Holy Spirit" that, indeed, we take action while the day is still with us.

70

> *"It seems that the major obstacle in resolving the present administrative disunity in North America is the absence of an agreed process by which the desired unity can be accomplished. Neither the Mother Churches nor their North American Daughters have taken the time to think out an acceptable procedure by which a solution can be found. Half-hearted efforts (and rightly so) do not count. In this respect, all are to blame."*
>
> *(September 1995)*

In 1994, the first plenary gathering of Orthodox bishops in North America was convened at Ligonier, Pennsylvania. We invite the reader to peruse His Eminence's own commentary on that historic meeting and its subsequent implications.

"To Be or Not to Be"

"Will There Be An Annual American Orthodox Episcopal Assembly Or Not?"

The first anniversary of the "Ligonier" Assembly will fall in a matter of weeks. In the Statement On The Church in North America, signed by 26 Hierarchs assembled at Ligonier in 1994, it stated: "We express our joy that in addition to the regular meetings of the Standing Conference of Orthodox Canonical Bishops in the Americas (SCOBA), this Episcopal Assembly **will convene on an annual basis** to enhance the movement toward administrative ecclesial unity in North America."

By now, the hierarchs ought to have had information about the date and site of the second assembly. As of this date, the

SCOBA has not called up the "annual Episcopal Assembly," nor is there any indication that it plans to do so.

As exhilarating as that joy was in 1994, it was short-lived, aborted, before seeing the light of another year.

Instead of issuing mild and apologetic statements, had the American Hierarchs at Ligonier proclaimed the reality of the Orthodox Church in America at that meeting, a kind of ecclesiastic "Boston (Ligonier) Tea Party" in good American tradition, the American Church would be in a state of "disagreement" with the Mother Churches for a while; and, in time, the "de facto" would become "de lege." But American-(here put in your favorite hyphenated ethnic people), prefer to follow the law and think themselves to be "law-abiding" people. But is there a "law"? Are there rules? What are they? Who knows them? Are they fixed or in a constant flux?

Of course, if there was an administratively united Orthodoxy in North America, the calling of an Episcopal Assembly and other problems would not exist.

Find An Acceptable Procedure And Follow It

It seems that the major obstacle in resolving the present administrative disunity in North America is the absence of an agreed process by which the desired unity can be accomplished. Neither the "Mother Churches" nor their North American Daughters have taken the time to think out an acceptable procedure by which a solution can be found. Half-hearted efforts (and rightly so) do not count. In this respect, all are to blame.

Where is the leadership in the Church?

The "Ligonier Tea-Party" did not take place; the "Mother Churches" offer no procedure. There appears to be apathy on both sides, some adherents of whom are content with the "status quo" and others who are caught between the "rock" of "loyalty" to their "Mother Church" and the "hard place" of knowing that an administrative unity in North America is essential to the nature of the Church.

As there was no sign of interest from the "Mother Churches," it behooved the SCOBA to seriously press forward to find a procedure to offer the "Mother Churches" for consideration in creating harmony out of the American Orthodox chaos. But a precious year has passed; SCOBA has been paralyzed; its state of moribund inactivity has disappointed the clergy and faithful. Perhaps the "Mother Churches" are, in fact, waiting for some "united" procedure proposal to come from SCOBA?!

Where is the leadership of the Church?!

Leadership Assumed and Leadership Surrendered

Indeed, whereat now lies the authority over the life of the Church in North America? In as many foreign synods as there are ethnic jurisdictions, one of which has denied (not simply objected to but denied) their hierarchs the blessing to attend another Episcopal Assembly. Is there a single authority over all jurisdictions in North America?

Where is the leadership of the Church?!

What about the other jurisdictions in North America? Does the absence of one group from the "Second Episcopal Assembly" necessarily mean the death of the decision to meet made by all "Ligonier" hierarchs? Apparently, yes!

As far as we know, most of the "Mother Churches" made no negative judgment on the "Ligonier" meeting. The Romanian Church, (the Patriarch and Metropolitans received Romanian versions of the Ligonier statements) did not condemn the SCOBA meeting nor object to a second one. Archbishop VICTORIN, who represents the Romanian Patriarchate in SCOBA, was present and signed the document, but he has not reported any repercussion nor interdiction.

In addition to Bucharest, no negative word came from the Patriarchates of Antioch, Sofia, Belgrade to express disapproval of the American Hierarchs' first meeting, let alone the decision to hold a Second Episcopal Assembly.

So, why is there no "Joyful Second Episcopal Assembly?"

Moscow, which recognized the autocephaly of its "Metropolia" in 1970, must certainly wonder why this "Autocephalous Church" took part in the Ligonier Assembly in the first place. The "Tomos" of Autocephaly is variously interpreted.

The Patriarch of Constantinople, however, did publicly criticize the "Ligonier" assembly, reprimanding the Greek Hierarchy in America, which caused much consternation in the

Greek Omogenia. Was the objection leveled solely at the participation of the Greek Hierarchy or at the SCOBA itself?

For sure, each "jurisdiction" is important and has a role to play, but because criticism came from Constantinople, let us ask some questions of the Greek Omogenia in North America.

Would the Greek Archdiocese ask Constantinople to release it to form an American Church? If all "Mother Churches" gave blessings for this and Constantinople held back, would it "take the matter into hand" and itself cut the umbilical cord? At this time, may the hierarchs of the Archdiocese take part in such discussion should it be on an agenda for a SCOBA meeting? What is the mind of the Greek Archdiocese? The "Greek American" Omogenia? Is there a consensus in the Greek Community?

In a letter to Archbishop IAKOVOS from the Archdiocesan (Greek) Presbyters Council, January 24, 1995, the clergy expressed their "overwhelming dismay" over the "misunderstanding" and "misinterpretation" which created the "consequent ire which is unwarranted" coming from Istanbul.

The letter puts partial blame on the Greek Press which has "slandered (Archbishop IAKOVOS), as well as our Holy Archdiocese. The Greek American news media does not and cannot speak for the One, Holy, Catholic, and Apostolic Church. Do they represent the Omogenia in America? Certainly not! Are we proud of our Greek heritage in America? Certainly, yes! Should our ethnicity overshadow our Orthodoxy? Certainly, not!"

Nevertheless, we have no clear picture of the meaning of the statement about what is meant by "ethnicity not overshadowing Orthodoxy." Does this mean that the clergy want an American Church but under Constantinople? Does it mean that the Greek Orthodox Omogenia would join others in forming an American Church? Does it mean a perpetuation of SCOBA as the only solution acceptable to Constantinople and the final solution (sic dictus) to the issue for the Greek Archdiocese, and the death of the reality of an American Autocephalous Church?

If the claims stated by Patriarch Bartholomew are true, then Constantinople should have been protesting the very existence of the various jurisdictions of "Mother Churches" in North America over the decades; since, she established the Greek Hierarchy in North America after the subjection of the Russian Church and its hierarchy to a Communist dictatorship causing the Russian Metropolia, with the blessing of Moscow, to "freeze" administrative relations with the "Mother Church."

Istanbul claims that due to the "seventy years of Soviet tyranny, the "Mother Church" of Constantinople, while painfully observing the un-canonical defiances or incidents going on here and there, ...co-suffered with you and judged with leniency." We are to understand that, due to the enslavement of the Churches in the Iron Curtain countries, she did not press certain issues, did not protest the "infringement" on her universal jurisdiction in the "barbarian lands."

The Patriarchate of Constantinople lays claim to the so-called barbaric lands. An official of the Church of Russia recently declared that Russia was not "barbaric" when Christianity was brought to Rus. So, too, American Orthodox should echo that neither is America a barbaric land and can remind others that the faith has been here for two hundred years, without the concern of Constantinople for most of that time.

"E Pluribus Plurus"

The search for the procedure for unification would be helped immensely if the "Mother Churches" would also show an interest in what is taking place in North America by issuing their stand on their right to exist in North America, by reacting to Ligonier and the proposed Second Episcopal Assembly.

It seems that the "Mother Churches" base their right to "subject jurisdictions" on the Gospel text of Matthew 28:19, **"Go, therefore, make disciples of all nations..."**. Their claim is that Christ was speaking of the conversions of peoples, nations, units, not of individuals. Perhaps this was considered so in the light of the concept prevalent among the Jews and among most ancient peoples of salvation through identity with an ethnic body. Their claim is that, wherever in the rest of the world outside the boundaries of their national state there are co-countrymen of the same ethnic origin, so the national church has the divine **command** to care for them as part of the "nation," in Greek "Omogenia."

Using this scriptural basis, the "Mother Churches" refute Constantinople's claim over the "barbarian lands" "in toto." Perhaps each "Mother Church" cares only about its own co-nationals and doesn't really care for the rest of the world. "E pluribus unum" is not according to the Divine Plan; "E pluribus semper et per omnia plurus" is. Thus, there is no reason for a local Church, because there is no "omogenia."

There is also the concept that North America is not a single "nation" but a composite of peoples; and therefore, it is necessary for each "Mother Church" to take great care that its own co-nationals do not "disappear or be assimilated" into the American melting pot. This "melting pot" theory has long gone the way of the dodo bird; no one is assimilated by force but by choice or lack thereof.

A word about Constantinople's concern about the ugly "ethnic" Medusa head in North America. We read in the Statement of the Church of Constantinople to the Church of Russia (July 1995) that "the Church of Constantinople, after rather immense jurisdictional expansion (during the Ottoman Empire), found that in these new times she had to strip herself...of her racially closest children, the Hellenes...".

Is this not an appeal to jurisdiction based on modern ideas of "nationality" and "ethnicity?" *"Racially closest children?"* This is the same claim as that based on Matthew and which is brandished at the "Mother Churches" who retain their jurisdictions in North America instead of recognizing the "ecumenical authority" of Constantinople in America.

The same questions posed to the Greek Omogenia should be addressed to all ethnic jurisdictions in North America.

A Possible Procedure

Let us consider a possible solution. Let each "Mother Church" follow the example of the Church of Russia by recognizing an autonomous state of "its jurisdiction" in North America. If the term, "autocephaly" is "incorrect," perhaps the Holy Spirit will inspire a temporary term, coined for the needs of this particular situation; call it "Pre-autocephaly" if you like.

"Pre-autocephaly" means the recognition of the "autonomous" state of each jurisdiction by its "Mother Church", and thus prepares the ground for a final "autocephalous" Church in North America embracing all "jurisdictions, recognized by the "Mother Churches," including Constantinople, and blessed by them to unite into a single administrative unity. Then, let us welcome the Ecumenical Patriarch to make the final and formal proclamation, "urbi et orbi."

Where Is The Leadership of the Church?

It should be obvious that the most important part of administrative unity, at this time, is not re-assignment of hierarchs and dismemberment of dioceses, the hasty and impractical undoing of almost two centuries of stability and effort. The basic need for the Church in America is for a single Episcopal Assembly, that is, for a unified Holy Synod composed of all hierarchs.

A unified hierarchy is the basis for unity of administration, a step toward the fulfillment of the canon of having one bishop in each city. The realigning of dioceses along strictly territorial lines would take place in the future. The financial stability of the Church must not be aggressively upset; a long-term, pragmatic program needs to be constructed rather than imposed.

The overlapping multiplicity of "synods" in North America under foreign Churches should cease. It is unreasonable to propose that hierarchs in North America sit on two synods: that of the "Mother Church" and that of the local American Church. That there could be a formal sharing of the status of the ethnic group in North America with the Synod of another Church is not unthinkable nor unreasonable; but, let the local Church, led by the Holy Spirit, fulfill its special mission to "all people," being responsible to itself through the hierarchal structure of the Church of God.

On the other hand, there is no reason why "Metropolitan Synods" in America, comprised of hierarchs in charge of a particular ethnic group concerned with the needs of that "mission" of the American Church, could not continue and co-exist within the Holy Synod. North America will always have immigrants, and the Church must always care for all of her "people."

With the apparent change of government in former Communist Iron Curtain countries, the Church has apparent freedom. It seems reasonable that these Churches, the "Mother Churches" should act now and quickly do what each can do: grant a status of independence to its North American jurisdiction which would allow for the immediate creation of a unified Orthodox Church in North America; and, which would take care of the ethnic needs of all jurisdictions in a unified and Spirit-directed way while reaching out to the American "Omogenia."

The leadership of the Church in America must meet! It must gather within the grace of the Holy Spirit and resolve this scandalous impasse which needs not the sword of Alexander to resolve but "one heart and one mouth" to bring to pass a unified witness to the Father, the Son and the Holy Spirit, the Trinity, one in essence and undivided.

Where is the leadership of the Church?

71

> *"This current administrative disunity, which is an anomaly from the Canons of the Church, must change. One day, every hierarch in North America will be part of a single Holy Synod of the Church in North America. The Mother Churches themselves and their "jurisdictions" in North America, under the guidance of the Holy Spirit, are working toward this goal of administrative unity, which would be expressed in the existence of a unique North American Synod of Hierarchs."*
> (May 1996)

As the question of the unity of the Church and of the Romanian Orthodox community in particular continued to gain prominence, Archbishop Nathaniel strove to shed light on these questions for his flock. This article places the Romanian question in the context of the universal Church and the hope of a united Orthodox Church in North America.

Thoughts on the Unity of the Church in North America

Preamble

The reason for which we have composed this document is our intention to put at rest some apprehensions related to us by our clergy and laity who were aroused by the promulgation of certain unofficial letters. These papers were written and dispersed to express the desire of some that a dialog between our Romanian Orthodox Episcopate of America (Vatra) and the Romanian Orthodox Archdiocese in America and Canada (Riopelle) be initiated to promote an administrative Church unity between the two jurisdictions.

The apprehension is that such unification might entail surrendering our autonomy, thereby placing the Episcopate under the authority of the Holy Synod of the Romanian Church. The Episcopate is not presently in dialog either with the Romanian Patriarchate or with the Archdiocese. Because there is nothing under discussion, there are no conditions to consider and no action to be taken. Nevertheless, we think it useful to offer our observations about the letters and the subject itself.

Orthodox Disunity and Unity in North America

We feel it necessary to preface our observations with some reflections about the present administrative disunity and also the general sacramental unity of North American Orthodoxy of which the Romanian community is a part.

The Church in North America rejoices in a sacramental unity which is evident in the concelebration of the Divine Mysteries by her hierarchs. Although there does exist a kind of gathering of hierarchs (the Standing Conference of Canonical Orthodox Bishops in the Americas/SCOBA), which in a broad way reflects the sacramental oneness of the Church; nevertheless, this is an informal and unofficial conference. At this time, there is no single Synod of which all hierarchs are members. A single Synod is the norm for an autocephalous (self-ruling) Church.

Due to past historical realities, such a unified Synod speaking with one voice and one heart in the name of the Church did not come into being. Nevertheless, it did grow roots in the past, and we anticipate its flowering in our day. In 1970, the Russian Church recognized the autocephaly of the Russian Metropolia in North America, and its Metropolitan Synod became the "Holy Synod" of the Orthodox Church in America. In that same year, our Episcopate joined the Orthodox Church in America, and Bishop Valerian became a member of that Holy Synod, that same body which later elevated him to the rank of archbishop. Today, we, too, are a member of the same Holy Synod, which also includes the hierarchs of the Albanian and Bulgarian faithful.

There are large numbers of ethnic Orthodox whose hierarchs are part of the Synods of their Mother Churches abroad and thus do not take part in the work of the Synod of the Orthodox Church in America.

This current administrative disunity, which is an anomaly from the Canons of the Church, must change. One day, every hierarch in North America will be part of a single Holy Synod of the Church in North America. The Mother Churches themselves and their "jurisdictions" in North America, under the guidance of the Holy Spirit, are working toward this goal of administrative unity, which would be expressed in the existence of a unique North American Synod of Hierarchs.

It is this acute awareness of the "unfinished unity" of the Church that troubles hierarchs, clergy and faithful of all jurisdictions in North America; and, through their unified efforts, they strive to work for universal recognition of an autocephalous Church of North America.

The SCOBA can be seen as one such effort on the hierarchal level. In many cities, there are "Clergy Associations" which represent similar efforts on local levels. There are also "Lay Societies" whose members are from various jurisdictions and who work together to bear a united witness to the One, Holy, Catholic, and Apostolic Faith.

The "Joint Dialog Commission"

It was in this spirit that, in the recent past, the representatives of our Episcopate and those of the Archdiocese, the "Joint Dialog Commission," worked together and came to the conclusion which they offered to the hierarchs, i.e., that there is no reason why our clergy and faithful should not be able to pray together and to serve as brothers before the Holy Altar. The Congresses of both dioceses agreed with the Commission. Along with Archbishop Victorin, we also embraced this proposal; and thus, between the two dioceses, sacramental unity was restored.

Some members of that Commission wanted to begin to consider ways for administrative unification between the two dioceses. The Archdiocesan Congress had empowered its members to move forward in this direction. Our Congress, however, had not yet discussed the issue. We felt that more time was needed to feel the pulse of the faithful clergy and laity of the Episcopate before establishing such a dialog for unity.

As a point of information, we remind you that the Antiochian, Serbian and Ukrainian jurisdictions in North America each suffered the pains of internal disunity; but in time, with understanding and good will, each group discussed the issues which separated them, and by the grace of God, settled them and united administratively in one ethnic jurisdiction.

The Unity of the Church in North America

A. The Ethnic Character of the American Church

The desire for Orthodox unity and the establishment of an American Patriarchate is among the foremost concerns of the Romanian Orthodox Episcopate of America. Being part of the Orthodox Church in America since 1970, along with Albanian, Bulgarian and Mexican faithful, we have the sense of fulfilling the spiritual needs of our Romanian brethren while at the same time being part of a unified Orthodox witness to North America.

We foresee the Church in North America fulfilling a specific responsibility to serve the spiritual needs of the ethnic faithful already here and those yet to come.

We perceive that the continued existence of ethnic jurisdictions and their existing particular structures are fundamentally necessary for stability of the Church at this point in the history of the Church in North America.

We acknowledge the rich variety of Orthodox traditions in North America and praise the Mother Churches for this variegated gift which was brought by immigrants to our shores and which has become an integral part of our common Orthodox witness and patrimony.

B. The American Character of the Church

It is clear that Americans born of ethnic origin are part of a new leavening which is shaping the Church from a purely immigrant presence to an American witness. Their particular talents and gifts for the Church must be utilized to the fullest. From them, in fact, ought to come the clergy of the future.

The faith in North America has been mightily blessed in the numerous converts to the faith, beginning with the native Alaskans who continue to use their own tongues in the divine services. Others have "seen the true light" and have further enriched the Church with their zeal and fervor to spread the Gospel of salvation.

Thus, the Church is not merely "ethnic" nor exclusively "American", but is truly "catholic" in her composition of all peoples in North America.

C. A Single Synod of Hierarchs in America

We consider that a unified synod of all Orthodox Hierarchs in North America is absolutely necessary: and, we are certain that by the recognition of the autocephalous state of the Church in North America and the establishment of an American Patriarchate, all present jurisdictional concerns will be speedily and satisfactorily resolved through the inworking of the Holy Spirit in the Holy Synod.

D. Spiritual Care for the Ethnic Communities

While we appreciate the Mother Churches' understanding of the message to "Go and preach to all nations" as being interpreted to mean that wherever ethnic people of their background live, the Church has concern for them, we promise that these spiritual concerns of each Mother Church for her "ethnic" children in North America will be satisfied by a unified Synod of Bishops guiding the Church in North America.

Therefore, we propose that each Patriarchal Church give a blessing recognizing a "pre-autocephalic" state for its own ethnic community in North America. After each community has been thus blessed, then the Ecumenical Patriarchate, in the name of the Sister Churches, will announce the unified autocephaly of the Church in America, which reflects the consensus of the entire Church.

We surmise that the Ecumenical Patriarchate in Constantinople has the most to gain by the recognition of an

American Patriarchate, which would have a strong unified voice in various arenas of American society.

We humbly offer the concentrated and unified talents and gifts of the American Church for the service of world Orthodoxy and her Sister Churches.

72

"We propose that the present jurisdictional administrative structures remain in existence in favor of the unification of all hierarchs into one Synod which, together with the clergy and faithful of the united Orthodox Church of America, under the guidance of the Holy Spirit, will determine the future territorial basis for dioceses."

(October 1999)

With the Ligonier conference now a five-year-old memory, His Eminence examines the many issues that are exacerbated by the state of disunity in North America. He proposes a structure that is surprisingly prophetic, when viewed in the light of the 2010 Episcopal Assembly.

One Bishop in One City or One Synod in One Nation

On reflecting on the reality of the multiplicity of overlapping Orthodox territorial dioceses in the United States, it is obvious that our Orthodox ecclesiastical household is in a state of disarray. Regardless of whichever historical circumstances of yesteryear shaped this reality, the Holy Spirit will guide us today into a better witness of the Gospel of Our Lord and God and Savior, Jesus Christ, through the unification of all arch-pastors into One Synod for the United States.

Administrative Unity

Does the Holy Spirit, who unites, uplifts, and fulfills, hear our pray for the **administrative unity of the Church in the United States?** We must examine our communal prayer-life to ascertain if, in fact, we are praying for this great gift. Are we beseeching God? Is the Psalm of Vespers the voice of our communal heart: "Lord, I have cried out to you? Hear the voice of my prayer when I cry to you!" Perhaps little has transpired to put our household of faith into good order, because our prayer before the divine throne has been weak, without fervor or even non-existent! It is possible that there are even those who not only do not share the desire for a unified Synod, but who implore the Almighty that such not come to be.

Beyond those many known suggestions as to how this administrative unification is to be accomplished, we propose a solution based on total trust in the Holy Spirit working through and in the Mother Churches. This would come about through our sincere explanation to the Mother Churches of the negative consequences born from the administrative disunity in the Church in the United States. We believe that each Church will respond to our explanation for the good of the Universal Orthodox Church, which welfare we would interpret to be to recognize and bless the reality of an Autocephalous Orthodox Church of America which embodies all Orthodox Christians.

Have Orthodox Christians in the United States fulfilled their filial duty to the Mother Churches by presenting a clear picture of the reality of the Church so that they can take an appropriate stance? What is this reality? Orthodox life in the United States is not unique to each "jurisdiction," but it is common to all. If one discusses with the hierarchy, the clergy, and the faithful their perception and concerns, one is immediately aware that these concerns which each jurisdiction thinks are unique to it are, in fact, the same for all jurisdictions and are best resolved "in common," for the common good.

Concerns and Perceptions

Among these concerns are: **"What is a balance in the use of ethnic languages and English in the divine services?"** Certainly, this cannot be determined outside the borders of this nation by those who neither live here nor experience the life of the communities. However, if the Mother Churches are concerned for the spiritual well-bearing of its ethnic children and are convinced that the Church in America can shepherd the particular ethnic sheep who are now grazing permanently in the New World, then that concern disappears. The spiritual ties will continue to exist to the benefit of both Churches, the Mother and the American Church.

"How to balance concern for the new immigrant as we reach out to America?" There is no doubt that immigration will continue as long as the government allows; and thus, the issue cannot be controlled nor resolved by the Church. The Church preaches repentance and salvation to all, regardless of political or social status: Immigrant and American-born, the unchurched; the Church reaches out to all and neglects none. She has learned from the Acts of the Apostles to offer her diaconia to all.

"How to preserve inter-faith marriages to lead families to peace and salvation?" The very high percentage of inter-faith ("mixed") marriages is a phenomenon which, numerically speaking, is unique to the American scene to an extent beyond that experienced by the Mother Churches. Only on a local level can the understanding of this matter be appreciated and shepherded, because the Church must take into consideration the social, political and other factors which move society.

"How to verify and weigh the value of imported ethnic culture to the benefit of local communities?" It is from Old World cultures that much of the faith was first transmitted to North America, and there are aspects of this piety which continue to nourish the faithful here today. Each people, however, is called upon to sanctify this land and create an Orthodox culture, even if it is an "orthodox subculture," but this can be done only by living the faith on this continent and not in imitation of others. There are those who insist that there is no such entity as an "American Nation;" they perceive of the United States as a collection of various peoples. Those born here and those who have become citizens, in general, consider that there is such a thing as an American culture, and thus a place and a need for an Orthodox American culture.

"How to reach out to the unchurched and to proselytize and to dialogue with non-Orthodox?" While most of the Mother Churches are only now experiencing a strong incursion by neo-Protestant and Roman Catholic zealots into their Orthodox flock, we have the experience of living in a poli-denominational society for 200 years. Just as we cannot tell the Mother Churches how best to respond to a non-Orthodox presence in their midst, so we, too, in the United States must respond to what we know from our experience of the past and in behalf of our vision of the future. These and other concerns are unique to the Church in America on a scale unknown to the Mother Churches and which are among the major problems which we must face on our own.

Results of Disunity

As serious results of administrative disunity, the Church in the United States is suffering from the fall-out which is exhibited in various forms. The first of these is in the existence of **"Local Clergy Councils."** These councils come into existence because of a vacuum, that is, the absence of a local hierarch and normal deanery organization. They exist across North America, with or without hierarchal blessing, sharing or not the knowledge of the activities, but in general living an existence "para-eparchial."

These councils are, *"de facto"* and *"de jure"* usurpations of episcopal responsibilities, prerogatives and authority. On their own, the clergy gather together and elect a priest to "preside" over meetings in which are discussed, decided upon and carried out, actions which are usual to be made by hierarchal authority. In these Local Clergy Councils, the president acts as a kind of supervisor (read "episcopos"), moderator, establishing communal religious services and activities, collections and distribution of funds, while speaking in the name of the "local Orthodox community" and representing it through his person.

We do not criticize the good which these councils have accomplished and admire their zeal for the Church, but we repeat that they exist as a response to a vacuum, the absence of a local hierarch. The culpability for this rests on the shoulders of the Mother Churches, who, by the fact of their reticence to bless autocephaly, are responsible for what this vacuum has created. That the clergy did unite into councils and did/do work in the name of the Church is commendable, but it must be acknowledged that these organizations are temporary, because they are not the norm, and the norm has been circumvented because of the lack of administrative unity in the land. The Church cannot gloss over the reality that these activities are the responsibility of a local hierarch, and the role of the hierarch is diminished and his responsibilities thwarted by the existence of these temporary 'para-hierarchal' organizations.

A second consequence of administrative disunity is **the confusion among the laity as to their role in the royal priesthood in the Church.** Each jurisdiction has created its own By-Laws to explain the responsibilities of the laity according to the historical development of each jurisdiction. There is no doubt that the administrative disunity of the entire Orthodox body in the United States has fostered this confusion and fomented vigorous debates among the hierarchy, clergy and faithful. Only a unified Church will be able to re-establish the Canons and assure the laity of their proper God-given role in the Church. While no one equates the priesthood of believers with the sacramental priesthood; nevertheless, the royal priesthood, too, is permanently active in the Body of the Church, and this priesthood is also Spirit-filled.

Another expression of this confusion about the role of the laity is a certain **congregationalism** which can be identified in every jurisdiction. It usually shows itself by the misunderstanding that the priest is merely an employee of the board, and the parish is perceived to be a legal, corporate entity apart from or even "independent" of the hierarch and the diocese. This comes from a confusion of equating the word "church," the local building of worship, with the totality of the local Church headed by the hierarch. In an aggravated form, congregationalism expresses itself through manipulation of funds to general control or alter actions on the parochial level. Taking the total administration of the parish and diocese into the hands of the laity alone is often seen as "the democratization" of the Church and is fostered as a normal step "forward" in the process of "making the Church American"; while, in fact, it distorts the image of the Church as established on Pentecost as an hierarchal body and not one ruled by the popular vote. One can hardly equate the "democracy" of the ancient Greeks with the democracy of universal suffrage we experience today, nor was the Church founded on "fallen human nature," but on faith in Christ, the new Adam, who restores our fallen nature, "carrying it back to the Father" for it to become God-like through the cross.

The parish itself is but one community within the Church, the Diocese, but it is not the Church. *"Ubi episcopus, ibi ecclesia -* Where the bishop is, there is the Church," **not** *"Ubi presbyterum ut concilium ibi ecclesia -* Where the priest or council is, there is the Church." From this attitude has arisen an underlying **"antagonism" toward diocesan administration** as a kind of external hegemony threat, as some kind of imposition of an extraneous power over the local entity. The diocese is tolerated. A Mafioso-type exertion in the form of an "ecclesiastical blackmail" to force certain conclusions at the communal level by circumventing eparchial authority promotes the idea that the parishes are mere free-will associations of the diocese. This is the case of most neo-Protestant denominations which have an ecclesiology based on local congregations and a loose form of confederation of these independent associations.

A third expression of this disunity, in addition to clericalism and congregationalism, is a form of **"papalism,"** or an hierarchal tendency to curtail or deny responsibilities of the clergy and faithful on the local level in favor a centralist control executed by a limited number of individuals surrounding the hierarchal person and executing that person's will, independent of and without responsibility to the entire Church.

Although none of the three tendencies dominates the life of the Church in the United States; nevertheless, there is enough of a presence of each to illustrate the absolute and essential need for a unified administration in the Church in the United States to put our household of faith in order as it is in every other Orthodox autocephalous Church.

Resolution

What will resolve these tendencies and will strengthen the spiritual life of the Church is **a unified Synod headed by a Patriarch.**

Inasmuch as the canons do not provide a solution to the ecclesiastical administrative disunity in the United States, under the Holy Spirit, we must proceed forward in the direction of creating a response to this situation.

There are those who would insist that the foundation of administrative unity of the U.S. Church rests on having one hierarch in one city; and therefore, they conclude that every jurisdiction, *"a priori,"* must dismantle its present administrative structure in favor of the principle of one bishop in one city. At the present, this appears to be an impossibility, nor is it absolutely necessary for this stage in unification. It seems that, in our present weak state, we are not ready for this step; but rather than just marking time, it is more beneficial to go forward in another direction.

What is essential is that all the hierarchs form one Synod for the nation, working together in the name of Christ and his Holy Church. The Standing Conference of Orthodox Canonical Bishops in the Americas (SCOBA), which is representation by "ethnic" principle, is incapable of becoming the Synod of the American Church. This was the reaction by His Holiness, Bartholomew, who saw in the meeting of many hierarchs in Ligonier, Pennsylvania, an abuse of the original scope of SCOBA as an unofficial, *"ad hoc"* committee of ethnic hierarchs representing their particular groups. This is, in fact, its contradiction, for it cannot be representational for the Mother Churches and at the same time be Autocephalous.

We propose that the present jurisdictional administrative structures remain in existence in favor of the unification of all hierarchs into one Synod which, together with the clergy and faithful of the united Orthodox Church of America, under the guidance of the Holy Spirit, will determine the future territorial basis for dioceses. There is no doubt that the Greek, Antiochian, Serbian, Ukrainian and Romanian dioceses would not be prepared, at this time, to disassemble their administrative structures as a *"sine qua non"* to have one bishop in one city nor for the formation of a unified Synod. Would it not be plausible, however, that they would accept the unification of all hierarchs into one Synod and that the present administrative entities continue under their hierarchs. As time goes on, this Synod will review and, with the entire American Church, shape future diocesan jurisdictions.

Thus, in place of an "Ethnic SCOBA" there would be a Synod of metropolitanates, working together in one Synod. With the formation of the Holy Synod, a Patriarch would be elected, and the Orthodox Church of America would bring to "self-resolve" the discrepancies which presently exist within her.

There remains that confusion over the term *autocephaly* as being an action granted *"ab extra"* or recognition of a state of being. We base our consideration on the latter, that the Church in America is mature and ought to be recognized by the Mother Churches.

Our Youth

A final chapter in our report to the Mother Churches must be about the **future of our youth.** It is normal that the government of a land lives in the land or it is in exile and is stymied in its activities by being absent from the land, thus rendering it ineffective. Young people understand that as citizens of a nation, they respond to the local government; that their spiritual authority resides far from the scene of their daily life is strange to them.

Obviously, this is not an argument based on the ecclesiology of the Church; nevertheless, it is an important factor which often times determines the adherence or separation of young people from the Church or their witness to others to embrace the faith.

In addition, the limited faith witness of parents to their offspring, the limitations imposed on the parochial "church school/Sunday school," present atheistic and antagonistic attitudes of public educators toward the faith, and the constant reinterpretation of the "intentions of the founding fathers" concerning the separation of Church and State, renders the public schools basically ineffective in shaping the ethical, spiritual qualities we want for our youth. To this and other factors, the appropriate answer is the **establishment of an Orthodox primary and secondary school system in each city.** This can best be accomplished through a unified Orthodox Church of America.

To some, these observations will seem subjective. In fact, they are observations made during the nineteen years in the episcopacy and twenty-nine after the declaration of Autocephaly by the Orthodox Church in America. We offer our report to our readers and to the Mother Churches during this "upbeat" frenzy of "Y2K," and pray "with our whole soul and our whole mind" for the Unity of the faith and fellowship in the Holy Spirit.

73

"There is a growing impatience among the majority of Orthodox Christians, clergy and lay, who vociferate or tacitly endure the silence of the Mother Churches as to why they do not recognize an Autocephalous Church in Canada and an Autocephalous Church in the United States. Silence is not golden - it is deafening, and deafening is unkind and unproductive and mistrusting."

(July 2003)

In this article, His Eminence again abandons indirectness for a "gloves-off" approach to the thorny problem of Old World control of the New World Church. He calls on the leadership of the Mother Churches to extend the same understanding and advocacy for the American Church that they offer to the world at large.

Old Europe & New World

Leaders of many major European nations bristled at a recently stated epithet, "Old Europe," flung at them by a high-ranking United States official. This title of dubious intent, it appears, implies to Europeans that they live in the past; and more offensively, Europe itself is "passé."

The retort was immediate. How arrogant of this "New World" to judge the "Old World"; and besides, Europe (the implication is there) doesn't care what the upstart continent of North America thinks nor does it need it. "We can exist very well without you, thank you very much!"

Transatlantic tempers boiled and are boiling and will, regardless of an occasional handshake and "photo-ops". Certainly, the US appellation will remain in the annals of history as a major gaffe, and the title will pepper diplomatic tete-a-tete "ad infinitum." Whatever ire and amazement the phrase raised, it bespeaks of two different existences which, nevertheless, are conjoined like Siamese twins. The development of North America is, for the most part, an unfolding of an extension of Europe beyond its borders; and on the other hand, it is a new entity different from and other than Europe (including by extension, Russia).

Both camps are correct to a certain degree. Europe is alive and well and tottering along a new course of unity in its history not too unlike the experience of the United States. Isn't it evident, after all, in the preeminence of the "Euro" over the once-mighty dollar? So who needs the new kid on the block? On the other hand, the United States has tramped onto the world stage either as a self-perceived sole super-power or is perceived as being a soloist super power-hungry entity which acts according to its own characteristic impulsive ways of the "Here" and the "Now" and the "Why not?" Rudyard Kipling once wrote: "East is east and West is west and ne'er the twain shall meet." Of course, he was speaking of other continents and other times. But is it not recognizable that Europe is Europe and North America, North America; and that although sharing certain historical experiences, each has its own "life to live?" Europe should cease considering this part of the world as "grown-up colonies run amuck," and the US should cease acting as though Europe is an anachronism, a mummy to be displayed but not heard from.

The United States, "contra mundum," or "in spite of" the opposition to US policies from some major European nations, although with the (willing?) support of others, moved forward to implement what it decided needed to be done according to its own estimation of the reality. What will be the results of these actions is still being played out; but, that there is definitely a European frame of mind and a United States frame of mind cannot be denied.

How does this affect the life of the Church? Recently, while on a trip to Germany at the invitation of the Metropolitan of the Romanian Orthodox Metropolia of Germany and Central and Northern Europe, His Holiness, Teoctist, Patriarch of the Romanian Orthodox Church, stated that Romania is part of Europe and her future lies within Europe. At these words, I wondered and then agreed, indeed, Romania is an integral part of Europe; and, the nation and her people must expand in sharing the experience of the continent of which it is part.

It seemed very logical, indeed, that the Church of Romania should understand and support the development of her faithful within the context of the European theater. What happens in the rest of Europe immediately affects what happens in Romania.

By extension, the United States is not part of Europe, and her peoples cannot share and shape what takes place in Europe, just as Europeans should not attempt to shape the life of North America. This applies to the life of the Church as the prime sanctifier of the nation in which she preaches the Gospel. There is a Romanian saying, "Omul sfințește locul" (It is the person who sanctifies where he lives). Although the Church is One, Holy, Catholic and Apostolic, history clearly shows that the Church adapts herself to local realities. Orthodoxy in Europe, the Middle East, Africa, Asia and the Americas, is the same sacramentally, theologically and morally; differing however, differing according to the social and political realities in which she is living the Gospel.

I applaud the Patriarch's observations about the role of Romania in Europe and ergo, the role of the Church of Romania in sanctifying its lands within the greater context of a united Europe. I would like applaud all the patriarchs who also understand the need for a united Church in Canada and another in the United States, so that the Church can sanctify these lands "according to the needs of each."

Canada and the United States long ago ceased to be colonies of Europe and have "made it on their own!" One ceased through warfare and the other through a longer process of change. Nevertheless, Orthodoxy has existed for over two hundred years in North America; and certainly, the Church is living the fullness of the faith and is united sacramentally. Sacramental union, however, is not the fullness of ecclesiastical union in the One Body of Christ.

Sometimes, no, most of the time, we speak of the Church "here" and the Church "over there." In this way, we are speaking about the administrative differences, because even "over there," each nation has its own hierarchy and administration and spiritual life. There is a growing impatience among the majority of Orthodox Christians, clergy and lay, who vociferate or tacitly endure the silence of the Mother Churches as to why they do not recognize an Autocephalous Church in Canada and an Autocephalous Church in the United States. Silence is not golden - it is deafening, and deafening is unkind and unproductive and mistrusting. May those voices who speak out for world peace and political unions speak out for the peace of God's household in North America and the sanctification of the New World.

At the High Place, Patriarchal Cathedral, Bucharest, 2008

74

"The true nature of the Church is, by her divine calling, missionary . . . If the hierarchs, individually, but much better in a synodal/collegial way, were to establish parishes for their faithful who no longer speak the ethnic language . . . the service to our Lord would be doubled!"

(January 2004)

In this article, His Eminence laments the exodus of faithful from the Church over the issue of language. He calls for increased mission to the English-speaking majority of Orthodox Christians and to the local, unconverted nation. In the twenty-first century, his view remains controversial rather than commonplace.

Double or Nothing

"A Word to the Wise is Sufficient!" - so goes an ancient proverb. The title of this article, however, is based not on a wise proverb but on a gambler's call. Does it speak of recklessness or of solid assurance of success? Laying aside any reference to gambling, this call could be aptly applied to the mission effort of the Church in North America in her service to her Christ.

The true nature of the Church is, by her divine calling, missionary. Mission can be within a nation and to the outside. The concern of this article is mission within the nation. In this regard, "nation" refers to Canada, as well as to the United States. Mexico has its own particular needs.

Orthodoxy was brought to North America both through the planned mission program of the Church of Russia and through the unplanned establishment of parishes by immigrant faithful from other Orthodox nations. In the first instance, the Church of Russia instituted an authentic mission program to reach the Native Alaskans. In the second instance, immigrants brought their faith with them to nourish and comfort them in the New World with little concern to reach out to others. One reached out to establish the faith, and the other turned inward to preserve the faith.

After two hundred years of the existence of Orthodoxy in North America, we find that these two missionary efforts continue: mission to the outside mostly through the work of the Orthodox Christian Mission Center (O.C.M.C.), while mission within is in the hands of hierarchs.

Every jurisdiction establishes new (mission) parishes. In most cases, mission means establishing a worshiping community for a particular ethnic group. In other words, it is the continuation of the activity initiated by the early immigrants to these shores and tends to be more conservative than missionary. Even those parishes which are established as "American" often have "ethnic" founders upon whom the new community was based, and this "patchwork" gives the mission a unique "flavor".

There is a particular mission recently established under the jurisdiction of an ethnic hierarch whose priest sends out postcards reminding individuals of the forthcoming service schedule. Around the edge of the postcard are invitations to "Greeks, Russians, Romanians, Serbians, Ukrainians, etc.," to attend. This is an effort to reach out to those who are already Orthodox but who have no 'ethnic' church to attend and who accommodate to a multiplicity of liturgical languages along with English.

The Greek-American community, unlike the former "Iron Curtain Nations" (ICN), has enjoyed continuous immigration over the decades since the Russian Revolution. Its ethnic identity remained strong while those of the ICN nations were weakened by the "shame" of belonging to a people labeled as "communist" and as the "Red Threat".

With the apparent change of governments in the former "ICN", "Orthodox" immigration to North America has increased greatly. A multitude of new missions for identifiable ethnic immigrants has been established for Romanians, Albanians, Bulgarians, Serbians, Russians, Ukrainians and others. Thus, the growth in certain ethnic jurisdictions is based on this "mission within" rather than "mission to the outside". The Church is taking care of her faithful wherever they may roam.

With the playing field of "Orthodox" immigration more or less leveled out, is the Church effecting mission with the nation or is it still merely maintaining and establishing communities for particular ethnic groups? How strong is the hierarchs' conviction to reach out beyond a particular ethnic pale? Is there a real concern? Only each hierarch knows his own conviction. We do suggest that not enough is being done to serve those of the ethnic groups who do not speak the language in which the Divine Liturgy is being served in their particular parish. Thus, the choice of the title, "Double or Nothing". Both language groups must be served. A hierarch who establishes English language parishes is acting in a pastorally responsible way befitting his role as shepherd of the "reason endowed flock".

Does it not make sense and is it not a responsibility to create new parishes using the English language for those faithful? Over the decades, every ethnic church has lost the majority of its faithful, because they no longer understood the language of the Divine Services. They were lost, too, because their non-ethnic spouses were not welcomed and the spiritual education of their children ignored. They were lost, too, because they were judged as not being able to fit into the "inner circle" of the ethnic parish. They were lost too, by the droves, swallowed up by those who did serve them in an understandable language, and large numbers enrolled in non-Orthodox churches.

How often has hierarch, priest or layman said, "If they can't learn the language, then let them go elsewhere!" Among the many stories reflecting this devastating attitude is that of a certain priest who, when approached by a small group of his faithful interested in learning more about the Bible in English, informed them that it was not necessary and they should spend time learning the language of their forefathers. Today, that group is enlarged and exists as a Pentecostal Community of Christians who study the Bible but are now bereft of the sacraments and teachings of the Orthodox Church.

Some of the leaders of the Church, of thrice-blessed memory, Metropolitan Anthony Bashir, Archbishop Valerian Trifa, Archbishop Theophan (Fan) Noli, published bi-lingual liturgical texts for use in their ethnic parishes. We can also glory in the efforts of our Holy Fathers among the Saints, Bishop Innocent and Metropolitan Tikhon who championed the use of the spoken tongue of the Alaskan Christians in addition to using Old Slavonic. Possibly the merit goes to the Antiochian Church in North America that first established English-speaking parishes, and most of the Dioceses of the Orthodox Church in America establish new missions with English as the liturgical language.

There is another story about the famous "Orloff" liturgical texts in English printed in St. Petersburg at the end of the 19th Century and shipped to North America. After the Bolshevik Revolution, the Church in America turned inward, became defensive, insisted on the use of Old Slavonic over English and stored those beautiful books in the recesses of some basement area. This "conservative" attitude can be observed in all the ethnic Orthodox groups in North America which were affected by control of their homelands by atheistic communist governments. They must have felt as if they would become the "remnant". Although new generations did not learn the ethnic and liturgical languages, neither did the Church learn the English language of the land to sanctify it.

Furthermore, is it not incumbent upon the hierarchs to reach out to the un-churched in a language they can understand? The most famous example of the Slavonic-speaking Greek brothers, Saints Cyril and Methodios of Thessalonika, bears witness to the absolute necessity for intelligible communication of the teachings of Christ. There is both the need to establish more English-speaking missions to serve our faithful who do not speak one of the liturgical languages, as well as to establish totally new missions to reach out to bring others into the Church.

If the hierarchs, individually but much better in a synodal/collegial way, were to establish parishes for their faithful who no longer speak the ethnic language or cannot understand an archaic form of liturgical language, the service to our Lord would be doubled! If the hierarchs also established new missions as an outreach to the nation, the witness would be quadrupled! Thus, there is a need for two kinds of English-speaking missions: those for the Orthodox who would be lost because of the incomprehensibility of liturgical language, and for missions to the nation.

If we plant nothing, we reap the fruit of nothing. If we plant not, others do and reap our faithful. Isolated from each, our left hand knows not what our right is doing. We duplicate; we exacerbate; we complicate. The Holy Spirit is economical and blesses that which is well planned. It is the same Holy Spirit, the Paraclete that gathered the hierarchs together 10 years ago in Ligonier. The two documents born of the unique SCOBA meeting held under the power of the Spirit of Truth are the touchstone to what was stated, what was promised and what has been implemented. We cannot gamble that which does not belong to us, the faith given to us by the Lord. We have everything to lose but also everything to gain! "A reminder to the Wise is sufficient."

75

"The quest for unity of Christians must be pursued and come to be. The world chooses not to accept Christianity, because it appears divided and thus, self-contradicting. Adherents of other faiths are puzzled by the apparent plurality of interpretations of Christianity. While most non-Christian faiths or philosophies allow for great divergences in themselves, Christianity claims to be unique, an answer to all and for all, and therefore, ought to represent a unity of dogma.

(March 2003)

Just as the unity of the Orthodox Church is imperative, so too is the unity of all Christians. Here, Archbishop Nathaniel reflects on the visit of Patriarch Teoctist to Rome and his plea for the unity of the Christian faith.

Unity Among the Followers of Christ

On Sunday, October 13, 2003, His Beatitude, Teoctist, Patriarch of the Church of Romania, attended a Mass celebrated by His Holiness, Pope John Paul II in the Basilica of St. Peter in Rome. At the invitation of the Pope, Patriarch Teoctist delivered a homily on the text, *"Make every effort to keep the unity of the Spirit, by the peace that binds you together"* (Ephesians 4:3). In his presentation, the Patriarch made clear that those Christians who believe in the Holy Trinity must unite due to **the almost total secularization of the Western World** [all bolds are ours]:

Today, a secular Europe which is very secularized tries, as much as it can, to be united economically, juridically, and culturally, often without seeking the direct support of Christian Churches on the Continent, perhaps exactly because our Churches from Europe are (themselves) too little preoccupied with the unity and cooperation amongst themselves.

This is also true regarding the international Christian ecumenical institutions which are not sufficiently convinced that the Churches they represent are deeply committed to the realization of Christian unity.

The secularized world **sanctions** today the disunited Churches of Europe, not through persecutions, but with **indifference** towards them, so much so that they become **marginalized**. The **spiritual crisis of our time** urges us to rediscover the relation between penitence-conversion or return to Christ, the humble one who suffers with us on the one hand, and the recovery of the communion among Churches, on the other. Contemporary secularization goes hand in hand with a fragmentation and a poverty of inner, spiritual life of human beings. Thus, secularization even further weakens the spiritual communion among Christians.

The Patriarch concludes his sermon with a prayer "...to Christ our Lord, the eternal High Priest and Head of the Church to bless and help our Churches, so that they may permanently listen to his prayer, 'that they may be one' (John 17:11), and to strengthen their willingness and work for the realization of full brotherly communion, to the glory of the Holy Trinity and for the salvation of mankind" (**The Romanian Patriarchate News Bulletin,** 7th Year, no. 7-9, October 2002).

The Patriarch's observation about the general secularization of Western Europe (he is speaking as a European) is not a new one. The Church has always carried out her mission to a world which is secular. Perhaps his concern can be explained, because now, after the collapse of the Iron Curtain, he is able to comprehend the extent of secularism in a Europe less than more Christian and more antagonistic than not to faith.

There is, however, a second reason for which the request for the union of Christians can be deemed urgent, and that is the rise of Islam in a great number of European countries and other parts of the world. Where once Islam was known as a religion "out there," it now is "among us."

In the German Evangelical Church magazine, "Ecumenical Dialogue," the following are titles of articles which reflect the state of this new religion in Germany, although they reflect what can be said about most of Europe and North and South America: "Germany - a country which accepts immigrants"; "Faint hearts and Scaremongers"; "Who's Coming, who's going, who's staying"; "Immigration and Religion"; "Acknowledging racism - coming clean." In the article, "Immigration and religion," the author states:

"The religious landscape is among the aspects of our lives (Germans' and other ethnic people living in Germany) which are being changed by immigration. Most non-Christian immigrants have been brought up to be devout and to practice their faith. Is this a threat to inter-religious peace? Hardly. Nevertheless, these immigrants pose a question to the largely secularized, traditional church religion which we take for granted....

Finally, the attitude toward religion in German society is a mixture of ignorance, indifference, and liberality: 'We have no objection to religion and religious communities, as long as they keep within normal limits and don't impose their messages and way of life too strongly on other individuals or the general public.'...

The recruitment of 'guest workers' from southern Europe led to a marked strengthening of the Orthodox presence in Germany. Today, it has become standard for Orthodox liturgies to be among the Sunday worship services broadcast on television. Today, Germany has the third largest number of men and women of the Jewish faith in Western Europe. By now, the Muslims have numerically become the third largest religious group in Germany after the Catholic and Protestant churches...".

Some of the facts to be drawn from this article are that the one-time influence of faith communities in their "traditional" countries is no longer as strong as it once was; that monolithic faith communities in a particular country are giving way to multi-faith realities; that there can be tension between the one-time "traditional" faith community and the newly-implanted faith immigrant communities as well as between these new communities and the secular society into which they have become transplanted. This development is for the churches, a "question"; for society, an "alarm."

While most immigration has been for economic reasons; nevertheless, the presence of these new people (it seems that they are not all that soon allowed to become and therefore be called, "citizens"), intentionally or not, creates tensions in the existing faith communities and in secular society. The one reflects on its minimal role in society, and society perceives that it is again being judged. The author seems to say that these people have a faith-centered life, the living of which is so important to them, that they intentionally isolate themselves from the rest of German society which they judge as without merit; and, that this separation is a judgment on the rest of society, faithful and faith-less.

Thus, in addition to the Patriarch's observation about the expanded secularization of society, the more urgent cause for Christian unity is the expansion of Islam in areas of the world where its presence was minimal. The Church, various Christian peoples, has experienced Islam, from the sixth century through today's Bosnia. Although Judaism and Islam are defined (as is Christianity) as being monotheistic, Christianity alone elucidates monotheism as Trinitarian. This remains today the source of the same tension between Christianity and the two non-Christian faiths as it did in the time of Julian the Apostate who tried to balance the religious tensions in his empire with the abolition of iconography. This is the same tension which is extending itself into most parts of the Western World.

The quest for unity of Christians must be pursued and come to be. The world chooses not to accept Christianity, because it is appears divided and thus, self-contradicting. Adherents of other faiths are puzzled by the apparent plurality of interpretations of Christianity. While most non-Christian faiths or philosophies allow for great divergences in themselves, Christianity claims to be unique, an answer to all and for all, and therefore, ought to represent a unity of dogma.

The disciples of Jesus Christ must go out into the world and share the Good News, so that that which is unique may become truly universal. Eastern Orthodoxy, Oriental Orthodoxy, Roman Catholicism and traditional Protestantism must sit down together and discover that the political maneuvering of the past, the manipulation of the spiritual by the secular is a thing of the past. The Church is freed from her bondage to the state, and in her freedom must put her household in order. The false unions of the past and the various "confessions" shaped on political, social and economic rewards are not applicable today. There is no papal army to bring liberation from foreign invaders; there is no threat of imposed "Hellenism" to dominate local cultures; there is no reason to be suspect of one another. There is only one faith, one baptism, one Christ who calls all mankind to salvation through the promise of the good things to come. What is needed is, indeed, "the unity of the Spirit by the peace that binds...together" (Ephesians 4:3).

Patriarch Teoctist was correct in saying, "the realization of full brotherly communion is to the glory of the Holy Trinity and for the salvation of mankind." We seek no "false ecumenism," but rather the fulfillment of the Lord's own prayer for his disciples, "that they may be one, even as we are one" (John 17:11).

Officiating in the Patriarchal Cathedral, Bucharest, 2008

76

"The Holy Spirit is the Source of Life, and Life is Action. The Holy Spirit moves us, not to revolution nor to remain in an embryonic state of infinite becoming. The Holy Spirit is act and action. The movement of the laity to help be a midwife to the birth of an administratively-unified Orthodox Church in the United States is to be admired as a gift of the Holy Spirit."
(November 2001)

Drawing on the image of the Holy Spirit as the Leader of the Dance, His Eminence calls on the Church to follow the Spirit's work of unity by taking action toward administrative unification in North America.

Not Revolution, Nor Indefinite Evolution, But Action

"Heavenly King, comforter, Spirit of truth who are everywhere and fulfilling all things, the treasury of blessings and source of life; come abide in us, cleanse us of all stains and save our souls, O good one."

This prayer/hymn of the church is found in the service of Vespers of Pentecost. Between Holy Pascha and this vesper service, the invocation is not offered. On the eve of the Day of Pentecost, it is sung in the sixth tone. It is a majestic paean of praise and trust in the Holy Spirit, the source of life. It is said at the beginning of most services of the Church. It is the appeal of each Orthodox Christian for all Orthodox Christians.

This is a case in point in which the power of words is most efficient in the language in which an original work is written. The Greek says of the Holy Spirit that he is "zois chorigos." The Holy

Spirit is the leader of the dance. A general rendering would be that this title is one given to the leader of a dance, the pace-setter, the one whose rhythm the others must accept to take part in the dance, the dance of life in which every human moves. That the Holy Spirit is the source of life, as most English renderings express this title, is certainly sufficient, but it does not emphasize the role of those who follow, the "line-dancers." The Holy Spirit, as the leader in this "Dance of Existence" of humanity, invites us to join or remain out of step. Even though man does have a human existence, the Christian exists in a new life, having put aside that of mere existence, which is rather like being part of the dance but out of step, into a life in Christ himself, in step with the Lord through baptism.

Sent to us by our Lord and God and Savior, Jesus Christ, the Holy Spirit is present in us through the seal (sfragis) at Holy Chrismation at which time our senses are consecrated to God. Thus, each of us has become a new creature through baptism and also a temple of the Holy Spirit who dwells within us, and thus among us as the Body of Christ. "Christ is among us! He is and ever shall be!" is the greeting and response. We ought to say as well, "The Holy Spirit is within us! He is and ever shall be!" We are told by our Lord, that it is the Holy Spirit within us who brings us to be able to say, "Abba! Father!" Thus, the presence of the Holy Spirit in our lives is the presence of "The Spirit of Truth, present everywhere and fulfilling all things."

Having stated all the above, it would seem obvious that the presence and movement of the Holy Spirit in the Church is one of synergy, a call of the pace-setter to the followers, an invitation to join in the Dance of Existence. Now the Church is not singularly the hierarchy nor the ordained nor the non-ordained but "all baptized in Christ," each having functions as members of the one Body.

The laity has now begun to respond to this dance in a special way, in synergy with the Spirit of Truth. This should be a cause of joy for the entire Church. Moved by the Holy Spirit, the non-ordained laity understands that there is One baptism, One faith, One Lord and One, Holy, Apostolic and Catholic Church which is localized in time and space. This local witness is one in Sacramental Life and one in Administration. Multi-mutual recognition of canonical authenticity of sacraments without full administrative unity is not the fullness of the Church. It is not "enough for now" to say that there exists "Sacramental Unity" among the jurisdictions. It is not responsible to say, "It is not the time!" When is the time and what are the conditions for reaching that time and fulfilling the conditions? Responsibility to the entire Church in America requests not only "trust" but action! As there is no action, there needs to be an explanation why there is none.

No one in the Orthodox Church in the United States favors nor promotes a "revolution" in seeking the recognition of the Church as autocephalous. We do not live in the times nor mentality of European peoples who were in quest of national recognition and ethnic identity as new national states forming out of the former Turkish, Austro-Hungarian and French and British Empires.

Americans know who they are, and no one is challenging their borders, language, history or self-determination. The unique composition of the citizenry of this nation does not necessitate an amalgamation of ethnic identities into one super "ID," labeled, "American." No one is prepared nor desirous of completely ignoring or rejecting or denying one's ethnic roots. One lives an existential life based on the reality of transfiguring the place and times in which that individual is living; and, this means that physically, existentially one can be in only one place at one given time. The transfiguration of the place in which we live out our lives is accomplished through God's grace working in us at that time in that place.

Nor do we speak of some kind of "independence" from the Mother Churches, because the Church is one and cannot be divided into equal or unequal parts totally separate or independent from the whole as a nation claims independence from its mother/fatherland. Even as all the "Mother Churches" make up the sum of the Church, so too, the Church in the United States must be a separate part of the whole. The witness of the Church speaks for itself, and when that witness is authentic in a new time and place, then that witness must be recognized by the Universal Church of all Mother Churches as a new entity in time and place, even as each of them came to be autocephalous at a definite time and place.

A new witness of the Church in a particular time and space must come of age in time; otherwise, the evolution of witness never arrives at being an authentic one. The Church in the United States has been in evolution for more than two hundred years, although her witness here is based on the witness of the two-thousand year witness of the entire Church. She has thrust her roots deeper and deeper into a new place and has born the fruit of saints, both canonized and those known only to God. An indefinite evolution lacks fullness. It is an ongoing process which is not recognized as whole, because it is judged to be in process. But what standards and what judgments or by whose standards and whose judgments is our Church considered to be not fully evolved? The laity, the clergy, the hierarchy of the Church in the United States must have a response to these questions. Upon what authority, by what power, is our Church so judged? Certainly, we are speaking of human decisions and not divine. We are not questioning the essence of the Church but her "accidental" witness in time and space.

The Holy Spirit is the Source of Life, and Life is Action. The Holy Spirit moves us, not to revolution nor to remain in an embryonic state of infinite becoming. The Holy Spirit is act and action. The movement of the laity to help be a midwife to the birth of an administratively-unified Orthodox Church in the United States is to be admired as a gift of the Holy Spirit. How much richer this movement will be when clergy and hierarchy participate whole-heartedly in this grand hour of celebrating and witnessing to God with one mind and one mouth. The Spirit of Truth, who brings to fulfillment the Orthodox Witness everywhere, will do so even in this nation of seven million Orthodox Christians. Administrative Unity is not a solution - it is the norm.

77

"Let us kneel before the crib of the newborn Only Son of God who out of love for us poured out his blood and sent the Holy Spirit upon his bride, the Church, to go forth to make disciples of all nations. Let us humbly ask for illumination to lead us out of this stagnation in which we find ourselves. Let us not continue along the path of equal but separate households, but rather unite to bear a single witness to the faith once and for all delivered to the saints."

(December 2001)

At Christmastime, His Eminence asks whether Orthodox Christians on this continent have adapted too well to American notions of independence and individualism. He reminds us that the Church is one, not many, and calls for an end to the separations that have given American Orthodoxy the appearance of division into separate denominations.

An American Orthodox Communion

In our American pluralistic society, citizens embrace a multitude of religious faiths and philosophies. The presence of the Christian faith in the United States is a strong one, even though the witness is subdivided into major and denominational, even "non-denominational," churches. Not to be dis-considered, however, is the reality of the many divisions within Judaism and Islam. There is no "faith community" of the three great monotheistic religions in North America which does not have its own variation of witness.

The major divisions within Christianity are most frequently identified as Roman Catholic, Protestant and Eastern Orthodox. Protestant America is often identified with the many denominational communities which broke away from "mainstream" Protestantism. One of those traditional "mainstream" churches, the Anglican, embraces various forms of witness, from "Low Church" to "High Church," encompassing them as a "Communion of Churches." The Church of Rome, which once was very monolithic, appears to also accept various witnessing, although it is not the "communion" of churches as is the Anglican Communion.

Founded on "rugged individualism" promoted by the Reformers, Protestantism as it appears in its "American" forms seems to promote churches which can include various witnessing under its umbrella. These witnesses may even be on the edge of mutual contradiction while still remaining in and participating at some kind of flexible ecclesiastical organization. It is a "communion of churches" which allows for such divergence for the sake of "unity" and which makes Christianity appear to some as "fuzzy."

Is Orthodoxy in the United States following a like path to "equal but separate" witnessing? Over the decades, each jurisdiction has developed independently of the others. The traditional Orthodox way of life brought over from Europe has been modified for the sake of "accommodating" to the New World. I am not referring to the adherence to a particular calendar, Julian or Gregorian. I am referring to the total sanctification of life through participation in the Holy Mysteries of the Church. Do we not project a distorted image about our claim to be One Church and of these many images, which is "orthodox?"

Having developed and presently living as "separate but equal," we have grown accustomed to variations of Orthodox witness to the one Lord, one faith, one baptism. This not only confuses our own faithful but makes us appear to our neighbors to be a **"conglomeration"** of churches. We are perceived to be a kind of **"federation"** based on good will. This does not reflect the true essence of Orthodox ecclesiology.

Although there may continue to be parishes and dioceses to serve the needs of various immigrant peoples (such a continuation of this particular witness does not diminish the unity of the Church, because it is on the basis of unity of these present units/jurisdictions that the Church in the United States will be formed); nevertheless, there must be one witness, one good order in the Church, and one synod of hierarchs. The longer we continue to remain separate, the further we go from one another in practice and witness. Clergy members in their associations ask, "Well, what do you do?" or "How do you do it?"

A peripheral reading of "Charters" or "Constitutions" of various jurisdictions verifies the wide interpretations of Church order. When compared one to another, it seems as though each charter is about a church (jurisdiction) totally unique from others. Because of this "low" and "high" interpretation, our external witness suffers, and our interior witness waivers.

Often one hears one of the faithful ask, "Are they (other jurisdictions) Orthodox as we are?" Ignorance of the oneness of the Church is the basis for the misconception among many American Orthodox Christians that, in fact, Orthodoxy is a **collection** of individual churches, a mere **communion** of individual and **separate** bodies which elect to cooperate one with the other. This "cooperation," they think, is not essential to the Church's witness. To many, the Church in the United States is an "American Orthodox Communion."

The existence of various traditions does add to the beauty of our local Orthodox witness, and these traditions may remain part of the American expression of Orthodoxy. Nevertheless, we have lived so long apart from one another, that we have created or allowed to exist or have not come to terms with the reality of the fragmented witness which we are living; and, this fragmentation may be more profound than we have perceived. We need unity to renew the gift of faith brought by our forefathers. In continuing on our separate jurisdictional paths, we are spinning away from the blessings of mutual support, stability and the good order which is the norm of the Orthodox Church and the fruit of an authentic witness to Apostolic Christianity.

It is long overdue for the Church in the United States to actually come together in a general assembly of laity, clergy and hierarchy of all "jurisdictions" to bear common witness to the unity of faith and the gift of the Holy Spirit.

Let us kneel before the crib of the newborn Only Son of God who out of love for us poured out his blood and sent the Holy Spirit upon his bride, the Church, to go forth to make disciples of all nations. Let us humbly ask for illumination to lead us out of this stagnation in which we find ourselves. Let us not continue along the path of equal but separate households, but rather unite to bear a single witness to the faith once and for all delivered to the saints.

With His Grace, Bishop Irineu,
Auxiliary Bishop of the
Romanian Orthodox Episcopate of America

78

"The Church exists locally, however, adapting to local government, while struggling to ever keep herself beyond secular control. To do so, however, she must be unique, able to respond quickly and authoritatively; and this demands a spokesman, a Patriarch."

(September 2001)

The election of Patriarch Irineos of Jerusalem is the occasion for His Eminence to point out the sharp contrast between the freedom of North American Orthodoxy and the relative dependence of the Old World Churches on secular authority. Again, he calls for immediate action to establish the united North American Church.

Jerusalem! Jerusalem!

Americans of all Christian denominations, as well as all Orthodox Christians around the world, hold Jerusalem to be the "Holiest of Cities." Last year, in December of 2000, the death of His Holiness Diodoros I, head of the Patriarchate of Jerusalem, the ancient but now small Orthodox Christian witness in modern-day Israel, made little impact worldwide. According to some statistics, there are less than 100,000 Christians in Israel, and the majority of these are Arab by ethnic identity. Thus, the passing of the head of such a small Church was not "newsworthy." Nevertheless, the Christian minority in its very city of origin, continues to sing the troparion: "Rejoice, O Zion, Mother of Churches, dwelling place of God. For you were the first to receive remission of sins, by the resurrection."

It took eight months from the falling-asleep of Patriarch Diodoros I for his successor, His Holiness Irineos, Patriarch-elect of Jerusalem, to be elected by the Synod of the Jerusalem Church. Since long-past December, however, the interest in the election of that successor grew enormously! Interest was not due, however, to pious concern as to who would spiritually head this ancient See whose first bishop was James, "Brother of the Lord." It was speculation over the temporal power, the financial clout and the position the new Patriarch would take toward Israel, Jordan and the Palestinian Authority which made news.

It was reported that, after an election by Church officials, the final approval of the vote rests on three States: Israel, The Palestinian Authority and Jordan, known to be "not Christian." This dependence for recognition by secular authority is almost as "about-face of Canossa"* as could be! This "right," it was claimed, was established by Emperor Justinian I in the 6th Century (apparently Justinian was not a prophet and could not foresee this fundamental change in the imperial rule). This peculiar state of affairs gives Americans something to think about. We are raised in the school of civic knowledge that there is (read also, "must be") a separation between Church and State, that the government cannot favor any particular religious formula nor interfere in the election of ecclesiastical leadership.

"Marriage" between Church and State or rather between government and religion, was prevalent in most ancient cultures. That is how the Christian Church inherited the Roman theory of the relationship between the governor and the governed. It was the European "Enlightenment," the rejection of faith, that brought down so aggressively the guillotine separating church and state. In our own day, it is the brutal efforts to eradicate religion in communist-dominated nations that also makes Americans cautious, queasy, and distrustful of government "partnerships" with "faith communities".

This kind of "arranged betrothal" is not new to the old-world patriarchates, not one of which escaped the gentle hand-in-hand, sometimes turned strong-arm, sometimes stranglehold government interference in the election of hierarchs and administration of the Church, from Saint Constantine the Great until Prime Minister Ariel Sharon today.

Our American understanding of the "independence" of faith communities from human government is one of the very fundamental differences and real causes of misunderstanding between Orthodox in North America and those living in Europe, the Middle East and Africa. We are uncomfortable and suspicious of government interfering in our religious administration. We enjoy the freedom to act and to evangelize and do whatsoever we deem acceptable to God without asking a definition from the civil authorities; and yet, we are still "good" citizens.

Americans do not have nor desire to experience a "Department of Cults." This is another reason why the Autocephaly of the Church in America is necessary; so that we are not dependent on the whims of foreign governments and their purely secular interest in using the power of the Church to serve mundane affairs, nor are we unaware of the possible pressures on the Patriarchates, which in turn may put pressure on Orthodox Christians in the United States.

The power of the Church and in the Church comes from the presence of the Holy Spirit within her, not from a position bestowed by external authority. This is true of the Universal Church. The Church exists locally, however, adapting to local government, while struggling to ever keep herself beyond secular control. To do so, however, she must be unique, able to respond quickly and authoritatively; and this demands a spokesman, a Patriarch. The election of the hierarchs of the Orthodox Church in America are strictly the concern of the Church here, clergy and lay, who elect without government interference or overtones of pressure, threats or intimidation. Such should be the same for the election of the head of the Church in America: full clergy and lay participation.

Four months have passed since the Second Conference of Hierarchs in the United States was held in Washington, D.C., the capital of the most powerful nation in the world. No government official was present, no Director of Cults, no one to be an observer on behalf of the civil authorities. The hierarchs were free to speak as they chose (although most chose not to speak). Four months out of twelve leave eight months, and still there is no announcement of the next Conference which was voted by the hierarchs to be held. (We would be amiss not to remind ourselves that the hierarchs voted this in the First Conference at Ligonier, too, and it took almost a decade to implement.)

So what keeps the Church in the United States from meeting? Not the governments under whose civil laws the Patriarchate subsist. Who then? Why? It took eight months for the election of the Patriarch of Jerusalem. Certainly, it should not take eight months to simply establish the date for the calling of the Third Conference of Orthodox Hierarchs in the United States.

In the meanwhile, we will watch with bated-breath to read the official government press releases from Jordan, Israel and the Palestinian Authority so that we may officially offer prayers for the new Patriarch of Zion, that holy of holy cities. Eis Pola Eti Despota!

Folklore states that Emperor Henry the Fourth stood in the snow at Canossa begging forgiveness from Pope Gregory 7th for thwarting papal edicts (Stephen Carter, "The Culture of Disbelief").

79

> *"The Church in the United States, her hierarchs, clergy and faithful, must continue to reassure the Mother Churches that she is capable of serving all peoples with her ministry as a unified Church with its own local Holy Synod and Patriarch, by her strong witness of common effort and actions at this time in her history."*
>
> *(August 2000)*

Archbishop Nathaniel's impatience with the pace of unity efforts comes out again in this article on the sixth anniversary of the Ligonier conference. Unflagging in his call for action, His Eminence addresses the topic of phyletism as it applies to the American context.

Phyletism or Ministry?

According to the late Ecumenical Patriarch Dimitrios, "It is truly a scandal for the unity of the Church to maintain more than one bishop in any given city; it contravenes the sacred canons and Orthodox ecclesiology. It is a scandal that is exacerbated whenever PHYLETISTIC (ethnocentric) motives play a part, a practice soundly condemned by the Orthodox Church in the last (19th) century."

We saw this quotation on the front cover of "An Orthodox Christian Church in the United States: Unified and Self Governed" (OCL, 2000, 30 N LaSalle St., Suite 4020, Chicago, IL 60602-2507). It does not state the source of the quote nor to which geographic area the patriarch is referring. He is, however, quoting from a statement made in the late 19th Century by the Holy Synod of the Patriarchate of Constantinople. It may be that the Synod was then referring to the shaping of national political entities in the

19th century and of the process of recognition of local (ethnic) autocephalous churches entered into by the Patriarch of Constantinople.

The repetition by Patriarch Dimitrios of this quote in a more recent time, brings to the foreground the reality of more than one bishop in a given city, a phenomenon which does exist in many cities in the United States. Because we do not know the context of Patriarch Dimitrios's statement, we can only wonder if His Holiness was referring to an "Orthodox" country, where there was more than one bishop in a city or to a number of countries. It would be a strange situation, indeed, inasmuch as the Church is governed in each country by a Holy Synod with a Patriarch as its head and by whose affirmation all hierarchs are enthroned. How could such a situation come to be? Where does it exist? In what "Orthodox" countries might one find "more than one bishop in any given city"?

If we apply his statement to the situation in the United States, we know that there is an over-lapping of jurisdictions and instances where there is more than one Orthodox hierarch having the title of the same city. Europeans are fond of stating that there is no such animal as "an American people," because it is a hodge-podge of peoples. We find it strange to identify the reality in the United States of "poli episcopii" in one city as being based on "phyletism." To accuse our Church of being "phyletistic" would be a contradiction to the assumed statement that "there is no such 'people' as 'an American people'." Perhaps Patriarch Dimitrios was aiming his statement at those Mother Churches which maintain ethnic jurisdictions in the United States? Is this the "Phyletism" to which Patriarch Dimitrios is referring? Inasmuch as a Holy Synod as a "Church in the United States" does not yet exist and therefore cannot be held responsible for this uncanonical condition, it seems probable that he is referring to the Mother Churches. But to what purpose? Was it not a clarion call from Constantinople to revise this unusual ecclesiastical anomaly?

The hierarchy, clergy and laity of the Church in the United States would, for the most part, state that the Church here is adequately serving the Orthodox faithful of all ethnic origins, the "American people." In the last decade, the Church in the United States has reviewed her ministry to serve a new influx of immigrants and has grandly responded to Orthodox from Albania, Bulgaria, Romania, Russia, Serbia and Ukraine. She cannot be accused of phyletism but rather should be lauded for being true to her ministry to the faithful born in North America and to those who have immigrated to the United States. The Church in the United States is fulfilling the command given her by her Savior to bring all nations to him.

No one should doubt that every jurisdiction in the United States is true to its mission to serve all Orthodox, in addition to sustaining a particular ministry to definable ethnic groups. This ministry to ethnic immigrants and to their offspring will continue, probably without end. It is a part of the fabric of the work of the Church in the United States. There will be a strong and necessary mission ministry in the United States as long as there is immigration. We do not mean by this to limit immigration nor mission to those solely coming from "Orthodox" countries. There is nothing un-Christian nor wayward in the Church ministering to particular groups, as long as she does not neglect the wider field to be harvested around her. In this arena, however, more cooperation is needed.

Those who insist that only English be used bear a burden of prejudice. The Church cannot fulfill her mission unless she uses the forms of communication necessary to her faithful; and, she is not obliged to "eradicate" the various liturgical languages now in use to the exclusivity of English, just because English is the language of the land. On the other hand, she must not neglect any of her faithful by refusing to hold services in English when the need is obvious. Children cannot learn a foreign language in the context of participating in the Divine Liturgy. Church leaders and others who want their offspring to learn an ethnic tongue need do so outside the context of communal praise of the Lord. "Lord have mercy" and "Grant this, O Lord" are not enough of a vocabulary by which children can learn the language of their ethnic ancestors.

The Church in the United States is actively ministering to others, offering them the gift of faith and salvation in Christ's holy Church just as the nascent Church took the Gospel into all the lands of the Mediterranean and Europe and offered it to those peoples. To bear Christian witness to non-Orthodox is the fulfillment of the Great Command by our Lord to his Church; it is her proper fabric; it is the "stuff" of which the Church is made.

In this manner, the warp of the Church can be likened to her infantile ties to the Mother Churches. This 200 year-old tie remains and ever will remain the basis of the founding sacramental life in North America. Ethnic Orthodox traditions came with the faith and are cherished in the ghetto parishes until this day. The weft can be seen as the local Church's response to being planted in a novel society. The accommodation to the use of English, reaching out to "non-Orthodox," bearing witness to a different society, the Church's adaptation to the "agora of the New World," all of these things represent the ability and maturity of the local Church to respond.

The warp continues as the authentic tie of "catholicity" with the rest of the Church. This is the "Holy Orthodoxy" which has been deeply rooted over the past two centuries. The weft is placed by the hierarchy, clergy and faithful, day by day, year after year, across the warp, thus creating a unique local witness as shaped by the Spirit of Truth who is present everywhere and fulfilling all things.

For this witness to develop and grow, however, there must be a unification of the hierarchs into one synod with a patriarch at its head. For the Church here to continue her ministry to the ethnic immigration, to the American-born, to those enlightened to Holy Orthodoxy, she must also reach out to others such as to the Afro-American, Asian, African, Hispanic peoples. To do this, to be true in the most profound sense of her mission, the Church must be unified. Ministries to these groups must be established by common consent and witness of a single unified Holy Synod.

The Church in the United States, her hierarchs, clergy and faithful, must continue to reassure the Mother Churches that she is capable of serving all peoples with her ministry as a unified Church with its own local Holy Synod and Patriarch, by her strong witness of common effort and actions at this time in her history.

On the other hand, it seems to us that the implementation of the canon directing having one bishop in any given city must be worked out here, locally by the Church, and in her own good time. Although the canons are clear, they do refer to different times and other circumstances. To "undo" episcopal sees at this time so that there would be only one hierarch in a city as a "condition sine qua non" for autocephaly is not necessary. Nor can a "fiat" from outside the United States enforce this canon before its time.

The Mother Churches are realistic and practical enough in facing the truth that the situation in the United States was not foreseen in the canons, and that the existence of more than one bishop in a given city can be phased out in time. Those who live in the United States and are living the life of the Church here know her history and her traditions. The Holy Synod of the Church in the United States, together with the clergy and laity, will be open to the prompting of the Holy Spirit to regularize the traditional ecclesiology of the Church when the time comes.

In the meanwhile, the Church in the United States continues her ministry and like the apostles preaching to the "hodge-podge" of pilgrims on the great day of Pentecost, ministering to everyone according to his own tongue and custom, working hard to bring in a harvest to her Lord and God and Savior. When should the blessing for this unified Holy Synod come? Without delay! From whom ought it be given and to whom? From each Mother Church to her own children! Who shall announce the formalization? Inasmuch as the regularization came from a Patriarch of Constantinople, let it be announced from his throne. When? Without delay!

80

> *"The Church is a unity of individuals working for individual salvation but through the communion of saints. Our American society promotes an individualism so radical that the very idea of being "a part of" a relationship, whether it is in the union of two in Holy Matrimony, or of more as in the unity of a family or organization, has almost become passé! Sometimes this radical individualism shows itself in certain statements which are not appropriate to the Church. The Church is not a "free-will" society or organization but is the Body of Christ himself."*
>
> *(July 2000)*

In this article, His Eminence stresses that the solution to the problem of Orthodox unity in North America must be pursued within the Church herself and within her Tradition. He warns us against adopting a separatist attitude toward the Universal Church and urges us to understand that we must do all things in good order and, ultimately, with the blessing of the entire Body of Christ.

An American Church? No! The Church in America? Yes!

The movement among Orthodox Christians in North America to fulfill the Canons of the Church which call for one hierarchy and thus one Church in a given territory grows daily and with notable growth. Active laity have established organizations to promote the education of others to comprehend the history of how this present canonical disorder came to be, so that all the faithful may be knowledgeable in participating in the furthering of the unification process of all jurisdictions into one Church. Articles and brochures are written, lectures given and associations are formed, all for the purpose of fulfilling the Canons. Dedicated clergy of various jurisdictions fraternalize with the scope of presenting a unified faith-witness in the Babel of the agora of their local communities. A limited few local Episcopal "brotherhoods" have arisen, and then there is the SCOBA. No one can deny that this movement is gaining momentum, and that clergy and laity expects an immediate resolution to this 200 years old canonical disorder.

Some Orthodox Christians are entirely ignorant of this disorder, continuing to live in a state of isolation from their fellow faithful. These live in a state of a pseudo ecclesiastical/cultural ghetto mentality which allows them to be a part of the general American society but favors withdrawal into an ethnic enclave when there is talk of a united Orthodoxy in North America. It appears that they are less fearful of becoming "American" than they are of becoming "American Orthodox." Others are fearful of alterations of jurisdiction, diocesan, parish establishments. They are content and retreat into a trite statement that "It is not the time!", but they do not say what are the conditions for this fullness of time. If the American Colonies had waited until a perfect political union would be established before they acted as united colonies, it seems reasonable that we would be singing, "God save the Queen!," rather than "The Star-spangled Banner!" But the Church already is living a unified sacramental life, needful however, of administrative unity.

We have become as that child's toy, an inflated, round-bottomed image that rolls around and back and forth but which makes no forward progress. According to the canons, three hierarchs are sufficient to represent an autocephalous Church. Obviously, we, the hierarchs have decided not to declare the obvious, that there are tens of hierarchs in numbers more than sufficient to auto-proclaim. We are obedient children, but we are adults who have outgrown the protective pouch of our Mothers. We vacillate between the reality of the maturity of our Church and our own immaturity to take the normal action of declaration of autocephaly.

Others are of the idea that there should be an "American Church." By this they mean that the Church in America needs radical reform as they perceive society demands; and these changes, they consider, are necessary because "we live in

America." These changes might even include questions of faith, the sacramental life, and profound administrative restructuring. Some of their primary concern is for changes in administrative operations. Among the various jurisdictions, there are differences of administration, much of which reflect the foreign origin from which these jurisdictions sprang.

Although it is true that Orthodox in America do live in a society different in some ways from those of traditional Orthodox nations, it must be understood that the Church must affect society, which means, the faithful sanctify their society and must guard against being "mis-shaped" by the pressures of a secular, hedonistic, divisive society. The faith, however, is the same in all societies throughout the world. On the one hand, each faithful, through living the sacramental life, must sanctify home, parish, city, state/province, and nation. On the other hand, this life is lived in common union/ communion, fellowship with others, within a special society, the Church, whose goal is to fulfill the will of the Lord as good stewards of his visible creation. This special society, the Church, must reveal herself as ONE to the society in which she is living; only in this way can the unity of the faith be preserved and witnessed. The present state of canonical disorder is a scandal to our faithful and misunderstood by co-existing faith-communities; our witness is badly shattered; our authenticity questioned. The Spirit unites.

The Church is a unity of individuals working for individual salvation but through the communion of saints. Our American society promotes an individualism so radical that the very idea of being "a part of" a relationship, whether it is in the union of two in Holy Matrimony, or of more as in the unity of a family or organization, has almost become passé! Sometimes this radical individualism shows itself in certain statements which are not appropriate to the Church. The Church is not a "free-will" society or organization but is the Body of Christ himself; and, to be part of the Body is essential to living a full human life on this earth as God himself planned and the enjoyment of eternal life to come. The Church is not a "pick and choose" affiliation as one does for clubs and service groups.

If there are grievances in certain areas of Church administration, these should be heard, weighted and acted upon under the guidance of the Holy Spirit. Americans have been indoctrinated with certain concepts which are correct in the political realm but which are foreign to the 2000 year life of the Church. When this time of the year comes around, the Fourth of July, flags, Mom, apple pie, and fireworks, and we bristle with patriotic pride which, however, mistakenly intrudes into the life of the Church, on the parish level and then on a Diocesan and "Jurisdictional" level, it is good to consider the difference between a political state and the Body of Christ governed by him and co-worked by his faithful, ordained and not ordained.

This unique Body, the Church, is not a democracy by which it governs itself by "majority vote!" She is not concerned with properties and laws of men, even though existing in the material world and possessing both property and co-existing with human established institutions. The life of the Church is a Spirit life, being enlivened by the Holy Spirit to do that which "seems good to the Holy Spirit and to us," but this "us" is the entire Body.

In this present movement for unity, there is a definable cry for stability in the Church. The Church must be stable to best bear witness to the faith and stability or "well-being of the Holy Churches of God" as is expressed in the Divine Liturgy, and is dependent on the one-mind, one-heart shaped by the presence of the Holy Spirit in the Church. For the Church to resist society, to alter society, to sanctify and transfigure society, her exterior life must express her inner unity. It is not enough to have "sacramental unity" and not have "administrative unity."

The faithful clergy and laity continue to express their concern for the undeniable need for immediate unity of administration in the Church in North America. To arrive at a common administration in which the talents of all of God's people will be utilized can happen only when all jurisdictions come together and review their respective "Constitutions and By-Laws" as The Church in America. While we are proud that this nation is a land of order and discipline, no less do the Apostles also demand order and discipline in the Church. In North America, there is such a wide variety of administration policies among the jurisdictions, that it is inevitable that certain variations exist which indicate contradictions in the administration of the Church.

The periodic review and revision of these documents of administrative operation will not be fruitful until the entire Church in America participates in creating what is good for the entire Body. Inasmuch as these revisions continue to be subject to approval by bodies which are outside North America, the knowledge of, the experience with, the actual witness to the faith by those living in North America is put to a subjective test. Certainly, the same Holy Spirit which guides hierarchs in other lands can guide the North American hierarchy?

Let us repeat that the Church is One in faith, but she can express herself in local modes of existence, thereby sanctifying the faithful and the land. The Mother Churches should recognize that the Church in North America will be responsible for shepherding Orthodox immigrants. They should be joyful to have a "Sister Church" in North America! For a period of time, the present jurisdictional administrations can continue, but the disunity of the hierarchy must be resolved without delay. There must be a single Holy Synod in the United States shepherding the entire flock of Christ on this territory.

To those who are looking for an "American Church," reshaped, misshaped, out of shape with the rest of the world, let us say, "No!" But to The Church in America, Orthodox, canonical, a reflection of the rest of the Church, let us say, Yes! And without delay. "How do we come to this? By a council of clergy and laity of all jurisdictions discussing under the grace of the Holy Spirit, the "syn-odos," the united road, the way established by the apostles and our holy fathers.

There will be **The Church in America** but not "An American Church.

81

"How can the One, Holy, Catholic and Apostolic Church have a multiplicity of jurisdictions overlapping the same geographical area? How can the Patriarchs of Constantinople, Antioch, Jerusalem, Moscow, Belgrade, Bucharest, Sofia, all claim universal, geographical, ecclesiastical jurisdiction in North America (and the rest of the world) based on the existence of their particular ethnic spiritual children living here? We are thankful that the Churches of Cyprus, Finland, Slovakia, Japan, etc., have not yet made similar claims to their ethnic compatriots in North America."

(February 2000)

His Eminence challenges the Mother Churches' assertions of jurisdiction over defined ethnic groups. He calls for a return to traditional Orthodox ecclesiology based on the local diocese and local Church.

Universal, Geographic, Ecclesiastic Jurisdiction: Is Such a Concept Orthodox?

When an Orthodox Christian is asked to state what is considered to be a major difference between Orthodox Christianity and Roman Catholicism, the response is: "We don't have a pope." In other words, Orthodoxy does not recognize the claim of the Bishop of Rome to have universal jurisdiction over the Church.

Jesus put a question to his disciples: " 'But you, who do you say I am?' Then Simon Peter spoke up and said, 'You are the Christ, the Son of the living God.' Jesus replied, 'Simon son of Jonah, you are a blessed man! Because it was no human agency that revealed this to you but my Father in heaven. So now I say to you: You are Peter and on this rock I will build my community'." (Mt. 16:15-18 NJB).

The Church of Rome interprets this to mean that the person, Simon son of Jonah, now called "Peter," would be the individual in whom would reside the fullness of Christ's own authority after the early mission of the Lord had been fulfilled. In other words, Peter's personal profession of faith gave him the authority to be the guarantor of the Christian faith.

From the Orthodox point of view, there was no such understanding among the Apostles. Orthodox interpretation of Saint Matthew's text is that Christ's statement refers to **Peter's faith** that Jesus of Nazareth is truly the son of God and does not refer to **Peter as a person** in whom will reside the gift of authority over the entire Church. The Orthodox interpretation is that everyone who confesses Jesus Christ as Son of the living God is a "rock," a witness of faith, and of these witnesses is the Church of God comprised. The so-called "Petrine privilege" is a late Roman invention and is not recognized by serious historians.

Perhaps due to the unification of Italy into a secular state in the last century at the expense of the papal estate and due to the decline of Catholic ecclesiastical power in Western Europe following the "Enlightenment," Pope Pius IX insisted on the declaration by the First Vatican Council (1870) that the Bishop of Rome is infallible when he speaks "ex cathedra," or "officially." In this moment in history, the Roman Pontiff was guaranteed a limited geophysical site, a "political state," complete with diplomats, its own currency, postal system, etc. The "City-State" known as "the Vatican" which did not in any way challenge his "right" to a universal, geographical, ecclesiastical jurisdiction.

The Pope of Rome claims universal, geographical ecclesiastical jurisdiction over all adherents of the Church of Rome (and implicit is a jurisdiction over all human kind because of the great command to bring all "nations" to Christ). By himself, he can define dogma, and he alone chooses who will be consecrated as bishop. Every hierarch is thus a "suffragan bishop" to the Bishop of Rome.

We have gone to some length to state what we understand to be the Roman Catholic teaching of the universal, geographical, ecclesiastical jurisdiction of the Bishop of Rome, not to herein refute it so much as to use it as a point of departure in contrast with Orthodox ecclesiology. Orthodoxy states that "where the bishop is, there is the Church." Orthodox ecclesiastical consideration is that every Bishop, Archbishop, Metropolitan, Patriarch has a particular geographic, ecclesiastical jurisdiction, but no one hierarch can claim a universal, geographical jurisdiction.

In the context of Orthodox Christianity in North America today, however, the status of the Church here is in an unusual state of being, in that numerous Patriarchs "de facto" claim jurisdiction over "their" people in the United States and Canada, even though this jurisdiction is outside their own national boundary and over another continent. Many of the same Patriarchates also lay claim to "their" people in other continents, as well.

It can be stated then, that identifiable, overlapping "Orthodox" universal, geographical, ecclesiastical jurisdictions exist in Orthodoxy today. This is not an Orthodox concept.

Whereas the Pope of Rome claims universal jurisdiction based on Petrine Privilege, some Orthodox Patriarchs are exerting universal jurisdiction based on ethnic priorities. We do not know where in the Canons of the Church or the historical experience of the Church it can be found that any Patriarch may lay rightful claim to universal, geographical, ecclesiastical jurisdiction based on ministry to a select **ethnic** presence, the so-called "diaspora" (not to be confused with the "Babylonian Captivity").

The word, "diaspora," at best meant the technical term for Jewish communities settled outside Palestine during the last century BC and the first century AD. These individuals regarded Jerusalem as their spiritual capital.

The use of the word "diaspora" by various Orthodox Churches to express the status of their faithful who have left their nation, willingly or unwillingly, and are living "beyond" the political, geographic borders of that homeland is strained. It is strained, because there is no geographical "center" for Orthodox Christianity; there is no "Rome," old or new which is the unique "touchstone" for the faith; the "new" Jerusalem is the heavenly one, yet to come; and, then it is the center because the Lord Himself will dwell there, and He is the source of life and truth. The guarantor of the faith is not a place nor a particular person but the indwelling of the Holy Spirit in the Church.

Can there be a multitude of Orthodox "centers/capitals," each claiming spiritual obedience but just for a determined ethnic few? How can one admit to a multiplicity of such centers of jurisdiction without creating a plurality of interpretations or variations of the truth? The Church is One, the faith is One, baptism is One; and, although it might have been useful to allow an elasticity of jurisdiction based on an assumed "temporary" status of the immigrant, surely that time is past. This temporary status has continued for two centuries. Orthodox Christians in North America, for the most part, do not consider themselves to be in a state of "diaspora," nor do they have any intention, nor desire, nor plan to "return" permanently elsewhere. Just as they are permanent citizens of North America and those nations of birth or naturalization, so too, their Church is permanent and not in diaspora.

It appears that the basis for the employment of universal, geographical, ecclesiastical jurisdiction rested on a particular interpretation of Christ's command to go forth and preach to all nations; that is to say, that Christ's reference is to the conversion of people being part of a national identity, not to the conversion of individuals. One is saved through being part of a people

This interpretation appears to have arisen in these latter times as a response to sustaining modern "national" identities, and has given rise to the "obligation" of the Mother Churches to care for her spiritual offspring around the political globe. If the obligation was forced by geo-political pressures, the Church can be excused, temporarily. This was the experience during the communist era. Now that the Churches are free to reestablish traditional Orthodox ecclesiology, they can also eradicate this un-Orthodox "universal, geographical, ecclesiastical jurisdictionalism."

How can the One, Holy, Catholic and Apostolic Church have a multiplicity of jurisdictions overlapping the same geographical area? How can the Patriarchs of Constantinople, Antioch, Jerusalem, Moscow, Belgrade, Bucharest, Sofia, all claim universal, geographical, ecclesiastical jurisdiction in North America (and the rest of the world) based on the existence of their particular ethnic spiritual children living here? We are thankful that the Churches of Cyprus, Finland, Slovakia, Japan, etc., have not yet made similar claims to their ethnic compatriots in North America.

We respond to the question: "Is the concept of universal, geographical, ecclesiastical jurisdictions an Orthodox one?" We believe it is not. Therefore, let the Orthodox Christians of Canada and the United States work with the Mother Churches and seek their blessings for the respectful "long-distance" shepherds and flocks to join into one administrative unity as is the Orthodox ecclesiastical principle. Let them elect patriarchs for Canada and the United States so that the Lord's work can continue with one heart and one mind to serve and thus give glory to the All Holy Trinity, Father, Son and Holy Spirit, to whom be all glory, honor and worship, now and ever. Amen.

Consecrating a Church, Romania

82

> *"Is anyone open to the movement of the Holy Spirit? Certainly, the Grace of the Holy Spirit, which assembles the Synods of other Churches, also assembles us in our worship and guides the Church in The United States and the Church in Canada. Is it such a bold step into the unknown for the Mother Churches to relinquish their pastoral concern for their children into the care of the same hierarchs whom they have elected and consecrated? Is it not the pleroma of trust in God that he will guide the Church wherever and everywhere?"*
>
> *(January 2000)*

Ten years before the historic Episcopal Assembly of May, 2010, Archbishop Nathaniel beseeches the Mother Churches to trust the very hierarchs whom they have chosen to shepherd the North American flock. Little by little, His Eminence's pleadings have come to fall upon ever more open ears.

"This is the Day which the Lord has Made! Today!" A Patriarch for the United States -- A Patriarch for Canada

Orthodox Christians are fond of remembering, bringing to mind, celebrating, the anniversary of meaningful events. In the liturgical services, many of the hymns begin with the word, "today!" Whether celebrating events in the life of our Lord or those of his All Pure Mother or the saints, the worshiper is invited to "be present," to participate in the event as a follower of Christ. It is a call to be not a mere observer but a participant, "today!"

It seems to me that Orthodox Christians failed to celebrate the anniversaries of some very important events in the life of the primitive Church in North America. I use the word primitive rather than nascent, because these events took place a good one hundred years after Holy Orthodoxy had first been planted in North America, in Alaska. The Church existed but was primitive, because the general grand wave of Orthodox Christian immigrants had not yet swarmed to these shores to swell the membership of the Church here to the point of its stabilization as a permanent institution in North America.

The events to which I am referring are the publications of liturgical books in the English language. An early English language work by John Glen King, **"The Rites and Ceremonies of the Greek Church, in Russia,"** was published in London in 1772 and appears to have become a classic for those interested in knowing something about the Orthodox Church. This was about the time when the missionary activity of the Russian Church already existed in Alaska.

"The Book of Needs" was also published in London but one hundred years later, in **1882,** translated by G. V. Shann who dedicated his work to the "Chief-Procurator of the Most Holy Governing Synod of Russia." The Church in Russia had not had a Patriarch for almost two hundred years but was ruled as a department of the state. Saint Tikhon was the first patriarch since the time of Peter "The Great."

The next two translations, the **1898 "Octoechos"** printed in St. Petersburg, and the **1899 "The General Menaion"** published in Moscow, were done up by Professor N. Orloff who dedicated the first to the Bishop of Aleut and Alaska, Nicholas, and the second to him as "late of Aleut and Alaska" and to Tikhon his successor. This is the same hierarch who since then has been counted among the saints by the Church.

Although the previous named volumes are perhaps less known to many of our clergy, it stands without challenge that the **"Service Book of the Holy Orthodox-Catholic Apostolic Church,"** published first in 1906 by Isabel Florence Hapgood in England, has become an almost universal standard in North America after World War II. This work is also dedicated to Saint Tikhon, who at the first printing was still Bishop of Aleut and Alaska but by the second printing, in 1922, was Patriarch of the Church of Russia.

In the 1956 edition of Hapgood, the Third Edition, Metropolitan Anthony Bashir of the then Syrian Antiochian Orthodox Archdiocese of New York and all North America, wrote in the introduction: "We have undertaken the present reproduction...also because of our continuing devotion to the advancement of our Holy Orthodox Church in America through the medium of the English language. ...In times to come, when the Church in America shall have realized more fully her ancient and glorious heritage, the complete wealth of our liturgical treasures will be set forth in English." This was forty-three years ago.

Of these English translations, one has been in existence for over two hundred years, 1772, and three for more than one hundred years: 1882, 1889, 1899, and the third has existed for 93 years! A sad commentary is that these books were not utilized to their fullest. What happened that these "liturgical treasures" were not put into immediate use? One plausible response has been that, because of the Bolshevik Revolution in 1917, the Russian Church in North America squirreled these "treasures" away so that the liturgical services would continue in Old Slavonic as a guarantee to the continuation of the life of the Russian Church outside of Russia. If so, what a sad response both to the missionary zeal and efforts of Saint Tikhon who himself promoted translations and their use in North America and to those who preceded him in the evangelization of these shores. There can be no doubt, that had the Church in North America had her own Patriarch at the time of the Revolution, as Saint Tikhon had suggested in 1905 to the Russian Church, this "ostrich-like" attitude would not have prevailed.

Our failure to celebrate these significant events is indicative of our negligence of, or indifference to, the efforts of the evangelization of this continent by Saints Tikhon, Herman, Innocent, the thrice-blessed Raphael Hawaweeny and others. Orthodox Christians used existing English translations of Holy Scriptures. These translated liturgical works, however, have an essential role in shaping our worship of the Holy Trinity. They are very important, and their existence in English ought to have been of great use and thus influence in the evangelization of North America. Could not our hierarchy have had a sense of respect for the past and fulfilled its duty to its predecessors by recognizing the value of these works and celebrated the publication of these translations as important milestones in the life of the Church in North America? Without a Patriarch, without a unified Synod to cradle the united history of our Church, there was no celebration, no common effort to bring it to the attention of the faithful.

The negligence to remember these works bespeaks of the reality that to express the consciousness of a unified Orthodox Church in the United States, the presence of a united Synod headed by a Patriarch is absolutely necessary. To synthesize all the traditions and all the events which are so very precious to the historical memory of the Church, there needs to be a unified body of the hierarchy. SCOBA was oblivious to these events and did not move to remember these events, because SCOBA speaks for particular ethnic entities and not the entire Church. The SCOBA is incapable of becoming the Holy Synod. Only a co-ordinated, unified Synod headed by a Patriarch can remember to speak for the whole Church concerning such events, calling the entire Church to give thanks to God for his blessings on his Church.

After two hundred years of witness, two hundred years and millions of faithful, thousands of clergy and hundreds of hierarchs, saintly men and women, the collective mind of the Church in the United States cannot yet be expressed by "one mouth and one heart." The Church in the United States and the Church in Canada must become participants, not observers, in the life of the Universal/Catholic Orthodox Church; and, this can happen only in a unified Church with each having her own Patriarch and Holy Synod.

We point out the papal centralism of the Roman Church, but there do exist local synods or councils of Roman Catholic hierarchs in every country. There is no such creature yet in the United States nor Canada nor Mexico. The English Reformers spoke about the "Italian" mission to England being ended with the establishment of the Anglican Church. Are Orthodox Americans the only ones not to be self-ruling?

We would like to address a question, but to whom? Even this is an unknown! Nevertheless, we ask: "When will the Church in the United States have her own patriarch? When will the Church in Canada have her own patriarch?" Today? Obviously, the word "today" is not a favorite one employed today in the language of the Church. "In the future. Not now. It isn't the right time." What is the reason or what are the reasons? There is no better time than today, not in some nebulous future. In Sacred History, there is no "right" time dictated by man but only God's time, the fullness of time, the "today." Is the issue that there are not enough faithful or clergy or what? Is the orthodoxy of our Church in question? What nonsense to say that there is no such thing as an "American" or "Canadian" people, and therefore there can be no "American" or "Canadian" Church!

Is anyone talking? Is anyone listening? Is anyone open to the movement of the Holy Spirit? Certainly, the Grace of the Holy Spirit which assembles the Synods of other Churches also assembles us in our worship and guides the Church in The United States and the Church in Canada. Is it such a bold step into the unknown for the Mother Churches to relinquish their pastoral concern for their children into the care of the same hierarchs whom they have elected and consecrated? Is it not the pleroma of trust in God that he will guide the Church wherever and everywhere?

One hundred years ago, the Church of Russia provided the primitive Church in North America with liturgical books. Twenty-seven years ago, in 1970, she recognized her daughter as her sister. Certainly, the other Patriarchates have the same wisdom and confidence in the Almighty to do likewise? Let there be a "today" on the lips of the Patriarchal Synods everywhere! Let there be a year of jubilee for two new sister churches. Let there be good order in the Church before the Lord of the Hour comes, so that he is pleased with us.

Come, dear Mothers, cut the umbilical cord so that the child you reared may be mistress of her own household and vineyard, today!

83

"The Orthodox faithful in North America are neither in exile nor diaspora, nor are they persecuted to surrender their ethnic identity. The Church is not in exile or diaspora, nor is she pressured to give up her 'coat of many colors,' her service to ethnic communities and North America. There are no reasons why the Church in North America cannot reconcile the different needs as the Apostles did, and there is no reason why there should not be, without delay, an administratively united Orthodoxy in North America."

(July 2005)

The example of Saints Peter and Paul, two Apostles with divergent missions in the service of the One Lord and God and Savior, is held up by His Eminence as an icon of the Church's mission in North America. He reminds us yet again that the Church must serve the ethnic communities with which she is often identified, and at the same time strive to transfigure the greater society in which she has been commissioned to labor. These two, divergent missions of the Church can be fully and fruitfully reconciled only by a united, autocephalous local Church.

St. Peter or St. Paul, or Sts. Peter and Paul? Orthodox Unity in North America in the Light of Apostolic Reconciliation

The feast icon of the two "Pillars" of the Church, Saints Peter and Paul, celebrated on June 29, portrays the two apostles standing upright and holding the depiction of a small church between them. This miniature building, of course, represents the universal Church of believers and not a specific church edifice. It is a very important representation of the fullness of the Church, the Body of our Lord and God and Savior, Jesus Christ.

In Acts of the Apostles, we read of some of St. Peter's mission to the Jews, such as Chapter 2:14, 22, when he addresses the "Men of Judea, and all of you who live in Jerusalem" and "Men of Israel, listen to what I am saying", and further on, "Brothers..."; and finally, in verse 35, "For this reason the whole House of Israel can be certain that God has made this Jesus whom you crucified both Lord and Christ."

There is no doubt that Saint Peter's primary mission was to the people of Israel. No doubt, he was also present when our Lord spoke about the faith of the Centurion, and certainly this experience must have made some impression on him as to the extension of salvation in Christ to all humanity. Furthermore, until the destruction of Jerusalem by the Romans in 70 A.D., the apostles preached and the community grew; and its presence and activities must have been known by the Roman authorities so that they, too, were aware of the preaching of salvation, even if they did not accept the message themselves.

Remember Cornelius the Centurion in Chapter 10 and how St. Peter had a vision of what was clean and what was not, and on meeting Cornelius said: "You know it is forbidden for Jews to mix with people of another race and visit them, but God has made it clear to me that I must not call anyone profane or unclean" (10:28); and, "The truth I have now come to realize is that God does not have favorites, but that anybody of any nationality who fears God and does what is right is acceptable to him" (10:34).

In Chapter 5, we read that the apostles were arrested, not by the Romans but by the Sanhedrin, because the apostles were preaching to the Jews. In fact, members of the Sanhedrin were so infuriated, that they wanted to put them to death (5:33).

In Chapter 6, were learn about a division in the apostolic community between the Hellenists and the Hebrews, both of which groups were Jews but expressing their culture and Judaism in different ways. Shortly thereafter, deacons were appointed, and among them Saint Stephen who became the first martyr. It was at the stoning of Stephen that Saul (later Paul), was present, and "Saul entirely approved of the killing" (7:8).

It was while Saul was "...still breathing threats to slaughter the Lord's disciples" (9:1), that he was converted to faith in Jesus Christ; and "after he had spent a few days with the disciples in

Damascus, he began preaching in the synagogues" (9:20). He, too, began preaching: "Men of Israel, and fearers of God, listen!" (11:17), and "My brothers, sons of Abraham's race, and all you who fear God..." (11:26). As Paul continued to preach, he was contradicted by some of the Jews. "We had to proclaim the word of God to you first, but since you have rejected it, since you do not think yourselves worthy of eternal life, we must turn to the pagans. For this is what the Lord commanded us to do when he said, 'I have made you a light for the nations, so that my salvation may reach the ends of the earth' " (13:46).

The title of this article is "St Peter or St. Paul, or Saints Peter and Paul?". It seems to me there are among us in North America those who would rather be bound by ethnic concerns as Peter was in the beginning of his mission. These are those who turn their backs to those who are not of their ethnic origin. Yes, one may say: "We need to take care of our own," but this is not according to God. Even St. Peter realized this and reached out to pagans, non-Jews. There are others who would be for the abolition of everything "ethnic" in the Church in North America: languages other than English, traditions and customs unique to various jurisdictions for the sake of becoming "American". St. Paul, in rejecting certain Jewish observances, did so to bring pagans into the community of believers, not because he did not respect that part of the Law which was still applied.

It seems to me that the Church in North America must reach out to all peoples while serving all peoples. We must not continue to isolate her from others, and especially from our brethren of the same faith! The Church in North America must be reconciled into one administrative unity which respects languages and traditions but which also founds new communities, that are shaped by the needs of North Americans. Strange that Orthodox are fond of saying that someone married an "American" or "Englishman," meaning someone not Orthodox, and even when the other party is born in the United States or Canada!

The Orthodox faithful in North America are neither in exile nor diaspora, nor are they persecuted to surrender their ethnic identity. The Church is neither in exile nor diaspora, nor is she pressured to give up her "coat of many colors," her service to ethnic communities and North America. There are no reasons why the Church in North America cannot reconcile the different needs as the Apostles did, and there is no reason why there should not be, without delay, an administratively united Orthodoxy in North America.

The Church is a light for all nations, but to be a strong light, it must be from a single source, the Gospel, which knows no nation above another and which brings salvation to all who fear God. Perhaps that is what is missing from our mix in North America, true fear of God and love for neighbor.

The icon of Saint Peter and Saint Paul **both** holding the Church shows us the universality of the Gospel and particular application. Orthodoxy is now present in Western Europe where similar problems exist, and is attempting to unite for the strengthening of the image of Eastern Orthodoxy in Western societies. Orthodox Christians in traditional "orthodox" nations are also aware that some ethnic peoples within their geographic areas are also looking for and discovering Orthodoxy and want to enter this way of salvation.

We believe that nations will be judged; Orthodox Americans will be judged as citizens of this nation and not of the ethnic land they or their parents left. Let those who have ears to hear, hear.

Appendices

Appendix I

The Address of His Eminence, Archbishop Nathaniel to the 2007 Episcopate Congress

"Blessed is the kingdom of the Father and of the Son and of the Holy Spirit, now and ever and unto the ages of ages."

Reverend Fathers and Lay Delegates, honored guests: Welcome to the 75th Annual Congress of our Holy and God-protected Episcopate. Some of you are "old-timers," like Mr. Avram Srbu who has attended as delegate or guest every Congress for the past 41 years! Many of the clergy and lay delegates have also been representing their parishes, on and off, for many years. Some of you are here for the first time; and therefore, we welcome you in particular.

Inasmuch as many of you are new, new delegates to the Congress, I will steal a little of our time to give some background into our position, our relationships and our activities as an Episcopate or, if you prefer, as a Diocese.

In order to understand these relationships, we must reflect on what it means to be "Church." By this, I do not mean the building in which we offer communal prayers to God, as we like to call our local parish place of worship.

In Canada, before 1902, immigrant faithful in Saskatchewan and Manitoba came together in homes, in the fields, witnessing to that same grace from God which unifies people into his witnesses and who acknowledge his presence in their lives. In 1902, St. Nicholas in Regina and St. Elias in Leonard were founded, and in 1903, Holy Trinity in MacNutt, and Saints Peter and Paul in Canora.

Recall what happened in Cleveland in 1904, when the faithful met on the shore of Lake Erie. They were "Church" even though they had no material structure. "Church" refers primarily to people and secondarily to buildings. "Church" is those individuals called together by God to be witnesses to his truth, to his actions in human history and to respond to him. Those few faithful individuals who met at the edge of Lake Erie were called together by God's grace to come together, to celebrate Pascha as much as they were able to recall; and thus, they remembered his mercy to them in Europe, and they implored him for his mercy in their lives in this "New World".

The Church is the unique Body of Christ in this world. She is not a mere human institution nor is she established by man-made laws, but she does respond to civil obligations. The Church bears witness to Divine Truth. I make this introduction as a reminder that the Church, being in this world, is always under some form of pressure to conform to the ways of the world, to the laws made by men, in different times, various places and even under various creeds.

The Apostolic Church began under the pagan Roman Empire, and spreading the good news throughout the world, also lived under other forms of government, including the aggressive Turkocracia and atheistic communism. She has lived in an exalted position under czars and monarchs, and more lately is experiencing life under "democratic" forms of government.

The universal Church outside North America has her own unique and varied historical experiences in living in some form of co-existence with various expressions of government. Historically, the Church and State each recognized the value of the other, and in "Orthodox" nations, there was some form of peaceful co-existence, although not without some tension.

Our Church in North America has her own experience of more than 210 years of witnessing, first in Alaska under the Czars, and then under the British Crown in Canada, and the Republican form of Government in The United States. These modern forms of co-existence, mutual respect for one another, Church and State, has allowed the Church to be relatively independent and free of government intrusion, and the State remains unassailable since it has not pronounced government preference for any particular faith community.

The universal Church, the local Church in North America and each diocese, continue to bear witness to Divine Truth. Even as North American societies become more and more complex due to recent establishments of faith communities new to this continent along with their particular forms of governance, the Orthodox Church continues to have her own historical place and influence on this vast continent, a presence which continues to grow and become a major voice.

Although the church in North American society has its own recognized and honored status, the governments of Canada and The United States have become more and more scrutinizing of the administrative operations of faith communities vis-a-vis civil laws. Although there are some who would say that governments are becoming "anti-religion," it is also likely that this scrutiny can be attributed to abuses by non-profit organizations.

The Episcopate parishes and mission are incorporated locally, that is, in the province or state in which the parish is established. The civil governing bodies must observe that non-profit organizations are following their own corporate by-laws and government regulations. It is to these bodies that the Church does owe vigilance and responsibility over her administration.

In the U.S., a parish can become a recognized 501(c)(3) body which means that individuals may receive the prescribed federal tax deduction for donations made to the parish. This also means that the federal government has the obligation and right to monitor the operations of the parish according to the standards established by the government for the 501(c)(3), as does the state or province have its own responsibility to monitor the parish/mission as a local corporation.

There have been and are, and one can suppose that there will be, financial mismanagement and abuses for personal gain in faith community operations. Read Acts of the Apostles, chapter 5, of the fraud of Ananias and his wife Sapphira. Fallen human nature is a universal reality, and it knows no faith community boundary, just as it is not foreign to the corporate and political worlds. Fallen human nature is universal, and its negative reality is found in all spheres of human life.

North American governments, in general, recognize two forms of ecclesiastical governance: hierarchal and congregational. No one would deny that the Orthodox Church is a hierarchal church. On the other hand, congregational churches are those which are totally locally governed. The uniqueness of Orthodoxy is that there is cooperation between the hierarchy, clergy and laity in the administration of the Church.

The annual Congress reflects this reality of cooperation. It is paramount that clergy and laity work together in the administration of the parish or mission. That is why we have elected and not appointed parish councils. Both clergy and laity are responsible to the entire local parish/mission and must work with "one mind and one heart" in the administration of the goods of the parish; goods which are, after all, God's goods which, in fact, we have offered to him.

Dioceses, parishes and missions are subject to civil government scrutiny in regard to how the organization is using the funds donated to it. Has the proper procedure been followed? The right checks and balances made and reported to the entire community? Have individuals, clergy and lay used the benefits of the non-profit status for personal or corporate gain?

Besides government supervision concerning non-profit financial operation, there is also scrutiny concerning possible abuse of immigration laws. Parishes and missions must not abuse the Religious Worker status. Government authorities do check to ascertain if a parish or mission is financially able to sustain an R-1 person and question the categories regarding bringing someone into North America through the Church.

Abuses of this nature, as well as financial irregularities, will bring about government investigations which could result in the loss of non-profit status and civil lawsuits. Our main concern, however, is to keep the image of the Church as the representative of truth, wholesome and free of taint.

As you know, each parish/mission is obliged to have an annual meeting within the first 6 weeks of the calendar year. At this assembly, reports are to be given by the parish priest, the elected council president, the treasurer and auditors as the principle officers of administration. The Episcopate receives a copy of these reports to preserve them and to know, according to the By-Laws, how the parishes are being administered. In reviewing the annual minutes and reports, it is obvious to us that there are parishes/missions which do not deliver written reports to the faithful. We know this to be true, because we do not receive them.

These written reports are part of the administration of the parish and are essential to the administration of the parish. Should there be a future need for evidence of these reports, it is the written report which will illuminate a given issue.

The purpose of the Church is to save souls. Here are some statistics for 2007 from the SOLIA journal. There were 46 conversions, 194 marriages, 118 deaths and 583 baptisms. This large number of baptisms is encouraging, and we rejoice that parents are aware of the necessity to have their children baptized into the Church. There were also some adult baptisms included in this number. Our concern as the Church must be to do all we can to be sure that in ten, fifteen, twenty years from now, these same new members of the Church are active Orthodox Christians.

In addition to participating in the holy services, the local parish and mission must have on-going religious education programs for adults and children. If the Church does not teach her faithful, secular, materialistic society and other faith communities will. We must be pro-active in teaching and sustaining the faith of our people. Church school for only one child is better than no education for that young soul. Parents must also be exhorted to take part in the home education of their children.

Most marriages in the Church are "mixed marriages," that is a marriage between an Orthodox Christian and a non-Orthodox Christian. Oftentimes, the non-Orthodox wants to know more about the faith and waits for an invitation from the priest and parishioners. In time, most of these "seekers" enter the life of the parish. Even after a person embraces Orthodoxy, he/she must be spiritually nourished by the priest to strengthen the new faith and must be accepted by the entire community to be fully integrated into the life of the Church.

The life of the Church is witnessing to God's truth and living his invitation to life eternal. We urge the parishes and missions to be more active in reaching out to neighbors and the North American public in general. Although it is true that most of our parishes and missions serve Orthodox Christians of the Romanian tradition, history has shown us that all people can be attracted to the faith through the witness of local parish priests and faithful. The real reason for outreach is that love for neighbor demands this of us, as we know from the Parable of the Good Samaritan. The Church must not live in isolation.

The younger generation becomes the older, and early on, it needs to be fully included in parish administration and social activities. It is this generation which will either continue in the parish or which will look elsewhere for spiritual nourishment. It is this generation which is also "turned off" by infighting and parish partisanship. This generation enters mixed marriages, and their spouses will either join them in the Church or lead them out of the Church to a new worship community or none at all.

Over the past few years, the Episcopate has celebrated the anniversaries of a number of her parishes rejoicing in 100 years of existence. Some of these continue with the same founding families. Others have experienced an influx of new immigration which, if welcomed, slowly enters into the mainstream of parish activities. There are new missions that are established for Romanian or English-speaking communities, and some of these serve all language needs.

The Episcopate is blessed and challenged by the recent immigrations; blessed, because these faithful bring the traditions of Romania, their piety, their excitement to enter into the long established Romanian Orthodox Episcopate of America; challenged, because the process of accommodating to a North American way of life and to church administration is different from that from which they have come. Yes, they may criticize, sometimes rankling established parish clergy and members. Yes, language can be an issue; and yes, some parish members need to take a leap of trust in the process of reaching out to this immigration which God has brought to North America. When this integration takes place with Christian patience and love, good fruits result.

It is also evident from the annual parish reports that most parishes/missions are on the tenuous edge of financial stability. A very few parishes have been recipients of large bequests; others have long-established building funds which mean that these are restricted funds. Most parishes just manage to make their budget. We intend to make a study of the financial stability of the parishes and may schedule workshops to review the financial needs, forms of income, operational concerns of the communities and to address them through experienced speakers in these areas.

We must be more concerned over the low level of some clergy salaries. Not a few clergy must work outside the parish and serve the parish "in between time." Many clergy-wives work out of necessity; and yes, others work because they are educated in a field of activity in which they find self-fulfillment using their talents. Over the past few years, we have released clergy to seek a better living salary in other dioceses. We have not hesitated to inform clergy from Romania to seek acceptance in these jurisdictions, because we ourselves do not have any openings for them and because of the limited salaries our parishes and missions offer. The clergy must receive better remunerations. We will resurrect the commission which studied and presented its proposal to previous congresses which rejected fixed salaries and benefits.

Our Episcopate is itself a local church comprised of hierarchy, clergy and laity, just as each Episcopate or diocese is part of a local territorial church based in a geographic area. Our Episcopate is a part of the local autocephalous Orthodox Church in America (OCA). The archbishop is a voting member of the Holy Synod. Some of our missions are hosted by OCA parishes. We are listed on the official OCA website. Each year, the archbishop reports to the Holy Synod on the administrative and spiritual status of the Episcopate. Our Episcopate is one of thirteen dioceses which cover Canada, the US and Mexico. You may want to look at the website for more detail and information: http://www.oca.org. Among the other dioceses are the Bulgarian, Albanian and Mexican exarchate.

Some of you are aware of an administrative crisis within the central administration of the Orthodox Church in America. This matter is limited to the Syosset administration and excludes any diocesan administration, although the dioceses are affected. An investigation is underway through an external audit by a CPA Firm and by a law firm. This action was initiated by His Beatitude, HERMAN, as the head of the Metropolitan Council. This was reported on page 6 of the September/October SOLIA 2006. In addition, our Chancery issued a letter to all clergy on April 2007, giving as much information to the clergy and faithful as was available and possible. At this time, the matter is in the

Spiritual Court and is still in process of being resolved; the results will be made known to the entire Orthodox Church in America.

The Episcopate is represented in external affairs, and in the Standing Conference of Canonical Orthodox Bishops in the Americas (SCOBA) through the Orthodox Church in America. This is a US-based Conference which includes only the heads of eight Orthodox jurisdictions and the Orthodox Church in America. In the September/October issue of SOLIA, 2006, a report on a special meeting of the SCOBA in Chicago was given. Other hierarchs of these nine jurisdictions had also been invited to hear reports on inter-Orthodox cooperation in The United States. Some of the other hierarchs attended, but not all, inasmuch as attendance is not obligatory.

The SCOBA endorses International Orthodox Christian Charities (IOCC), Eastern Orthodox Committee on Scouting (EOCS), Orthodox Christian Education Commission (OCEC), Orthodox Christian Fellowship (OCF), Orthodox Christian Mission Center (OCMC), and Orthodox Christian Network (OCN). SCOBA also endorses Project Mexico and other charitable organizations.

The Episcopate, through various publications and websites, is known throughout the world. But this can be said of most Episcopates which are made known through modern day technology. Keep in mind that the Episcopate, our Diocese, although part of the local Church, is an integral part of the universal Orthodox Church, sharing the same mysteries, sacraments and teachings.

Worldwide Orthodoxy is affected by immigration from "Orthodox nations" into all parts of the globe. The ongoing migrations mean that new dioceses are being established in nations where Orthodoxy was merely a name. Thus, in some west European nations, a multiplicity of jurisdictions has been established, creating a status like that of the Church in North America. These recently-established dioceses, still dependent on their Mother Churches, are also striving to create local territorial churches which would include all Eastern Orthodox Christians under the care of one local synod of bishops.

Since 1990, Orthodoxy has spread to almost every European nation and beyond. Orthodoxy or any form of

Christianity is not acceptable in Muslim nations, and no immigration can be found there - certainly not the establishment of parishes or dioceses. Islam is, however, now evident in those same European nations and in North America. Thus, Orthodox Christianity and various forms of Islam are now present in nations where neither has historically been prominent. Through extensive immigration, both are now reaching out to the people of de-Christianized European states.

This means that just as in North America, so in western and northern Europe, the issue of ecclesiastical order is the most pressing issue relating to effective evangelization. There exists in world Orthodoxy an ongoing debate as to the good order of the Church and as to how this order is made manifest. Some say it is through Constantinople; others say it is by a universal council of the Church; others express neither concern nor urgency in resolving the matter; and some (primarily foreign governments) continue to inappropriately entitle this spread of Orthodoxy "the diaspora."

How does this ecclesiastical disorder affect the Episcopate? In theory, we are considered to be part of this problem "diaspora," just as are all Orthodox jurisdictions in North America, Europe and elsewhere. Is the Church in North America to be under a foreign Patriarch in Constantinople? - Under the multitude of foreign Mother Churches? - Self-existing or autocephalous?

The issue is also a political one, because the Church, abroad and here, does not live in a vacuum. Here, she exists and evangelizes North American societies and is aware of the needs of the local Church. From another aspect, if the Church is under the authority of a foreign Patriarch who claims authority over all Orthodox parishes and institutions, it is a precarious matter for us and is a form of papalism foreign to the Church. Most Mother Churches lay no claim to the goods and properties of their colonies in North America, but all of them retain the right to choose or confirm the election of the primate of their colony in North America. This persists in North America for all jurisdictions except for the Autocephalous Orthodox Church in America.

We are aware and rejoice that the Russian Orthodox Church Outside Russia, also called the "Synod Abroad," is now in communion with universal Orthodoxy. This group has made peace with the entire Church through a concelebration with the Russian Church from which it had been estranged for almost a century. Although the Holy Synod of the Orthodox Church in America expressed its interest and concern as to how this might impact the image of autocephaly of the OCA, the action of restored communion is still new, and time will tell how this plays out. The blessing of the re-communion is in the re-integration of this body into world Orthodoxy.

Unlike the Synod Abroad, the Episcopate was never estranged from world Orthodoxy. The existence of two Romanian jurisdictions in North America is not unique: there are two Bulgarian and two Albanian jurisdictions, two Ukrainian jurisdictions and even the Serbian resolution remains with separate administrations.

Some would reduce the matter to stating that now that communism has apparently (our subjective observation) been eradicated from those Orthodox lands, all North American jurisdictions should return to the free Mother Churches. The matter cannot be reduced to stating that since government has apparently changed, everything can return to a pre-communist status. It is a matter of canonical order that on the North American continent, there must exist at least separate and autocephalous Orthodox Churches, one in Canada and one in The United States.

If the issue is that government interference influenced or at least hindered the Church in the past, there is no reason that such may not happen in the future; God knows. We have written to His Beatitude TEOCTIST to request a dialogue directly with the Church of Romania concerning its perception of the Episcopate. In the meanwhile, the Joint Dialogue Commission (JDC) continues to meet on a regular basis, as you will see in its report, and prepares for this possible dialogue with the Mother Church.

To recap our presentation, the Episcopate is a sovereign body; it is part of the local autocephalous Church; clergy and laity must work together, mindful that the Church is one; we participate in pan-Orthodox activities in North America; we are known in world Orthodoxy; and, we are moving forward in dialogue with the Church of Romania so that some kind of reconciliation may be blessed by God for the good of Orthodox unity in North America.

This evening, a special tribute will be given in honor of the late and thrice-blessed Archbishop Valerian D. Trifa whose 20 year anniversary of falling asleep is being observed this year. We urge every delegate to be present, not only to honor the memory of the archbishop, but to come to know something more about his work in the Episcopate which he shepherded for 33 years. After his retirement in 1984, the Episcopate continued on the solid basis which he left behind. For this and future generations not to know the sacrifices, dedication and great pastoral love of this unique individual would be a reproach to those who knew him and supported him in his dedication to Orthodoxy in North America. Memory eternal!

Dearly beloved, as Orthodox Christians, we know that we are not living merely in secular time but primarily in the kingdom of God. Let us acknowledge that as God's stewards, our proper administration of the goods of the Church is an important part of our divine mission in that kingdom; let us add our own "Amen!" to the words with which we begin the Divine Liturgy and every Holy Mystery: *"Blessed is the kingdom of the Father and of the Son and of the Holy Spirit, now and ever and unto the ages of ages. Amen!"*

Appendix II

Resurrection Pastoral Letter 2010

To our beloved clergy, monastics and pious faithful of our God-protected Episcopate, Grace, Mercy and Peace from God, and from us our fatherly love and hierarchal blessing.

"The Lord God says this: I am now going to open your graves and raise you from your graves, my people. And I shall put My spirit in you, and you will live ... it is the Lord God who speaks" (Ezekiel 37: 12, 14).

Christ is risen! Truly, he is risen!

Dearly Beloved:
What a glorious day this is! The mercy of God is great and his love is everlasting! He has looked upon his people and smiled on us and put his spirit into us to celebrate this day of brightness which surpasses the light of the celestial bodies. Today, darkness is no more, and death has been crushed and annihilated, for God has opened our graves and raised us into unending life! For his love is everlasting!

In the Book of Genesis, we hear it stated that *"God said, 'Let us make man in our own image, in the likeness of ourselves...'. God created man in the image of himself, in the image of God he created him, male and female he created them"* (Gen. 1:26, 27). This man, made in the image of his Maker, however, chose to think of himself as self-sufficient (he and his wife); and thus, putting themselves in place of their Creator, they found themselves, in fact, insufficient and mortal.

Having turned from God who is Life and the Source of life, man and his wife found that the result of turning from the source of life is death. Hearing from the mouth of God these words, *"For dust you are and to dust you shall return,"* man travailed his days on earth under the quest of restoration with his Creator, God (Gen. 3:19). God, however, did not leave man alone in his quest but bowed the heavens to come and carry this burden for his children.

The Messiah, Christ the Eternal Word of God, came to restore that image of God in all humanity and to raise mankind up from the dust from which it is taken, to eradicate, to pull out from its roots, the "sting" of death, and to bestow on humanity a new and unending existence in the presence of him "through whom all things were made." The Resurrection from the dead of our Lord and God and Savior, Jesus Christ is the true triumph of Life over death. Jesus, Only-begotten Son of the Father, born of the Holy Virgin Mary, took on our human nature, so that he could *"refashion in us the image broken by passion,"* meaning, the passion or failing of the first man. *"And finding the wayward sheep lost in the mountain, he (Jesus) took it on his shoulders and carried it to the Father."*

God, through his prophet Ezekiel stated: *"I am now going to open your graves and raise you from your graves."* Saint Constantine the Great, the first Christian Emperor, in the early 4th Century *(To the Assembly of the Saints)*, reflects this prophecy of Ezekiel when he speaks about the "renovation of bodies long since dissolved." He says: *"That light which far outshines the day and sun, first pledge of resurrection, and renovation of bodies long since dissolved, the divine token of promise, and the path which leads to everlasting life ... is arrived ...and the predictions of the prophets were all fulfilled."*

Saint Ambrose of Milan in the same century, reflecting on the death of his brother, says: *"What grief is there which the grace of the Resurrection does not console? What sorrow is not excluded by the belief that nothing perishes in death?...So, then, if death frees us from the miseries of this world, it is certainly no evil, inasmuch as it restores liberty and excludes suffering....For now we know in part, and understand in part, but then it will be possible for that which is perfect to be grasped, when not the shadow but the reality of the Divine Majesty and eternity shall begin to shine so as to be gazed upon by us with unveiled face."*

The Divine Majesty is of course the Holy Trinity in whose image we were made and to which we shall return in the presence of God in the reality of his "unveiled face"; and, we will "live again, it is the Lord who speaks." Through his boundless mercy, this fellowship with God is an unending relationship in love. This is the relationship which the first man and woman rejected. This is not simply a restored relationship, but a new relationship based on the obedience of Christ to the Father.

Saint Cyril of Alexandria in his 4th Lecture *(On the Ten Points of Doctrine on the Resurrection of the Lord)*, says: "*Did Jonah come forth from the whale on the third day, and has not Christ then risen from the earth on the third day? Is a dead man raised to life on touching the bones of Elisha, and is it not much easier for the Maker of mankind to be raised by the power of the Father?*"

The reality of the resurrection of Jesus Christ is hereto testified in reference to the Old Testament experiences of the Prophet Jonah and to the raising of the dead man through contact with the bones of the Prophet Elisha (2 Kings 13:21). Both of these events took place not through any power of the prophets but through the power of God working through them.

In a long poem *(On Pascha)*, only a few lines of which are here quoted, Melitios of Sardis makes the analogy that there is only one perfect sacrifice to God the Father: Jesus Christ the "Lamb of God who takes away the sin of the world". . . *"a speechless lamb was precious, but it is worthless now because of the spotless Son; the temple below was precious, but it is worthless now because of the Christ above. . . . The Jerusalem below was precious, but it is worthless now because of the Jerusalem above; the narrow inheritance was precious, but it is worthless now because of the widespread bounty."*

The sacrifices of the Old Law are no more; the one and only ever true sacrifice, the Lamb who came forth from the Virgin's womb, once and for all time, for all the "ends of the inhabited earth." Who is most precious to the Father but the Son through whom the Spirit of Truth came upon the apostles on the Fiftieth Day after the Resurrection? Jesus reaches into the earth, into the graves to raise our fallen nature to the heights of heaven. When God promised to open the graves and to empty them, he was promising in Christ Jesus who is the "first fruit of those rising from the dead," whose grave was the first opened to the universal resurrection. Look at the icon of the Resurrection! See the Lamb of God, Christ the Destroyer of Death reaching down into Hades, grasping out of its clutches Adam and Eve and the righteous as he tramples greedy Death!

Leo the Great of Rome (Homily 71: *On the Lord's Resurrection, Great and Holy Saturday)* reminds us that we must all become partakers in Christ's Resurrection life. *"We must strive to be found partakers also of Christ's Resurrection, and 'pass from death unto life' while we are in this body. We must die, therefore, to the devil and live to God: we must perish to iniquity that we may rise to righteousness . . . . As we have borne the image of the earthly, so let us also bear the image of Him Who is from heaven; we must greatly rejoice over this change, whereby we are translated from earthly degradation to heavenly dignity through His unspeakable mercy, Who descended into our estate that He might promote us to His."* Thus has Christ fulfilled Adam's quest for restoration.

Being thus encouraged by the words of the prophets of old and being satisfied by the reality of the empty tomb, confirmed by the witness of the apostles and great cloud of saints through the ages, we are called by God to remember daily that we are individual and collective witnesses to the Resurrection and graced to live a new life through baptism in the death and resurrection of our Lord, anointed by the Spirit and sustained by his glorious and precious Body and Blood.

St. Leo continues: *"Let God's people then recognize that they are a new creation in Christ, and with all vigilance understand by Whom they have been adopted and Whom they have adopted. These thoughts, dearly beloved, must be kept in mind not only for the Paschal festival, but also for the sanctification of the whole life ... so that rising ever anew from all downfalls, we may deserve to attain to the incorruptible Resurrection of our glorified flesh in Christ Jesus our Lord . . .".*

This day's celebration of the Resurrection must be a daily celebration for those who put their hope in God. This hope gives us joy in our daily lives. Our daily lives lead us to eternal life. Eternal life is bestowed on us by him who said: *"I am now going to open your graves and raise you from your graves, my people. And I shall put My spirit in you, and you will live ... it is the Lord God who speaks."* Amen!

Christ is risen! Truly he is risen!

Accept our fatherly love and archpastoral blessings on those near and those far away.

+NATHANIEL
By the Mercy of God, Archbishop of Detroit and the Romanian Episcopate

Appendix III

Letter to the Editor: Archbishop Nathaniel
By Alexandru Nemoianu
(November 1999)

On October 20, 1999, the Holy Synod of the Orthodox Church in America decided to elevate the Rt. Reverend Bishop Nathaniel to the rank of Archbishop. That was a very wise and right decision that recognized the merits of one of the leading personalities of American Orthodoxy. But its significance is much larger and is of historical proportions.

In his essay, "The Five Deaths of Faith", G.K. Chesterton said that during the centuries, Christianity has encountered numerous crises, and several times (he mentioned five to which a sixth, the end of communism should be added) it appears that the Faith was near death or anyhow seemed almost irrelevant. However, those crises ended, and the Faith was again not only relevant but able to renew a world in confusion. All the crises, all the persecution, all moral relativism were able to prove one thing: "Heaven and earth shall pass away, but my words shall not pass away". The same dangers were encountered by the Romanian Orthodox Episcopate of America in its seventy year old history.

Among those mortal crises, I will mention just a few: when Bishop Policarp was stopped from returning to his flock; when Archbishop Valerian was viciously attacked and finally forced into exile; when the Episcopate's financial resources were shamelessly embezzled. But during and after each of those crises, the Episcopate recovered miraculously and rose again more powerful, more beautiful and more relevant.

I mention all the above facts just to point out that Archbishop Nathaniel could not have started his pastorate under more critical circumstances; but against all odds he has prevailed, and this is a miracle and a proof that this Episcopate is defended by a Power that is mightier than that of man. It is not in the scope of this article to enumerate the achievements of Archbishop Nathaniel's pastorate even if they are many: the new missions, the new churches, the new administrative center of the Diocese and many others. What I would like to emphasize is another fact.

Most of the time, we have a tendency to characterize a person or to describe a person as the sum of his deeds, the sum of his acts. In fact, a person is defined not by the sum of his acts but by the consistency of his actions, and the values under which those acts were fulfilled.

Archbishop Nathaniel is a spiritual person with a special charisma. It just happened that he started his pastorate when I moved to the Heritage Center, and in this context I can confess that when he is at the office, everything is fine and an atmosphere of security and serenity is present. Archbishop Nathaniel is a person of fantastic humbleness. Only his persistence and power of work probably match his humility, which are definitely signs of his Romanian heritage. Archbishop Nathaniel cannot be outworked, and still he is always available to give advice, to receive confessions, to hear and heal human pain, for hours if necessary.

Archbishop Nathaniel is a wise man and also a leader in this world. In such a context, he is fully aware that on this earth there are pestilences, pain, suffering and victims. In such a context, he decided to take, in every predicament, the victim's side in order to reduce the damage done by the victors and by the "movers and shakers" full of conceit and empty of compassion. What Archbishop Nathaniel has tried to do or rather tries to teach us is that each of us has to accumulate good deeds while we still can. The memory of good deeds is our only treasure, and the only thing we can lean on when in captivity, exile, sickness and need. That is the lesson which Archbishop Nathaniel teaches us all, his beloved flock.

We should be grateful to God for the shepherd He provided for us. In the meantime, we should also be aware that in this world, joy and happiness are not "rights" to be taken for granted, but rather are gifts and privileges; however, "this is the Day the Lord has made; be joyful and glad in it."

Appendix IV

Archbishop Nathaniel Popp
By V. Rev. Fr. Vasile Hategan
(December 1999)

We no longer have a bishop! He is now Archbishop NATHANIEL Popp. He was raised in Episcopal rank by the decision of the recent meeting of the Orthodox Church in America (OCA) Synod of Bishops in New York. We who know him, have worked with him and have followed his activity throughout the years, were not altogether surprised by this decision, because we felt it was upcoming and well-merited.

The life and work of an Orthodox bishop in the New World is difficult and heavy. Territorially, his jurisdiction covers the vast North American continent. He is on the road much of the time, traveling by various means, carrying burdensome baggage with Episcopal vestments and appointments, officiating at various services, giving speeches, attending meetings, conferences, consultations, appeasing dissidents, smoothing ruffled feathers and generally being a factotum. All this and running an office and staff. There are not enough hours in the day to attend to all the diocesan functions.

Much is expected of Archbishop NATHANIEL, but he has more than met the exigencies of his office. It is not easy. You have to be superman. Moreover, you never can satisfy everyone, but Archbishop NATHANIEL sincerely tries and is successful in most cases. Whatever the outcome, he never bears ill feelings and animosities towards anyone. He can talk with love, openly and sincerely with anyone, friend or foe.

Archbishop NATHANIEL has his own unique personality and style. Each succeeding Romanian Orthodox bishop in America was somewhat different from the others. Bishop

POLICARP came to America in 1936 and was of the so-called old school, finding it difficult to adapt to the precarious conditions here. He gave it his best and managed to cope with the many problems.

On the other hand, Archbishop VALERIAN, during his 30-year troublesome and hectic tenure of office, in spite of all adversity and obstacles, proved to be a leader, innovator, builder and achiever.

One thing Archbishop NATHANIEL is not, is an imitator. He has his own way of getting things accomplished, which is proving to be most effective in the long run. Born and raised in America, he embraced Orthodoxy with conviction and determination. Though proud of his cultural heritage and roots, he is American in thought and ideals. He combines all these traits in a symbiosis of values, which is worthy to be followed.

Fate would have it that he was elected during a time of political turmoil in Romania and that he would have to spend much of his time and efforts to meet many problems of these newly arrived Romanians, though he always looked beyond them, visualizing a united and autocephalous Orthodox Church in America with its own patriarch. As such, he finds no conflict in belonging to the Orthodox Church in America (OCA), which is dedicated to these ideals. At the same time, he never neglected or belittled his Romanian aspirations. He welcomes newly-arrived Romanian priests and laymen, organizing new missions for them, helping them to resettle and supporting them through the beginning stages. Personally, he has polished his Romanian language abilities, though he urges them to become more Americanized, without forsaking their Romanian heritage.

Like his predecessors, Archbishop NATHANIEL runs a well-organized and efficient Episcopate office. He continues to expand the physical facilities of the Vatra. No letter goes unanswered. No problem is too small to be neglected or brushed aside. No suggestion is entirely ignored. Everyone – young and old, learned or simple – has his ear, is taken seriously and given proper and due attention.

Time marches on. The youthful hierarch is graying. The awesome responsibilities of his office are taking their toll. The Archbishop could very well use an assistant to take some of the heavy burdens off his shoulders. We sincerely hope that this, too, will be forthcoming.

In the meantime, the good intentioned and loyal members of the Episcopate most heartily congratulate Archbishop NATHANIEL on his elevation and pray that God continue to endow him with love, patience, wisdom and good health. Above all, we hope that he will continue the crusade to unify the Orthodox Church in America, consolidate its standing and eventually have an Autocephalous Church with its own Patriarch.

Întru Mulți Ani Stăpâne! Unto Many Years, Master!

Appendix V

A Celebration of Our Faith: Archbishop Nathaniel – 10 years of Apostolate
By Fr. Remus Grama
(September 2000)

Romanian Americans in the parishes of Ohio and Western Pennsylvania are now blessed with the opportunity to rejoice in their Faith by celebrating 20 years of Apostolate of their Archpastor, His Eminence Archbishop Nathaniel. Both clergy and faithful contemplate assembling in prayer and a festive banquet on Sunday, October 22, at St. Mary Cathedral in Cleveland to celebrate their Faith, by recognizing and appreciating their spiritual leader for 20 years of blessed episcopacy.

When a Bishop – who is the servant of all – is honored, the Church unveils her essence, which is all about love of God and philanthropy (love of man). They feel that the best way to recognize the service of their Archbishop is to personally participate in the celebration and bring or send a generous offering to the Archbishop's Charity Endowment Fund. The Ohio – W. Pennsylvania parishes did not have the chance to get together in an event of such proportions since 1984, when they said farewell to the late Archbishop Valerian. It was due to the clairvoyance of the latter that – through the election of then Fr. Nathaniel Popp – the Episcopate's sorrow, generated by the departure of their Archpastor, was turned into joy.

Fr. Nathaniel Elected Bishop in Cleveland

On September 20, 1980, the Congress of the Episcopate, assembled in a special session at St. Mary Church in Cleveland, elected Fr. Nathaniel Popp, a celibate priest in Hermitage, Pennsylvania, to be the Auxiliary Bishop of our Episcopate. The 1981 *Solia Calendar* indicates that a total of 102 delegates, clergy and lay people, had to choose from a slate of well respected candidates. Emotions ran high since the Episcopate did not go through the election of a bishop for almost 30 years. Archbishop Valerian himself describes that moment in the following words: *"When the newly-elected entered the church during the bell ringing and singing of* "God is with us", *it was a deeply moving moment and one of great joy".*

Archbishop Valerian Writes About His Successor

Archbishop Valerian also published perhaps the shortest and most clear biography of our Hierarch in the above-mentioned source. For the benefit of the youngest readers, I reproduce it in its entirety:

"Father Nathaniel Popp is the son of a Romanian from Transylvania, having been born on June 12, 1940, in Aurora, Ill, where he spent his childhood. After the elementary school, he studied at East Aurora High School and then St. Procopius College, in Lisle, Illinois. With a College Diploma (Psychology), he was enrolled at The Gregorian Pontifical University in Rome, where he earned a "Bachelor in Theology". After his studies, in 1966, he was ordained a deacon and priest by His Grace, Vasile Cristea, the Romanian Greek-Catholic Bishop. Having been attracted by the teachings of the Orthodox Church, upon his return to the United States, he petitioned and has been accepted as a priest in the Romanian Orthodox Episcopate of America. As a celibate priest, he remained for five years near "Vatra Romaneasca" (headquarters of the Episcopate), planning to establish an American Orthodox Monastery and, at the same time, helping His Eminence, Valerian with the religious education programs, translations and editing of liturgical books. Beginning with December 1975, Fr. Popp has served the Holy Cross parish, in Sharon/Hermitage, Pennsylvania" (Solia Calendar, 1981, p.93, in translation).

Auxiliary Bishop, Ruling Bishop and Archbishop

On November 15, 1980, His Beatitude Metropolitan Theodosius and several American Orthodox bishops consecrated Fr. Nathaniel to the Holy Episcopacy, in St. George Cathedral, Detroit. Until 1984, he served as an Auxiliary Bishop, residing at the "Vatra" and assisting his mentor, whom he loved and whose work he has steadily carried on, perpetuating his memory, through his actions, deeds and writings. After the departure of "the Archbishop", a special electoral Congress was again convened on October 20, 1984, at St. Mary Cathedral, to elect him as "the ruling Bishop". After this, the enthronement services and festivities took place in the St. George Cathedral, in Detroit. After 19 years of dedicated labor in the vineyard of the Lord, presiding over an Episcopate of continental and international proportions, the Holy Synod of the Bishops the Orthodox Church in America in its autumn session elevated His Grace, Bishop Nathaniel to the rank of an "Archbishop". The faithful of the diocese rejoiced in this timely recognition, because he is, after all, presiding over the largest Romanian Archdiocese in America and Canada, being the spiritual Father of the majority of Romanian Orthodox on this continent. His involvement and unrelenting efforts for and contributions to the growth and coming to maturity of Orthodoxy in America is now an acknowledged reality, beyond the borders of our jurisdiction. In this respect, at our last Vatra Congress, Fr. Jim Kyriakakis (IOCC) spoke in unequivocal terms about his image.

"Come and See": Our Charity at Work

Since 1984, His Eminence Archbishop Nathaniel has led his Church into an unprecedented growth, adding 25 new missions and parishes to our roster. Immediately after the fall of the "Iron-curtain", he obtained canonical recognition from the Church of Romania, inaugurating a new era of hopes of reuniting the two Romanian jurisdictions in America. Through the 1990's, he opened many doors in Washington, D.C. to facilitate a more favorable treatment of Romania and acceptance in the western structures. Supported by many generous faithful, Archbishop Nathaniel spearheaded the "Help For Romania Program", which generated Christian charitable assistance of goods totaling more than $60 million.

The exposure by the media of the tragedy of the "orphanages", "elderly asylums" and hospital problems of Romania indicated, however, that much more was to be done, and that we only scratched the surface. Our charitable investments through "Project Hope" and "Brother's Brother Foundation" brought much change and comfort to many. Besides this, the needs here, "at home", pointed to the fact that our Christian Charity must be endowed. The Archbishop's Charity Endowment Fund became a reality to which many of our readers have positively responded. When so many have done it, the faithful in Ohio and Pennsylvania feel that they cannot remain indifferent; and, they wish to honor their leader by supporting Him to carry out the work of Christ. His Eminence once told me that there is no greater way to honor him than to do the work of Christ in "washing the feet of the least of our brethren". Therefore, institutionalizing "Charity" is truly one of his many dreams for our Church in America. On his 20th anniversary, this would also be a great way for all of us to say *"Thank You, Your Eminence!"*

We appreciate the leadership and blessing Archbishop Nathaniel has brought to all of us, as one large family in Christ. It is he who led us to have a new "Vatra" Administrative Center, which brings us into the 21st century, and the new St. Andrew's Center of Orthodox Christian Studies, which offers us hopes for a brighter future. Recognizing the fact that the Church is not at all "a one-man-mission", but rather the communion of faith and action of all Christ-lovers, we see in our Hierarch the Apostle of our times, who embodies to us the evangelical image of the Lord. For this reason, in honoring him, we actually celebrate our own Faith and offer honor to God. But, on the human level, we wish to joyfully say, as one family – with one mind and one heart – *"We thank you, Your Eminence! Your life in Christ inspires us to do what we do and even more, for God's glory! May God grant you many more years in the Holy Apostolate, Master!*

Escorting kings, (date unknown) . .

. . . And Princesses, Akron, 2010

LODGINGS ALONG THE APPALACHIAN TRAIL
New England